Professional Communication in International Settings

Professional Communication in International Settings

Yuling Pan, Suzanne Wong Scollon, and Ron Scollon

BLACKWELL
Publishers

First published 2002

2 4 6 8 10 9 7 5 3 1

Blackwell Publishers Inc.
350 Main Street
Malden, Massachusetts 02148
USA

Blackwell Publishers Ltd
108 Cowley Road
Oxford OX4 1JF
UK

Library of Congress Cataloging-in-Publication Data has been applied for.

ISBN 0-631-22508-0 (hardback); 0-631-22509-9 (paperback)

British Library Cataloguing in Publication Data

A CIP catalogue record for this book is available from the British Library.

Typeset in 10.5 on 12.5 pt Ehrhardt
by Best-set Typesetter Ltd., Hong Kong
Printed in Great Britain by
MPG Books Ltd, Bodmin, Cornwall

This book is printed on acid-free paper.

Contents

List of Figures   vi

Preface   vii

1   Analyzing Communication in the International Workplace   1

2   The Telephone Call: When Technology Intervenes   27

3   The Resumé: A Corporate "Trojan Horse"   53

4   The Presentation: From Dale Carnegie to Ananova the Avatar   79

5   The Meeting: Action or Ratification?   106

6   The Reflective View: Seeing Ourselves as Others See Us   137

Appendices: Reflective Self-Assessment   159

   1   The Communication Display Portfolio Exchange Planner   162

   2   Presenting Across Cultures   164

   3   Suggestions for Users   206

Further Reading   223

References   228

Index   234

List of Figures

2.1 Technological transformation of communicative style   39

4.1 The "Dale Carnegie" model   84

4.2 The "Dale Carnegie" model with visual aids   85

4.3 Presentation with voice-over model   88

4.4 The Avatar model   88

4.5 The double relationship model   90

4.6 The multiple relationships model   91

4.7 Presentation faces   93

5.1 Power in Chinese meetings   122

5.2 Power flow in Chinese meetings   124

6.1 The CDP exchange process   151

Preface

The globalization of activities in business, government, marketing, and even entertainment has made us aware of how interconnected our world now is. But globalization has also made us aware of how fundamentally different we are in different nations, cultures, and even organizations. This book has been written to help individuals and organizations deal with professional communication when communication takes place across the frontiers of international, organizational, and even interpersonal relationships.

While the international world of communication is based on uses of common technologies of communication, we are all still participants in very different cultures, societies, and organizations. A technology such as the mobile phone, for example, is used very differently in Finland and in Hong Kong. Other books which address cross-cultural communication, or, as we prefer to call it, intercultural communication, focus on how communication works when two or more people from different groups are in communication with each other. In our own books we take this approach. For example, in Scollon and Scollon's *Intercultural Communication: A Discourse Approach* (Blackwell 2001, revised edition), which is addressed to both researchers and students in the field who are primarily interested in the analysis of intercultural communication, we lay out the theoretical groundwork for understanding how communication across cultural and social boundaries works. Pan's *Politeness in Chinese Face-to-Face Interaction* (Ablex 2000) focuses more specifically on how different situations within a single cultural group, Mainland Southern Chinese, are very different from each other and how, therefore, we must not make broad analytical categories such as "the Chinese" or "North Americans" in doing intercultural analysis.

Our focus in *Professional Communication in International Settings* is more practical. Here we are writing for the individual or organization that wants to begin to learn directly how to be a better communicator when engaged in professional work in international settings. This book grows out of research projects which were undertaken by the authors together with several other colleagues: "Professional Communication Across Cultures" (Yuling Pan, Ron Scollon, and Suzanne Scollon) and "Identity Claims in Oral Presentations" (Andrew Taylor, Becky Kwan, Ron Scollon, Suzanne Scollon, Vicki Yung, and Rachel Lai). Our purpose in these projects was to develop a practical method by which ordinary people who were actively engaged in professional communication could learn for themselves the most important aspects of intercultural communication that would be relevant to their own concrete circumstances. In our thirty years of experience as consultants, teachers, and trainers in intercultural communication, we have found that while it is very useful and interesting to give people a broad background in the theory and methods of intercultural analysis, in practical cases this analysis is not really very helpful. A person might know a great deal, in theory, about how a German businessman might communicate with an Indonesian counterpart or how a French-Canadian account representative might need to adjust culturally to work successfully in Brazil, but still not be able to bring any of that knowledge to bear on his or her own need to make a presentation of company products to a company in Denmark. The world is simply too complex for any book to even sketch an outline of all the things to be taken into consideration for each and every different situation a person might encounter.

Even if there were only a few cultures we needed to consider, the world is changing so rapidly that any encyclopedia that could somehow encompass all varieties of intercultural encounter would soon be out of date. One of us had a conversation with an architectural products representative on a flight from Chicago to Seattle just before this manuscript went to press, describing our research interests and the book. The person could immediately see the relevance and potential usefulness of our approach. She said that with the formation of the European Union many French people were having to use English to do business. One representative for an American cosmetic firm, a woman in her fifties, was not at all competent to make sales presentations in English. She had her daughter, who is fully bilingual, coach her in the niceties of presentation in English.

Not all of us are lucky enough to have a daughter competent to coach us in the many aspects of professional communication in this period of escalating change. What we have designed instead is something all of us can undertake. In the research projects upon which this book is based we have developed a method for cooperative and comparative exchanges of professional communication products – we call these *Communication Display Portfolios* or CDPs – which individuals or organizational groups can use to get the information they need directly from their counterparts without going through the lengthy and not completely effective route of extended intercultural training programs. This book, then, represents the outcome of thirty years of consultation experience as well as six years of research in Hong Kong, Finland, and Beijing, which was undertaken to specifically develop the method which we present here for the first time to a public reading audience. While we take a practical focus, our method combines critical and methodological approaches well established in the fields of cultural anthropology and interactional sociolinguistics and lends itself to discussions of communication theory. Thus, though designed for use by individuals and organizations, it is also suited for use in courses such as organizational communication, discourse analysis, applied linguistics, socio-cultural approaches to language, and of course intercultural communication and international business.

We attempt to overcome the ethnocentric approach of most textbooks written in English by referencing not only textbooks written in Chinese but also the work of Japanese scholars writing in English, looking at American business practices from a Japanese point of view. Of course these sources are very limited, which is another reason why we show readers how to go directly to the source of living people with whom they need to interact in their professional dealings.

Long before we imagined the projects on which this book is based, two of the authors taught what may have been the first university course using audioconferencing, computer communication, and videoconferencing some twenty years ago. Students in "The Social Impact of Instructional Telecommunications" spanned four time zones and over a thousand miles. They ranged from city dwellers sitting in a university conference room or computer lab to a rural teacher who rode an hour by snowmobile to the nearest village where she could talk over the phone and use a computer with a modem hook-up. We evaluated the use of these instructional communications technologies, finding for example that videoconferencing could not be effectively used until the speakers learned to make use of the visual channel when the audio channel failed. In chapter 2 we show that ways of using the telephone evolved over decades. Similarly, it will be decades before the use of videophones will be effortless and taken for granted.

Any project of this complexity owes much to many people. First of all we would like to acknowledge our gratitude to our colleagues on the research projects which have been the basis for the ideas presented here. Besides the investigators named above, we are indebted to Hu Wenzhong of Beijing Foreign Studies University and Liisa Salo Lee, formerly at the University of Jyväskylä, Finland, and now director of the Finnish Institute in Madrid, who as consultants on the Professional Communication Across Cultures project helped shape the research at three sites. Li Ming at Beijing Foreign Studies University was most helpful in all aspects of the project in Beijing, and Li Zhenyi of the University of Jyväskylä helped make contacts with Finnish business professionals and students. All of these people visited Beijing and Hong Kong during the course of the project to discuss procedures. We are further indebted to the focus group participants whose comments appear throughout the pages of the book, and especially to the professionals who offered material for the Communication Display Portfolios. Finally, none of this would have been conceivable without our assistants at the City University of Hong Kong. Cecilia Leung, the senior assistant on the project, and Beatrice Chan, who took charge of several concurrent projects, mobilized student assistants and worked out the format for the Communicative Display Portfolio, then edited, translated, and distributed copies to all three sites. Yvonne Tse summarized textbooks on nonverbal communication, conducted focus groups, and transcribed and translated comments that are part of chapter 5. Rachel Scollon pointed us to sociohistorical sources on telephone use and translated from Chinese sources. Natalie Richter furnished us with a case study of corporate communication, and Ulla Ladau Harjulin provided helpful insight and materials. Barbara Craig and students at Georgetown University tested parts of the appendices at a workshop on Presenting Across Cultures, and Barbara read a complete draft of this book. Anonymous reviewers provided helpful comments. While we are indebted to all of these people, the conclusions and recommendations are our own.

1

Analyzing Communication in the International Workplace

What's a Meeting?

Recently we attended a meeting of a professional association in Budapest, Hungary. Delegates from all over the world were present. A key point in the five days of meetings was the business meeting of the association, in which a rather delicate issue was discussed having to do with a conflict between a delegation from Israel and their supporters and another delegation sympathetic to Palestine and their supporters. Shortly after the meeting we met a colleague who is a Brazilian now resident in England. We asked about the meeting and she said, "Oh it was very good. There was a bit of discussion and everything was resolved amicably."

This conversation took place in the main hotel reception area. Our Brazilian colleague was called away to deal with something at the reception desk and another colleague, a South African, sitting close by said, "Were you at that meeting?" We said that we had not attended. She then went on to say, "It was terrible. They were shouting at each other and very threatening. If something like that happened in our country, they'd be arrested!"

Two of our colleagues had attended the same business meeting. One felt it was an outrage to sensible business meeting practices, that things had very nearly gotten out of control, and that, on the whole, the behavior of the delegates was very improper. The other felt that it was quite a good discussion and that a sensible conclusion had been achieved. Two people from very different cultural backgrounds attended the same meeting far from their own homes and together with many others from equally different cultural backgrounds. All of them were members of the same profession and yet their idea of how a meeting should be conducted was so different that they came away with very different impressions of the meeting and of their professional colleagues. One felt they had behaved very appropriately; the other that they had not.

Our purpose in writing *Professional Communication in International Settings* is to give the reader a useful means of learning how to survive in such a complex international environment in a very concrete and personal way. We want the reader to be able to discover through his or her own resources how to be most effective in such complex international settings, as well as how to interpret the behavior and communication of other colleagues in these settings most effectively.

There are many books on the market about cross-cultural communication or, as we call it, intercultural communication. Such books can be very useful in providing you with general concepts of how intercultural communication works and even give specific details for how people in different cultural groups approach such common business and organizational events as meetings. For example, in the case of this meeting in Budapest, it would be useful to know that Brazilian meetings can be quite chaotic from the point of view of, say, British people. A colleague in São Paolo told us recently that at meetings in his organization "everyone talks at the same time." He described a British colleague who has been in Brazil for almost twenty years, and yet at each meeting he waits patiently to get his turn at the floor, and as time goes by he gets more and more agitated until he finally just blows up and begins shouting quite angrily. As our colleague put it, "He still hasn't been able to understand how we do it."

In Rio de Janeiro we watched a "Meet the press"-style program on television. The norm for North American programs would be to have two or three guests and a moderator. We have seen French programs of this type with up to five or even six guests. On the program in Rio there were ten guests seated facing each other, five on each side of a U-shaped desk with the moderator seated at the top of the "U" facing the camera. There were two moving shoulder cameras as well to track the discussion. While at the beginning one or another speaker would talk at a time, within five minutes or so, there were many side conversations among the participants as well as two and usually three of the speakers speaking at the tops of their voices, even shouting at each other in a sequence so rapid that the moving shoulder cameramen could not track the exchanges of turns. Finally, as the program neared the end the moderator faced the camera and used exaggerated mouth and lip movements and nonverbal signals to conclude the program, because she could not be heard at all in spite of the fact that each speaker was wearing a separate lapel microphone.

If we *know* that a typical Brazilian "meeting" will consist of a lot of simultaneous speaking as well as a lot of side conversations, then we can easily interpret how one South African woman can describe a meeting as almost scandalously uncontrolled and yet a Brazilian woman can describe *the same meeting* as a "good discussion" with an amicable outcome. The problem arises when some people interpret simultaneous speech as "a good discussion" and other people interpret it as "very threatening." Of course it would be best if a person could simply know all of these particulars of how people in different cultural or even organizational groups are expected to behave. Unfortunately, very few people who are not research specialists have time to develop this rather complex body of knowledge. What is the ordinary business person supposed to do when he or she receives an assignment to go to Brazil, Indonesia, or Hungary, Hong Kong, Germany, or Egypt?

The Changing International Workplace

In this book we take the position that the international workplace is now so complex that we cannot solve this problem by just assuming that there are only two cultures involved in an intercultural interaction. After all, the case we have just mentioned involved a Brazilian woman who has lived for years in England, another woman who is a South African, and still other colleagues who were Belgian, Israeli, American, and Dutch, and the meeting was taking place in Budapest. Where would one find the book which could give simple guidelines for dealing with such levels of complexity? It would have to be an encyclopedia of cultural communicative behavior and then all one would have would be examples of pure cases, not the incredible mixtures of experience we see around us in our daily lives. The mixtures grow increasingly complex with migration of populations from continent to continent as well as increasing global trade, diplomatic, and nongovernment organizational contacts. The entry of Finland and other Scandinavian countries into the European Union, for example, has been viewed as shifting the balance from French to English. The development of new interpersonal communication technologies also makes the prospect of effective communication in international settings bewildering. We have yet to see the effect of the use of Chinese domain names on the World Wide Web.

We also believe that it is not a viable solution to try to standardize professional communication practices around the world. In preparing this book we have reviewed dozens of books on professional communication. While there is some very important and useful advice in such books, most of them take the mistaken view that it is possible to standardize professional communication. There are two problems with the idea of standardization we will elaborate in the following chapters. The first of these problems is that most of these so-called standardizations are not really attempts to develop an international standard that everyone can accept as workable. Instead, they are attempts to get everyone to accept the cultural and communication practices of one group of people as "the standard." Mostly, of course, these "standards" are simply the cultural communication practices of North American business people. For example, it is the custom among business people in North America to speak to each other on a first-name basis wherever possible. This gets translated in the "Dale Carnegie" tradition of "winning friends and influencing people" into the rule that you should always focus on learning a person's personal name and then use that name to address the person.

Using the practices of just one cultural or social group to try to standardize communication in international settings does not work simply because it can only be achieved by doing violence to very important cultural practices within other groups. For example, there are at least three options in addressing others in a business encounter: simple first name, as in many North American meetings; title plus first name, as for instance in Brazil; and title plus last name, as in Asian cultures. Many very successful business people around the world are insulted when they are addressed by their personal names and the sales representative who is going by the book is not likely to have even guessed that he or she is being insulting. Furthermore, practices change, so there is no way of knowing from books or past experience whether or not a given person will find being addressed by personal name insulting. For example, with the recent change in Japanese government policy of listing family names first in foreign publications, it will not be easy to know which is the family name and which is given.

There is a second and more practical reason why standardization does not work in international settings, and that is simply that there are too many players on the international scene now and no one group can be said to be in a dominant position. We know, for example, that the long insistence that the ability to speak English is enough to be able to work anywhere does not suffice, for the reason that there isn't just one *English*. There are many *Englishes* in use throughout the world, and the fact that one might grow up speaking "English" in Iowa is no guarantee that he or she will understand a word of a conversation in London's East End, much less in Sydney, Hong Kong, or New Delhi.

We believe that a really effective and practical approach to professional communication in international settings is the one we present here: we need to learn how to learn *directly from the people with whom we need to interact*. That is, we do not need to read a book on how Brazilians run meetings. If we are going to a meeting in Brazil, we need to learn how Brazilians run meetings from our Brazilian counterparts themselves and we need to learn from them how they perceive the way we do our meetings, whether we are Chinese, Australians, or Israelis.

The Communication Display Portfolio (CDP) Exchange

We can describe our method quite simply here, although it will take the rest of the book to make it clear why we believe this method works well, and how to actually begin to do Communication Display Portfolio (CDP) exchanges. Our method is to exchange best-case examples of one's own professional communications with counterparts in other countries, cultural groups, or organizations for reflective discussion and feedback. The purpose is to find out as directly as possible how significant counterparts perceive our own communications and to tell them how we perceive theirs, so that we can make whatever adjustments are needed to simply get on with the other tasks we are trying to accomplish. Our thesis is that successful communication in the international workplace requires a self-reflective understanding of the processes of communication.

To give an example, we could imagine that we have a small team of buyers based in Frankfurt who have established contact with producers of supplies in Guangzhou, China. The buyers will be going to China and the Chinese team will be visiting Frankfurt, as the relationship is expected to last over a period of at least several years. A traditional approach to the intercultural aspects of this program would be to provide training to the German team in Chinese communicative and cultural practices and also, if at all possible, to provide training to the Chinese team in German practices. Of course, this is already extremely idealistic in that it would be quite difficult to find effective trainers and training materials to conduct this training. We know of only a few experts who could work with German–Chinese intercultural relationships, and in those cases, their expertise is focused on Mandarin-speaking Chinese, not Cantonese-speaking Chinese.

Our approach, in contrast to this, would be for at least some members of each team to put together a professional CDP, which would include things already at hand such as product brochures, business cards, letters, faxes, and resumés and also, wherever possible, videos or other materials which would show how a meeting was conducted, or a sales presentation, or whatever other sort of communication might occur frequently in future exchanges. These CDPs would then be exchanged between the two teams. Each team would then conduct a "focus group" discussion of the materials from the point of view of their communicative effectiveness. That is, they would say what seemed confusing to them, what was missing, what seemed excessive or unnecessary, or whatever other adjustments might be needed to improve on their ability to understand. These comments and reflections would then be returned to the other team for them to consider and digest.

To give just one example from our own research projects upon which we have based this book, we found that a representative of a computer company in Hong Kong provided a very lengthy and detailed resumé which included all of his past employment and even information about his nonprofessional life and interests (see appendix 2). His counterpart in Beijing provided a very brief resumé that focused much more closely on a particular job assignment. Their counterpart in Finland did not provide a resumé at all. It was very clear upon reflection that these three counterparts – all of them were representatives of computer or other high-tech manufacturing companies – saw the resumé as a different kind of communication. One saw it as a way of making a rather broad personal introduction, another saw it as a way of presenting credentials for a specific task. The third, as we were to learn, felt that personal contacts were the most effective way to make self-introductions. As to credentials, he believed that other means – particularly third-person evaluations – were the best and most reliable way of handling that question.

Perhaps most important is that when the Beijing group saw the Hong Kong resumé they felt it was very exaggerated and they tended to mistrust the person because of the length of the resumé. Also both Beijing and Hong Kong participants were doubtful about the Finnish participant because a resumé was absent. This was taken to mean that he had no credentials which could be displayed. Once all parties were able to see these differences, however, and especially once they were able to see that the resumé was really serving a different function for each group, they were able to focus on those functions and set the resumé aside, as it was no longer so relevant to the question. Chapter 3 discusses the resumé in more detail.

From the point of view we are taking in this book we do not really care whether the differences participants find in CDP exchanges are thought of as cultural, national, or simply personal. In fact in our research projects the participants almost never mentioned cultural or national backgrounds, as we will describe in the chapters that follow. It does not really make any difference at all *how* the participants explain the differences as long as they come to see *that* their own practices and those of their counterparts are different, and therefore they are able to adjust their own practices somewhat to become more effective. If they find that their Finnish counterparts do not emphasize the resumé but feel strongly about third-person endorsements, they could focus on having some third-party person speak on their behalf. On the other side of it, perhaps the Finnish participants would feel that for the comfort of their counterparts a brief resumé might carry a lot of weight in establishing good relationships.

Our overall goal in *Professional Communication in International Settings* is not to tell the reader how to communicate in any particular setting. Instead our goal is to show the reader one proven way to establish good relations with colleagues in other settings and to begin the learning process together toward establishing their own best means of communicating. We believe that since each case will be largely unique, the best source of knowledge about how to communicate within that setting will come directly from the participants themselves. In a sense all that is required is that the participants become reflective about what they are doing and how, and the learning process can begin. We believe that the CDP is an effective tool for establishing the process of learning to communicate professionally in international settings.

Not only is social and cultural change occurring extremely rapidly in our contemporary globalizing business environment, but also technologies and practices for communication are changing so swiftly that the only way to stay current is to keep your eyes and ears open wherever you find yourself. Cellular phones, for example, are proliferating so fast that there has been time to conduct only a few studies on their use in professional settings. Our research, however, indicates that major changes are taking place in the ways people answer the telephone. With fixed-line phones the opening must focus upon the identification of *who* is calling and *who* is answering. With mobile phones the first primary question is more often *where* the callers are located. Just this simple difference makes most of the research and textbook manuals for business calls on telephone calls in business and private obsolete. Because of the rapid pace of change, we have made no attempt to provide analysis of current practice but rather concentrate on exemplifying the process of learning from one's associates. In Finland, though everyone owns a mobile phone, people use them only when necessary and would not think of bothering people with casual calls. Professional people go to lunch leaving their cell phones at the office so they can enjoy their meal in peace. In Hong Kong, on the other hand, one constantly hears people telling friends or family members where they are and where they are headed, and people are even scolded for not answering their calls quickly enough.

Though we collected messages sent by e-mail and fax in our research, these were not regarded as significant by any of our participants. For this reason we have not discussed these media in any detail. Rather than evaluating the use of particular technologies, we noted the attitudes of participants in different settings toward technology in general by paying attention to their comments on particular uses of technology. One Finnish professor of organizational communication, for example, refuses to use videoconferencing technology for lecturing at a distance. Instead, he combines slides of graphs and other visuals with audio presentation.

The Research Base

The field of intercultural communication is developing rapidly in tandem with changing international business alignments. As, perhaps, the world's largest undeveloped player, China's business potential is widely recognized. At the same time, with European unification, formerly less central business players such as Finland are taking on a much more significant role. Our own consultation and training projects, with companies including some of the world's largest mobile telephone producers, have shown a significant underdevelopment of the research and training literature on intercultural professional communication dealing specifically with Hong Kong Chinese and Mainland Chinese organizations. We began to try to address this lack while at the same time providing solid research support to professional training programs.

Many aspects of intercultural communication might have been considered. One of the problems with materials now available is that they cover too broad a range of intercultural differences, including religion and philosophy, table manners, or how to buy train tickets in a foreign country. All of this is interesting and important, but we wanted to focus more closely on situations which would be most useful for people involved in professional communication. We assumed that they could buy a standard travel guide to assist them with the more practical day-to-day matters of getting around, exchanging currency, or finding entertainment. Thus we focused on the problem of how professionals present themselves to others, both in first contacts through letters and resumés and in meetings and formal presentations. These contacts are being made by e-mail and fax as well as by telephone, fixed-line or mobile. The participants in our study did not notice differences in e-mail and fax communication. Nor did they comment on the use of mobile phones, though some of them worked for manufacturers of these products. Generally technology was not viewed in cultural terms but rather as a neutral tool for doing business.

Many of the crucial sites at which professional communication across cultures takes place involve formal presentations. In product presentations, contract negotiations, and many other such interactions it is important for members of one corporate or governmental group to communicate with people in another similar group. Details of presentation, from business cards and dress to the use of computer technology and gestures, as well as language, can affect the course of the interaction through participants' perceptions of each other's intent, confidence in their product or company, competence, or sincerity. Yet it is not easy for persons involved in communication to be aware of the reactions of members of another cultural group to their presentation style. There is a large body of research in this area which demonstrates that perceptions of how other people are performing are responses to subtle cues that are habitual and largely outside of conscious awareness.

For example, as we learned in our research, a Finnish participant's formal style was "read" by Chinese as too stiff and even as possibly incompetent. The Finnish participant delivered his presentation by reading a text, and we believe that he did so in order to show his sincerity and careful presentation. Nevertheless, the Chinese felt that only high-ranking officials who do not write what they read or people who do not know their material would read. A truly knowledgeable person should be able to speak directly to the audience without relying on texts.

This book is based on our research in many countries over the past decade. The research project upon which we will focus our central attention was designed to test the concept of the exchange of professional CDPs in three sites: Hong Kong, Beijing, and Jyväskylä, Finland, so that we could elicit perceptions of presentation effectiveness of each site in each of the other sites. We were trying to get answers to two main questions:

1 What do members of a corporate group select as crucial aspects of their self-presentations? That is, how do they present themselves when they are trying to put forward their best image?
2 How do nonmembers, especially those from another cultural group, respond to these presentations?

We asked members of corporate groups – in each case high-tech computer or communications companies – to develop CDPs, which were then comparatively examined and critiqued by corporate members within each of the three sites. This was to determine the corporate group's own self-assessment of their communicative image and self-presentations. Members of three unrelated high-tech corporate groups in Beijing, Hong Kong, and Finland were asked to prepare videotaped and textual documentation of some significant event, possibly an internal communication such as a meeting or an external communication such as a sales presentation or a negotiation. Corporate documentation such as memos, letters, product catalogs, or annual reports were added to these video materials to form a professional CDP of normal, day-to-day corporate communications. In focus groups and through interviewing, corporate members critiqued their own CDP indicating their own assessment of strengths and weaknesses. This was the first phase of the project.

In the second phase of the project, each of the groups sent their CDPs to the other two groups, and focus groups at each site viewed and evaluated the CDPs of the other sites. Summaries of the evaluations were then circulated to each site to elicit secondary responsive reflections and perceptions of these primary perceptions. Even though our focus in this book is on the use of the CDP for self-development and training across culturally different sites, we also found that the CDP was an effective tool for reflective self-analysis of the effectiveness of presentations even internally within the sites we studied.

The Three-Culture Reflective Model

In the international corporate environment, successful communication depends upon understanding how clients and business partners perceive each other's positions and interpret their messages. When businesses work across international or cultural boundaries, it is important to tailor corporate communications to the interpretive frameworks of clients, suppliers, and partners so that both contractual clarity and clearly projected corporate images can be achieved.

The methodology of our project was based on the classical interactional sociolinguistic method of recording actual instances of language use – real resumés, messages, videotapes or audiotapes of actual telephone calls, and presentations – analyzing that data, and then returning that material including the analysis to original participants for cross-checking. We have found, for example, that many of the most important insights come from this final cross-checking or "playback," when the original participants were able to discuss with the researchers their own interpretations of the situations in light of the researchers' analysis.

To this research method we added a further triangulation by having the data and analyses of each site cross-culturally compared in two other sites and then having the responses in those sites returned to the original locations. By adding this methodology to standard interactional sociolinguistic methodology, we believe we were able to provide a second level of perceptions which greatly enriched both the theoretical and practical training perspectives of this project.

Our methodology went beyond linguistic analysis. In international settings everyone is normally aware of differences in language, which are often handled through simple translation. Unfortunately, much research in interactional sociolinguistics and intercultural communication has shown that more often problems arise from aspects of communication other than language itself. As we will discuss in the chapters which follow, there are many features of communication that research has shown to set the stage for communicative difficulties. Among them are:

- body language, dress, tone of voice
- use of space, layout, and design of both physical spaces and publications
- the use of colors to reflect subtle impressions
- timing at the face-to-face level as much as the degree of punctuality in meeting deadlines
- the use of meetings for negotiation as opposed to ratification of already agreed positions
- leading with main topics as opposed to leading with social relationships
- talking vs. silence
- formal agendas vs. open discussion.

The purpose of this research project was to construct a productive environment in which self-assessment and self-reflection on these aspects of corporate life could be achieved without risk to either corporate or individual identity while providing researchers with rich direct and interpretive data. The three cooperating groups were chosen so as not to be involved in direct contractual negotiations with each other or to be direct competitors in the same markets. At the same time, by participating in the project, members of each group received support from the other two groups in contrastive self-assessment to enable them to increase their own capacity for reflective communicative development.

One of our goals in this project was to extend the scope of interactional sociolinguistic research to move beyond simple two-way comparisons and to enrich the crucial concept of contextualization cues to include nonverbal communication in its broadest sense. Research in interactional sociolinguistics has focused to a large extent on data of two types: (1) intracultural face-to-face social interactions and (2) bilateral intercultural interactions. By adding a third group we overcome the limitations of two-party comparisons. Contextualization cues are forms of metacommunication that tell the participants what kind of situation they are engaged in and how what they say is to be interpreted. Participants in sociolinguistic studies have been audiotaped and sometimes videotaped, with linguists analyzing transcriptions of what was said. What is noted on the written transcriptions tends to be the content of what is said, with some marking of tone of voice, pausing and interruption, and other paralinguistic aspects of communication. Intonation, for example, is a kind of contextualization cue that tells a listener whether the speaker is being ironic or serious. Differences in conventions or habits for using intonation often lead to misinterpretation of what people say. Only rarely have other semiotic systems such as proxemics, the study of how people use space, or kinesics, how people move in time, been considered.

Through triangulation we tried to overcome binary or two-way comparisons which easily lend themselves to the reinforcement of stereotypes, whether negative or positive or simply exotic. Through self-reflective analysis we felt we were able to bypass the narrow loop of external analysis by researchers, which is reported as "findings" in the literature and later gleaned by practitioners for application. Because of the time lag between the analysis and publication of results and the limited range of observations reflected in research reports, not to mention intervening social change, applying research literature can be of limited value, as we have suggested above. There is also the danger of misapplication if the context in which data is gathered is not taken into account, especially if commonly held stereotypes remain.

Personal vs. Professional Knowledge

Our colleagues from Brazil and South Africa reacted to the meeting we described in the opening of this chapter on the basis of perceptions that grew more out of their personal than their professional knowledge, though both play a part in making people from the same country react to a situation in ways that may not be shared by colleagues from another country. Although all are in the profession of studying how people communicate with each other using language, in the business meeting of the organization they were acting as human beings, not as professionals reflecting on their communicative practices. In the international business meeting, participants were discussing the affairs of the organization in light of their own personal views shaped by their nationality, ethnicity, gender, religion, political orientation, and other factors.

We believe that it is important to keep in mind that there are two orders of knowledge: one which we might call "human knowledge" and another which we can call "the institution's knowledge." The first of these is the basis of all of our interpersonal relationships. From birth we have been getting to know people. First we have come to know those who are most like us, normally, because these are the people who bring us into the world and nurture us into our first habits. In due time, however, we begin to learn the institutional order of knowledge through formal institutions such as churches, clubs, schools, and employers. As two of the authors (Scollon and Scollon) have said in the book *Intercultural Communication: A Discourse Approach*, our human knowledge derives from being members of groups that are based on who we are, where we are born, our gender, who our parents and immediate intimate relationships are, the age or period of our birth, and so on. Because we have little or no choice of these identities, at least initially, these memberships are largely involuntary. By that we just mean that they are presented to us as "given," though, of course, we often do much to try to change aspects of this form of personal background knowledge. We take up this question of personal knowledge again in chapter 3.

In contrast to these involuntary memberships, our memberships in institutions are voluntary. They are governed by purposes – the institutions' purposes and our own. We join a company to earn a living. The company exists to make a profit. From this point of view, institutional knowledge is dominated by these goals and motives. We join international professional associations which have goals which may differ from those of our company. Our behavior as members of voluntary groups is largely conditioned by our socialization as members of involuntary groups such as family, church, class, and nation, though we may not be consciously aware of the sources of our responses to the communicative behavior of members of different involuntary groups.

In professional communication it is sometimes crucial to separate personal knowledge or human knowledge from professional or institutional knowledge, though the unconscious, taken-for-granted nature of knowledge embodied in habits formed as members of involuntary groups makes it difficult to distinguish. In families or neighborhoods we assume we know who is married to whom and how long they have been together. Although people move about a lot more than they used to, associates at the workplace often act as if they have access to the same sort of personal knowledge about their professional colleagues, though they may in fact be quite mistaken. A friend of ours has been married for decades to the same man, but not everyone in her office knows this. When a bouquet of flowers was delivered to the office with a card saying "from your first husband" and her husband arrived to meet her for lunch, office personnel took great pains to conceal the flowers. They felt it was necessary to protect the husband, her one and only, from embarrassment. It is comical if you know that the man was playing a joke, and the incident reveals how much personal information is assumed to be shared by co-workers in an institution, in this case an American university.

Expressions of love are often mingled with professional communication in the workplace, whether in the corridors, over the phone, or on the Internet, and employees are not always careful to monitor their personal communication in the office, although some workers have to be circumspect in using e-mail on the job. Thus an e-mail message with the subject header "I love you" and an attachment carrying a potent virus was automatically opened by countless office workers in the United States, shutting down operations for hours. It is difficult to determine how many clicks on this attachment were automatic, how many were made by workers expecting a message from their loved ones, and how many were cynics knowing any virus shutting down company computers would give them paid time in which they could not work.

In professional communication, whether dealing with e-mail, having meetings, making phone calls, or preparing documents or presentations, it is necessary to decide how much personal information to include. This judgment is difficult enough to make within a familiar cultural setting, but when crossing national, cultural, or other boundaries, one's behavior becomes highlighted, especially if it is inappropriate. Having others react to one's communication is essential in facilitating critical self-reflection.

The C-B-S Style

Whether it is personal or professional, many people expect information to be presented in a clear, concise, and sincere manner, what Lanham, a professor of English at UCLA, calls the clarity-brevity-sincerity or C-B-S theory of composition. He traces this theory of rhetoric to Aristotle, but points out that composition texts are always full of contradictions. He says, for example, that, "Students of style are bombarded with self-canceling clichés, giving 'a quintessence' published in the last century" (Lanham 1974:16). He seeks to get beyond these exhortations: "Anyone who dips into The Books soon sees that their advice runs to a dreary sameness. Yet successful prose styles vary as widely as the earth" (Lanham 1974:17). Lanham is writing about prose style, but we would say that any form of professional communication has styles that vary "as widely as the earth" as well.

In this book we first give a "quintessence" of guidelines for business and professional communication. Our reason is not so that readers can follow these guidelines. Quite the contrary: our purpose is to show just how difficult it is to follow these "essential guidelines" in daily practice. That is, we go through what the "experts" say about professional communication style. Then, we show by using examples from our research how styles vary widely across the earth. We conclude as Lanham and many others do: "No absolute norm of 'clarity' prevails" (Lanham 1974:34), "For clarity is not any single verbal configuration but a relationship between writer and reader" (Lanham 1974:32). Whether talking over the phone, sending e-mail, preparing a resumé or presentation, or meeting face to face, clarity in communication depends on being aware of the requirements of the audience, not necessarily on being brief. Our method of exchanging CDPs helps us to pay attention to the participants in professional communication who are most likely to resemble the ones the reader of this book will enter into relationship with.

In Scollon and Scollon's earlier book (*Intercultural Communication: A Discourse Approach*) the development of the C-B-S style was traced to the ideology of the Enlightenment of the seventeenth and eighteenth centuries. There they developed the argument that this C-B-S style represents the preferred style of what they call the utilitarian discourse system. This is the dominant communicative system in the business and governmental world, which began with the Utilitarian philosophers but is now seen wherever Euro-American utilitarianist values are present. Clarity and brevity demand that the speaker or writer answer these questions: Who? What? When? Where? Why? How? For our purposes in this book, we critique the idea that communication *must* follow these norms. We will try to show how while they may once have seemed appropriate, changes over the course of the last century have made them questionable. In order to sort out to what extent people assert this ideology and to what extent they follow the C-B-S style in professional communication, we take different perspectives on communication in various international settings.

Four Perspectives

In our research and in this book we approach professional communication from four different perspectives. These might be outlined as:

- *members' generalizations.* This is what the members of a group say they do. Of course, people will often tell others, especially researchers, what they believe they should say or what they think others want to hear.
- *the objective or neutral view.* This is what an uninvolved or external observer would say about the behavior in question. Normally some form

of objective record is made, such as a video/audiotape recording or a photograph.

- *individual case histories.* This is what an individual member of a group will say he or she does. Quite often this is very different from the members' generalization.
- *contrastive studies.* This is a comparison with how people in other groups do the same thing, and could also include a contrast between the analyst's explanation and the member's explanation of a particular behavior.

Members' generalizations (what the members of a group say they do; another term for this might be "conventional wisdom"). Members' generalizations may be found in many places. For our research on this book we found these in textbooks on professional communication, in in-house style sheets and other policy and procedures manuals, and in what people would say about their own corporate or organizational practices. This is the sort of statement you find when a textbook on professional communication says, "It is most effective to always state the 5 Ws – Who, Where, What, When and Why." Throughout the world of organizational communication, as we will show in chapter 2, it is emphasized that effective communication is *clear*, *brief*, and *sincere*.

The objective or neutral view. Our own research and the research of many others has shown that there is often a huge gulf between what members of a group *say they do* or *say they should do* and what they actually do. Many researchers call this distinction the difference between a normative (or prescriptive) view and a descriptive view of behavior. Organizational personnel handbooks are filled with the normative or prescriptive view, but only experience within the organization will tell the new employee what one should really do to succeed. In questions of international communication we have found it is extremely important to distinguish between what people say they do and what they actually do.

Individual case histories. One reason both the normative standards of members' generalizations and the objective findings of research are ignored in actual practice is that each individual knows that much of what one does is highly idiosyncratic and allows for a display of individuality and personality within the corporate environment. This perspective keeps alive the concept of pragmatic flexibility and individual creativity, and shows how in many cases what is supposed to work (members' generalization) or what is theoretically right (objective view) has little relevance in the day-to-day complexity of successful communication.

Contrastive studies. Finally, it is most important to realize that what may seem natural and logical in one cultural or corporate environment is interpreted very differently in other environments. Simultaneous and energetic talk is both the norm and the practice in Brazilian meeting environments, though we know that our colleagues from Brazil are able to shift into British practice when they are in those environments. What is important to know is how one's own behavior is being interpreted by others. That is the only basis upon which we can build a choice of communicative action. Contrastive studies are the best means for learning how the same action can be interpreted very differently in different settings. Our main goal in this book is to provide the reader with a practical means of developing his or her own contrastive perspective on professional communication.

We believe that all four of these perspectives are very useful in coming to understand communicative behavior. It is essential to know not only what people are doing but what they think they are doing. When what they are doing conflicts with what they think or say they are doing, we need to be able to understand this conflict as well. Our strategy in what comes in the following chapters is to bring in observations, examples, and analyses from each of these four perspectives to try to produce as broad as possible a view of professional communication in international settings.

Nonverbal Communication: Conflicting Members' Generalizations

To illustrate these four perspectives, we first summarize what textbooks on business and professional communication say about nonverbal communication; these present the conventional wisdom or members' generalizations. Because this is also a textbook on professional communication, the familiar format may mislead readers into thinking we endorse these guidelines. As we said above in describing the three-culture reflective model, problems in international communication often arise from different conventions of nonverbal communication as well as from differences in language. Such guidelines constitute members' generalizations, in other words generalizations agreed upon by experts who conduct training seminars and write textbooks, most of them in the Anglo-American tradition. Because they have been widely translated into most major languages, they have the appearance of universality. Further, because of the hegemony of Britain and the United States, they are uncritically accepted around the globe. People naively believe that American business has flourished because American business people follow these guidelines.

We will use the other three perspectives to show that these generalizations, while familiar to everyone who reads books about or has had training in professional communication, represent the ideology of a particular group.

Outside of the United States, the same society in which Dale Carnegie wrote his books, these assumptions about communication are not widely shared. Though professionals in Beijing or Finland may express some of these maxims, what they actually do is at variance with some of this very same conventional wisdom. They also evaluate other professionals not according to this conventional wisdom, which arises from another tradition, but according to the conventional wisdom of their own social, cultural, and historical circumstances. We must take these guidelines, therefore, with a grain of salt.

Here is what the textbooks say you should do:

1 Use space for successful communication.
   (a) The person seated in a position to have eye contact with the most people should be able to exert the most control or power.
   (b) Rectangular tables are best used in conference rooms when there will be a designated leader controlling the discussion.
   (c) Round tables encourage equality of participants.
2 Use time for successful communication.
   (a) Some people may perceive the failure of another person to keep appointments promptly as a personal insult and an indication of irresponsibility.
   (b) Some people rarely arrive at the appointed time and this may convey the impression that the person being waited for has higher power.
   (c) Interruptions are a part of the use of time and may also be interpreted in terms of power.
3 Plan your physical appearance to affect communication favorably.
   (a) It is best to avoid fashion extremes in a professional setting.
   (b) Jewelry and other accessories should not distract from the message or impression the speaker intends to convey.
4 Use appropriate gestures and other body movements.
   (a) People use gestures or body movements that reinforce the content of verbal messages.
   (b) People also use body movements and posture with energy that can indicate meaning without using any words at all.
5 Use touch with caution.
   (a) Touching another person may have a decidedly positive or negative impact in communication.
   (b) Avoid any touch that may be perceived as coercive and an unfair use of status or power.
6 Use objects with caution.

(a) Speakers frequently use objects as an extension of their gestures in making a forceful statement or in pointing to something.

(b) Accessories in the office may communicate status, just as accessories on a person influence the perception of a listener.

7 Understand what facial expressions reveal.

(a) Affect displays may be a form of self-disclosure.

(b) Facial expressions should reinforce the content of the message of the speaker.

(c) The most important aspect of facial expression is eye contact with others.

8 Use appropriate voice and paralanguage.

(a) Paralanguage refers to the way the speaker uses vocal inflection, vocal quality, and the rhythms of language.

(b) Use the pronunciation that most educated people use.

These rules of thumb or members' generalizations are so general and vague that it is difficult to know just what they might mean. To gain a more objective or neutral view, we and our associates have videotaped professionals interacting in different settings and analyzed these videotapes for non-verbal elements of communication. This provided a second perspective. To take just the first item, the use of space, we have many videotapes of people sitting around both rectangular and round tables.

For the third perspective, individual case histories, we asked people how they arranged seating. Though round tables are said to encourage equality of participants, one of our Chinese colleagues said that sitting at a round table reminded her of family dinners where children were expected to be silent. One of the authors regularly went to a restaurant with members of a group that practiced *taijiquan* together in Hong Kong, and was told by group members that the leader of the group preferred the seat of honor in the corner of the room. Though all the tables were round it was obvious that he, like many patriarchs, controlled the conversation. In this setting it may be true that the person in the position to have eye contact with the most people should be able to exert the most power, but the textbooks we have consulted do not consider the social roles of people outside of the particular situation. In most cases, they assume that professional communication takes place in conference rooms with typically only one rectangular table.

This leads us to the fourth perspective, contrastive studies. The different reactions of individuals to the same spatial arrangement led us to compare how members of different groups communicate around round and rectangular tables. Our colleague who said that round tables reminded her of family dinners declared that she and her friends would not talk when seated at a round table except to the persons right next to them. She found in analyzing focus group discussions held in Hong Kong that people would not speak to strangers. In presenting her findings to European colleagues she found that they had very different norms for communication around a round table. That is, she found that members' generalizations were different depending on whether they were European or Hong Kong Chinese.

Four Situations

In this book, we cannot deal with all aspects of the use of space, time, physical appearance, body movement, touch, use of objects, and facial expression. Therefore we restrict our focus to the use of these means of nonverbal communication in common business contexts where our focus groups raised them as issues in discussion. Voice and paralanguage are salient in telephone communication as well as oral presentations. The use of time and space are significant in meetings as well as in oral presentations, as are gestures and facial expression.

In order to make our discussion as concrete as possible, we have chosen only four rather typical contexts in which professional communication takes place – the telephone call, the resumé, the presentation, and the meeting. Of course we realize that there are many other situations, such as business lunches and dinners; there are business letters and other forms of correspondence (e.g. e-mail, fax); there are business cards, and literally hundreds of other types of documents, reports, and events. Our purpose is not to provide full coverage so much as to show how the reader can think about and analyze typical environments of professional communication.

We begin in chapter 2 with a consideration of the telephone call from four perspectives. First, we begin by bringing an additional historical perspective to bear on the members' generalizations found in commonsense views of how to make phone calls in textbooks on professional communication. We argue that commonsense views are holdovers from the era when primitive phone technology necessitated brief, clear, and loud speech. Like the QWERTY keyboard (with letters on the third row of a keyboard laid out as QWERTYUIOP from left to right), these tenets of effective communication are no longer the most effective means. Using neutral, objective recordings of phone calls made by participants in different businesses, we contrast individual case studies and our own analysis of phone calls with the interpretations of these calls formed in discussions of audiorecordings among participants in different geographical settings. Our comparative perspective suggests that there is no universally accepted way of speaking on the phone either as a caller or as a respondent. In light of conflicting views, individuals can only resolve for themselves what is most likely to work in their particular circumstances by observing and interacting with those most like the people they will be communicating with in their daily work, and getting other perspectives on their own communicative behavior.

Chapter 3 begins by pointing out that even though the resumé has become a fixture in our lives – it might be something to be tinkered with, but not eliminated – there are many people alive today even in industrialized nations who seldom or never read or write resumés. This is true even where those industrialized nations are proud of their cutting-edge information communication technologies. The resumé (or curriculum vitae, as it is still known in English outside of North America) has no agreed-upon standards for how to present information. Again we take a historical and comparative perspective to critique the members' generalizations or conventional wisdom found in dozens of books and word-processing wizards offering guidelines for writing resumés. Because this genre is relatively new and the demands of the international workplace are in such rapid flux, even the conventional wisdom contains contradictions. There are also contradictions between the generalizations of members of focus groups about their national or cultural tradition and what they say they do or strive to do.

Data from our case studies demonstrates that not only do the form and function of the resumé vary across professional and national settings, but whether or not they are used at all cannot be taken for granted. Within the world of transnational computer manufacturing companies operating in Hong Kong and China, standards of length, focus, categories and their order of presentation, and details to be listed vary widely. Correspondingly, specific resumés or objective records were evaluated quite differently not only between but also within different sites.

A major point of contention was the inclusion of personal in addition to professional information. Focus group participants in both Hong Kong and Beijing insisted on the value of personal details such as age, gender, and recreational interests, though these were not included in the resumés presented for discussion. As we found in the dispute over identifying oneself over the telephone, which we discuss in chapter 2, there are broader considerations having to do with geopolitical circumstances. In the case of using the telephone these were considerations of trust and security which vary from city to city, while in the case of resumés there are legal considerations which make the presentation of personal information problematic in the United States and other western countries. In China, on the other hand, there are no legal constraints on personal data as such, but the listing of chronological details of work and residence reminds contemporary people of the social and political demands of the Cultural Revolution (1966–76), which makes the chronological resumé distasteful. The functional resumé that emphasizes personal achievements seems to present difficulty to Chinese, who are disinclined to brag, in the same way as preparing a resumé at all is problematic for many Finns.

The conflicts over how much personal information to divulge and how to best present one's professional accomplishments underscore the differences between conversations and documents as ways of communicating on the one hand and between personal or human knowledge and institutional information on the other. In telephone calls as well as resumés there is a tension centering on how much information to volunteer, not only in the way of verbal disclosure of names and institutional position but also in nonverbal cues such as voice quality and pitch, or photographs that may provide clues to gender, age, or ethnic identity. It is these details of professional communication that bridge personal human lives and institutions that often fall between the cracks when national boundaries or other sociopolitical factors separate professionals in the business of communicating. In order to compensate for the interacting participants' lack of years of shared history, we have developed the CDP exchange.

In chapter 4 we turn to a discussion of the presentation, which has evolved with changing technology since Dale Carnegie taught Americans *How to Win Friends and Influence People* over sixty years ago. In our contemporary world, presentation styles that vary as widely as the earth are being homogenized through the use of standardized presentation technology.

Though Windows 98® offers a wizard that helps users make successful presentations using PowerPoint®, it is difficult to follow the advice of maintaining eye contact when the audience's eyes are focused on the screen covered with PowerPoint® slides. Here we have a competition between information conveyed by the person of the presenter and the professional or institutional information which is projected on the screen.

We review several American sources which are widely used overseas on making presentations in business and professional organizations. We summarize the features of the "friendly American style" which was outlined by Carnegie and is still considered essential for successful presentation, especially the feature of maintaining eye contact with the audience. The introduction of visual aids complicates the direct interaction between presenter and audience. Because the presenter must manipulate the machines which are producing the images, and in doing so divide his or her attention among visual aids, speech, and audience, his or her movements are constrained by the technology. A Chinese textbook on public speaking adds to this the relationship of the speaker to his or her material as well as the knowledge the audience has of the material. Besides these considerations are the relationships among speakers presenting at the same event and between them and the organizers of the event.

From place to place relationships among participants, materials, and presentation technologies as well as complex verbal and nonverbal styles vary. Some presenters use effusive gestures and facial movement but others are very still. Our research shows that people negatively evaluate presenters that violate either the unarticulated norms of the social group that is viewing the presentation or the standard norms repeated in textbook after textbook. Because of the contradictions between assumptions and practice, we believe that the most effective way to get useful guidance on how to prepare presentations is through feedback obtained in an exchange of Communication Display Portfolios.

Finally, chapter 5 rounds out the study of four types of professional communication with a discussion of meetings. As we indicated at the beginning of this chapter, these take different forms and are judged differently by professionals from various international settings. We take a functional approach to meetings. Even though they are an inevitable part of professional communication in international settings, meetings take different forms which are shaped by the functions emphasized by the social group that holds them. A meeting can be primarily a place where group members exchange views on issues that arise in conducting their business, or it can be primarily a means of developing group cohesion and team spirit. Whichever function is viewed as primary, social relationships and relative positions among participants are always negotiated and ratified.

We summarize studies of American, Japanese, and Chinese business meetings to add to our opening comments about Brazilian meetings, in order to illustrate some of the different assumptions about how to conduct a meeting and how to behave as a participant as well as to illustrate the complexities that arise when these assumptions come into conflict. For example, these studies, conducted by Chinese and Japanese researchers, highlight the unusual nature of American bank meetings, which are shown to operate according to C-B-S ideology, with speaking turns allocated according to a rationale of egalitarian division of labor. In contrast, Japanese bank officials seem more concerned to create a nonthreatening environment within which consensus can be reached. Personal ties assumed more importance than setting or following an agenda, resulting in a looser, less restrictive conversational structure than in the American meeting.

An analysis of a negotiation between an American expert and a Japanese telecommunications corporation shows the tension and frustration that can arise out of significant differences in assumptions about the function of business meetings. Both functions of exchanging information effectively and establishing good social relationships are important in organizational relations in Japan and America, but Americans give information exchange priority within the boundaries of meetings and relegate maintaining social relationships to casual encounters and other social events.

Chinese organizations achieve these functions in a manner that differs from either the American or Japanese norms exemplified by meetings of small groups of bank officials. In the government and bank meetings analyzed by one of the authors (Pan), the primary role of speaking was neither to develop rapport nor to allocate speaking turns equitably but to ratify power relationships in discussing and announcing decisions. According to our research, the display of official status before, during, and after meetings appears to be much more prominent in China than in Japan or the United States. However, this impression may arise just because we are more familiar with studies in China than elsewhere. As we said in comparing Japan and the United States, the display of status and other social relationships among professionals in America takes place largely outside of meetings and has been comparatively little studied. An exchange of CDPs may reveal that functions that seem exaggerated in other societies are dealt with by ourselves in ways we simply have not paid attention to.

These contrastive studies, which make use of objective analysis by outsiders as well as members' generalizations, demonstrate that the tension between the display and exchange of personal and professional or institutional information in different settings is resolved differently in different societies. The existence of different forms of power and different ways of displaying status and authority make communication in international settings complex indeed. We present a detailed analysis of phenomena found in official meetings in Beijing which would be recognizable to officials and business professionals anywhere on earth.

We end chapter 5 with an individual case history and focus group discussions recorded among professionals in Hong Kong that illustrate conflicts in perceptions of how meetings should be conducted. We feel that the linguistic, social, political, and cultural complexity of a city like Hong Kong gives a good illustration of the difficulties and also the rewards of taking our approach to understanding communication in intercultural and international settings.

The Communication Display Portfolio

In chapter 6 we give a brief summary of the four chapters in which we have presented analyses of specific types of presentations. These chapters all point to the same conclusion: successful communication in the international workplace requires a self-reflective understanding of the processes of communication. We recommend the use of the CDP as a tool for self-assessment to be exchanged with counterparts from other cultures, nations, organizations, or professions. We present the language audit as a part of an individual's CDP as well as a communicative profile of the salient ways of functioning within an organization. This may be useful, for example, for a Chinese businessman who has just taken a job in a Norwegian corporation and needs to know which aspects of his job will require speaking or writing in Norwegian, English, Mandarin, Cantonese, or other languages and how his skills match the job requirements. Phone calls may be more difficult than face-to-face or written communication in Norwegian than in his first or second language, as visual cues cannot compensate for what he lacks in words and tone of voice.

As the final chapter, chapter 6 provides a detailed outline of how to produce a CDP and how to set up a CDP exchange, with a discussion of important issues to keep in mind and possible difficulties in following the outline based on our own experience in our exchange across three cultures. We then enumerate the items in the appendices, which start with a checklist called "The Communication Display Portfolio Exchange Planner." This is followed by a handbook that we have used in training personnel to conduct a CDP exchange. The third appendix provides suggestions on carrying out a CDP exchange. We provide suggestions on using these appendices for various readers, whether trainers, professionals, researchers, or students.

This book has been written to enable the reader to increase shared knowledge between himself or herself and peers in international settings, by suggesting ways of exchanging concrete examples of communication and reflecting on them. In this way differing perceptions can be discussed before they interfere with effective communication. The CDP exchange emphasizes relatively nonthreatening ways of increasing shared knowledge across the boundaries of nations, languages, professions, organizations, and the many other entities that shape the way we communicate.

Chapter 2 deals with a technology (telephone) everyone either loves or hates or both. It illustrates our basic approach to analyzing communication, narrowing the focus to one universal medium, the audio channel. Chapter 3 focuses on a printed document (resumé) whose use arose in the latter half of the twentieth century and is changing with the use of the Internet. Chapter 4 focuses on gestural elements of communication in conjunction with new technologies of presentation. Chapter 5 presents detailed research findings on an elusive phenomenon, the meeting, and illustrates different approaches to eliciting information in focus group discussions.

Readers who want to find out more about the theoretical and methodological bases of our approach will find useful sources in the lists of further reading and references, especially the revised edition of *Intercultural Communication: A Discourse Approach*, by Ron and Suzanne Scollon (2001). The present book concentrates on the practical aspects of enhancing information exchange and increasing self-awareness. If we are successful, most readers should not have to read every page in order to accomplish this purpose, nor should they need further reading material.

2

The Telephone Call: When Technology Intervenes

The "Common Sense" on How to Make Business Calls

It is almost impossible to find a textbook treatment of business telephone calls which does not say that the caller should have his or her main point(s) in mind before calling – usually jotted down on paper by the telephone. It would be hard to argue with this in principle; of course, it is always common sense to be prepared before talking to clients and other customers. These same books will also say that you should state your purpose or open your main topics immediately so that the person called will know why you are calling. This is the conventional wisdom, which is just one perspective that we argued in chapter 1 needs to be supplemented by other perspectives in order to be effective in international settings.

We will show in this chapter how limited this commonsense view is in a world where companies serve immigrants from several regions and professionals deal internationally with multiple technologies in tandem with phone calls, including faxes, e-mail, pagers, and voice mail. We argue that the norms articulated by textbook writers grow out of the limitations of early telephone technology and may not always be appropriate. With mobile telephones proliferating and restructuring phone communication practices, textbook advice on making a phone call may be as outmoded as instructions for writing a business letter a century ago. Rather than offer advice, we provide objective illustrations of a few of the many kinds of calls made by professionals in Hong Kong and show how they were evaluated there, in Beijing, and in Finland, in order to show the reader how to find out for themselves what people think is appropriate telephone behavior by obtaining contrasting perspectives. The common sense offered in textbooks is partly a result of early technology that has been greatly improved on and partly an outgrowth of a population that takes as natural the C–B–S style of communication we introduced in chapter 1. We describe situational and relational as well as cultural differences which affect the use of the C–B–S style. In short, telephone practices are governed largely by technology, situation, type of relationship, and cultural practices. Conflicting norms can only be discovered and resolved by observing and engaging in interaction with the people with whom one needs to do business.

The procedures set forth in textbooks on international business communication are based on a kind of utilitarian principle which emphasizes clarity, brevity, and sincerity in style. Along with this C–B–S style goes what two of the authors of this book have called "the deductive presentation of concepts" in an earlier book, *Intercultural Communication: A Discourse Approach*. The "deductive presentation of concepts" means you present your main points at the beginning and then follow this with your arguments, explanations, and clarifications. This can be contrasted to an *inductive* presentation, which would begin by warming up or softening up your listener before coming to your main points. Of course, we know that often when the topic we wish to introduce is a difficult or embarrassing one, this is exactly how we will proceed. If we want to borrow $300 from a friend, we are likely to avoid bringing up our reason for talking to her until we see how she feels. This would be an *inductive* approach, and all the standard texts on communicating in business tell us to avoid being inductive.

To give an example, Bateman and Sigband's book, *Communicating in Business*, stresses the theme of speed and efficiency in telephoning. Under the heading of sending calls it has the following (1989:260):

> Here are some hints for effectively initiating calls:
> **Plan**: Prepare your calls just as you would outline a letter or memo.
> **Identify**: Immediately give your name, your organization, and your place (if long distance).

When they write about receiving calls, Bateman and Sigband say (1989:260):

> Because there can be a direct relationship between the calls received and sales, it is important to handle incoming calls courteously and efficiently.
> **Promptness**: Answer quickly; people don't like to wait while the phone rings or to wait long after being placed on hold.
> **Identify**: Quickly indicate who has been reached.

Of course the question of identification is rather different with mobile telephone calls, where the crucial question is not usually *who* has been reached – mobile phones are usually personally owned and carried. The question is *where* the known person is located.

Bateman and Sigband do not actually say anything about the issue of the topic at this point in their book. Earlier in the same book, however, they make it quite clear that the first principle of successful communication in their view is knowing and being able to state your purpose in initiating the communication. That is, they strongly emphasize *deductive communication* throughout their textbook. To their credit they not only say that one should always overtly state this purpose as a topic, they further clarify that there are multiple means of arranging one's points, including deductive, inductive, and chronological orderings.

One further consideration is that this textbook treatment of telephone calls says nothing about how to disconnect and get off the phone. We believe that this indicates that they see nothing of interest in ending a telephone call. This was not always the case, however. In the 1920s there was some discussion about who should end the telephone call, the caller or the receiver. It seems at that time it was felt it was best for the caller to close a call, unless the receiver were a woman, in which case she should signal the end. In any event, there were no specific instructions about how this should be done. Perhaps this reflects an assumption that all that really needs to be taught regarding telephone calls is two things:

1   know your purpose in calling, and
2   be quick in getting to your main point.

A second textbook, Jones and Alexander's *International Business English*, also takes this business-efficient utilitarian view of the process of telephoning. Students are advised (1989a:28):

make sure your call is BRIEF, and
make sure that you sound EFFICIENT.

In the workbook that accompanies the first text, students are asked to fill in the blanks on the following entries (1989b:17):

1.   State your name and your _____ in the company slowly and clearly.
2.   Make sure you're talking to the _____.
3.   Say right away what you're calling about, the other person shouldn't have to _____ this or work it out.
4.   Be _____, remember that the other person may have other things to do than talk to you on the phone.

We can assume that the blanks are to be filled with something like "position," "correct person," "guess," and "brief," respectively. The point of this exercise, of course, is to emphasize the main features of the deductive tele-phone call. As in the case of the Bateman and Sigband textbook, as well as many others, there is no consideration given to the endings. Again, we believe that the absence of any advice about endings indicates that the authors see nothing particularly teachable about how telephone calls should be ended.

The practical skills presented in textbooks such as these treat business telephone calls as unexceptional social events with clear, learnable struc-tures. Furthermore, they treat the person of the caller (and the receiver of the call) as equally unexceptional and unproblematic social entities. The grounding assumption is that the only issue at stake is language – learning the wordings in a new language for accomplishing taken-for-granted tasks. As we will discuss below, as soon as we think of several different types of business calls or as soon as we consider making telephone calls across lines of nations, cultures, and histories, or even across lines of personal differ-ences, many of these commonsense ideas about how to use the telephone evaporate and we are left not knowing what might be the most appropriate way. We will begin this reconsideration by looking at the history of how the telephone entered into our business worlds.

Hello?

A Canadian notice in 1896 had these instructions on using the telephone:

> To Listen: Place the telephone fairly against the ear, with an upward motion, so that the lower extremity or lobe of the ear is gathered in, into the cavity of the telephone; in this position it will be found to fit snugly and comfort-ably – the lobe of the ear acting as a cushion and at the same time closing out all ulterior sounds, thus enabling the voice to be heard with clearness and precision. (Fischer 1992:70)

The telephone is so much part of our lives now that we can hardly imagine that there was a time – not so very long ago – when users had to be told how to use the telephone. Not only that, the technology was so bad by present standards that we were told to jam our ears into the earpiece so that we could receive the wonderful benefits of this new technology. Even the word "hello" is so common now that we do not realize or remember that it was the telephone that gave us the need to have this regular formulaic phrase to use in answering it. It has not always been so. A winning essay in *Tele-phone Engineer* from a 1910 contest began:

Would you rush into an office or up to the door of a residence and blurt out "Hello! Hello! Who am I talking to?" No, one should open conversations with phrases such as "Mr. Wood, of Curtis and Sons, wishes to talk with Mr. White . . ." without any unnecessary and undignified "Hello's." (Fischer 1992:70)

Before the telephone, "hello," a variant of "halloo," was associated with shouting to urge dogs on, to call attention, or to express surprise. Thus it was natural for someone surprised by the loud ring of a bell to respond "hello!" Chinese, Koreans and speakers of other languages use a similar interjection ("wei" in Mandarin Chinese) to attract attention and begin telephone conversations. For example, in Beijing we heard a shop clerk berate a customer for shouting "Wei!" at her: "We're not in the village!" She apparently also felt the telephone opener was undignified. A Dutch phone book printed in 1925 admonished, "In case of a call, one says his name and does not shout 'Hallo.' The call should be answered immediately" (Houtkoop-Steenstra in press).

Communication in international settings is highly technological and depends vitally on information and communication technology, what some analysts now call ICT, such as the cellular telephone, PDAs (organizers), internet, and e-mail. Successful communication depends on being able to use this technology *as technology*, but more importantly, it depends on being able to use ICT in ways that are *culturally* and *socially* appropriate for specific situations. Naturally, this is the difficult part; we probably all have known how to use the telephone since we were children. One recent research project showed that children know all the routines of picking up the receiver, saying things into it, and hanging it up – sometimes angrily – long before they know that there should be another person on the other end speaking. In fact, when a "real" set of telephone booths were set up for these children to use so that they could actually talk to another person, they would look at the other booth first to make sure there was nobody else in it, so that they could do their own routine without being bothered by what somebody else would say.

We realize that many of our friends and colleagues do not act much differently from these children on the telephone or at meetings – simply saying whatever is on their own minds, and not paying any attention to what others are saying – but we will work with the assumption throughout this book that effective communicators *do* want to know two things:

1 what others are saying to them (in a meaningful way, that is, not just the words but the real intent), and
2 how to speak to others so that their own meanings are clearly communicated.

Being clear about our own meanings and understanding those of others depends not just on mastering the technologies, especially the new media technologies, but also on learning how those ICT are being used by others who have different social, cultural, or personal histories from our own. This is the central problem of professional communication in international settings: we cannot take it for granted that our own ways of doing things carry the same meanings for others who have different histories and backgrounds.

In this chapter we will show how the things we take for granted about telephone use are really quite specific social and cultural products. To put this another way, we will give examples from history and from our own research that show that many of our ideas about how to use the telephone, such as being brief, clear, and stating your purpose at the very beginning, are actually the historical outcomes of the poor technology of the telephone when it entered into the workplace. We were encouraged to use the telephone briefly and politely, for example, and then these "proper" ways of using the telephone rapidly spread along with the use of the invention within English-speaking industrial countries. Now with new telephone technology, many of these so-called commonsense ideas are not really common sense at all. In fact, they go right against common sense and in the world of new ICT they need to be revised.

From this we conclude that the best way to be effective in using the telephone and the other new ICT in international settings is to begin to set aside our most common assumptions about how we *should* communicate and to examine what people actually do in real situations. This will show us that actual practice is a more effective learning environment than prescribed procedures. In other words, the most effective place we can go to learn about communication in international settings is those settings themselves. To do this, we follow John Dewey's axiom:

Learn to do by doing.

The C-B-S "Business Style" and the Telephone Call

We now use the telephone without thinking how we learned to do it. We are quite accustomed to requiring service and training contracts for new ICT packages when they are being installed in our businesses or government offices, but we have largely forgotten that when the telephone was first introduced, people required very explicit instruction on how to use it, as this quote from a social history of the telephone points out:

Through circulars, ads, and notices on telephone directories, companies instructed subscribers on the operation of the machine. In the nineteenth century companies advised customers first to turn the crank three times and then to lift the receiver, and in the twentieth century to lift the receiver, put their fingers in dial holes, turn clockwise, and so forth. (Fischer 1992:70)

The first official guide of the Dutch Bell Telephone Company in 1881 instructs users that on hearing the bell "one takes the telephone off the hook, pushes it against the ear, makes clear he is present, and listens" (Houtkoop–Steenstra in press). A Californian instruction warned, "Speak directly into the mouthpiece keeping mustache out of the opening." Other notices cautioned users to answer promptly, speak directly into the transmitter, avoid banging the receiver when hanging up, and so forth. A notice run by the Pacific Telephone and Telegraph Company showed the profile of a man's face with his lips an inch away from a primitive mouthpiece. Headed, "Speaking Directly Into The Transmitter," the notice advised:

> The transmitter of the telephone is the result of years of study and experimentation by telephone engineers. It is of delicate adjustment and its fullest efficiency can only be obtained through proper use.
>
> The lips should not be more than an inch from the transmitter, and the voice should be clear, not loud.
>
> Speak distinctly and directly into the mouthpiece. This will mean your satisfaction and that of the person with whom you are talking. (Fischer 1992:162)

This notice reminds us that, in spite of the years of engineering that went into the development of this remarkable machine, it was in fact primitive by today's standards and required a delicate adjustment of frequency and volume for efficient transmission. Users who did not understand the principles of sound engineering would instinctively speak louder, just as we speak louder to children or foreigners who do not seem to understand the inconsequential things we say. In the early days of telephones, some businessmen and professionals refrained from using the instrument because it did not allow for quiet conversation. One observed, "A telephone caller had to shout as if he were speaking to another person 80 feet away."

With today's technology it is not necessary to pay particular attention to diction in order to be understood over the phone. In other words, we do not need to speak with exaggerated clarity but can speak normally, as if the person being addressed were a few feet away in the same room. But because of the imperfect technology, early phone users had to be instructed to speak clearly and distinctly but not loudly, directly into the transmitter. In other words, because of imperfect technology, phone professionals sought to cultivate a style that would compensate for the shortcomings of the machines. That style of clarity, brevity, and sincerity is now taken for granted as ordinary or acceptable business style. That is, it is advocated as the way to communicate with business associates, not only over the telephone, even though technology and society have changed so that there is no longer any need to unquestioningly follow this style.

When telephones were installed in new territory, the instruction in the business style of C–B–S was transported along with the technology. In a book published in Hong Kong on the art of conversation (Jin Ren 1940), the author instructed the reader on how to make a phone call, making the following points:

- The telephone user should not yell loudly over the phone.
- He/she should speak slowly and clearly.
- The user should avoid aimless chatting, stick to the business of the call, and refrain from prattling about personal matters.

These instructions on telephone use were based on the belief that the telephone line was a place for the purposeful, quick transmission of information, not a children's playground or a women's hairdressing salon, and that the user should establish brisk, straightforward business habits when using the telephone. About the same time, in 1935, a Dutch author wrote, "One does not answer the telephone with 'Hallo,' but mentions name or telephone number." The reason given was in keeping with the C–B–S style: "in order to prevent loss of time, and in case of a wrongly dialed number, to give the caller the opportunity to put back the receiver and disconnect."

When Bell invented the telephone, his goal was to facilitate the transmission of information and increase labor productivity. He did not anticipate that the introduction of this new technology would have such a great impact on social interaction and interpersonal relationships. Before the telephone, communication channels were either face to face or in writing. Telephone technology introduced a new channel for communication from which followed new social practices. Because the visual channel was missing, callers and receivers had to develop means of identifying one another and assuring each other of their goodwill. This was especially true when switchboard operators were replaced by mechanical equipment. People who would refrain from rude language to a human operator would make all manner of unconscionable utterances to receivers they could not see.

Telephone companies began to undertake not only mechanical but also social education to deal with the complaints of profanity, yelling, and abuse over the telephone registered by many industry people. Through notices, direct chastisement of customers by employees, and occasional legal action, the companies sought to improve telephone courtesy. AT&T distributed cards labeled "The Telephone Pledge," to be attached to instruments and reading, "I believe in the Golden Rule and will try to be as Courteous and Considerate over the Telephone as if Face to Face." Companies cut off service to abusers and obtained legislation that fined or even jailed profane customers.

Telephone etiquette was thus elaborated from the standard uses prescribed by the telephone companies. People were told to use good manners on the telephone, to employ such general courteous phrases as "Please" and "Thank you," in part to compensate for visual assurances of goodwill and the perceived rudeness that might be brought on by what seemed like shouting. According to Martin (1991), at first AT&T actually wanted to suppress "hello." They considered it to be vulgar. Obviously this suppression didn't work. Martin notes that AT&T turned around and even referred to its operators as "hello-girls."

Receivers were instructed to answer calls promptly themselves, in order to avoid making the other party wait for them, and to apologize when they did make callers wait. This was necessitated by the nature of the technology, first because available lines were limited and also because the caller could not see what the answerer was doing, whether he or she had registered that there was a call for him or her, and how long it would take the person to walk to the telephone.

Now of course where the call is placed to a cell phone it is assumed that the person called will have the telephone somewhere close on his or her person. A new impatience is setting in where callers become frustrated by an answer that takes longer than three rings. Even greater annoyance is expressed about those who turn off their cell phones. With fixed lines we could assume an "always-on" status of the telephone and so could interpret no answer as meaning there was no person within the space in which the ring could be heard. A turned-off cell phone signals a person who does not want to communicate – quite a different assumption than simply that the person is elsewhere or otherwise occupied. These matters are further complicated by answering machines and services, which many now use as buffers to determine whether or not they wish to be contacted.

Feminist scholars see the earlier standards as prescribing behavior considered normal for business men, as the following passage shows:

> Failure to follow telephone etiquette was seen as a matter of gender, as women were presented as the main offenders in terms of telephone manners.

Operators reported that women callers "have an exasperating way of asking, 'Who is this?' when some one answers their call whose voice they do not recognize." "Girls" were accused of unduly using their employers' telephones during business hours. (Martin 1991:159)

The telephone introduced a measure of time consciousness that was not universally welcomed. It was considered a "nerve-racking" technology because of its capacity to intrude on privacy at any time, and anxiety was increased by injunctions to answer the phone promptly. With time the usefulness of the telephone in doing business began to be taken for granted, and companies started to expand the range of phone contact by exploiting the use of the networks by women who made social calls that annoyed their employers. Companies began to emphasize personal contact in addition to the use of the phone to optimize efficiency in business communication. Ads like the following became common:

The Southwestern Bell Telephone Company has decided that it is selling something more vital than distance, speed or accuracy. . . . The telephone . . . almost brings [people] face to face. It is the next best thing to personal contact. So the fundamental purpose of the current advertising is to sell the company's subscribers their voices at their true worth – to help them realize that "Your Voice is You," . . . to make subscribers think of the telephone whenever they think of distant friends or relatives. (Martin 1991:76)

There is always a relationship between an ICT technology and common practices for the use of the technology. Many people are familiar with what has been called the QWERTY phenomenon. The original reason for this layout was because of the technology of the early mechanical typewriter. Keys which are frequently typed in sequence had to be separated physically so that they would not jam with quick typing. In English "Q" is always followed by "U," and so these two letters had to be placed away from each other, preferably where typed by two different hands. With that layout it was possible to achieve relatively high typing speeds without having the typewriter keys get jammed on the platen.

Of course the QWERTY layout became entirely irrelevant as soon as the electric typewriter with the rotating ball was invented. In fact, the QWERTY layout was then really an obstruction to faster typing. This is because the QWERTY keyboard was not optimized for the human hand. Keys which are very frequent, such as "a," "s," "w," and "o," as well as the full stop (.) and the comma (,), were located under the weakest and least mobile fingers of the hand. A number of alternatives were invented and it has been said that the world speed records for typing have all been set on non-QWERTY keyboards. So why do we continue to use it? The reason is simply custom. A new layout would require everyone who now knows how to use the QWERTY keyboard to learn another pattern, and it would require changing all of the textbooks and computer software packages now in existence for teaching the QWERTY layout. Most users of keyboards resist the days or weeks of retraining it would take to make the change, and the loss of productivity during the changeover time. So the keyboard remains the same, even when it is not the most efficient way of entering text with our new word-processing technology.

All of the authors learned to type on mechanical typewriters before these changes took place. Ron Scollon was a clerk-typist in the US Army and learned to make originals with five carbon copies on mechanical machines. He still bangs away at a delicate laptop computer keyboard as if he were making five copies with each stroke. The power of technology to transform our practices is sometimes very weak in relation to the power of custom and habit to make the technology suit our conventional ways of doing things.

The same could be said about sound recording and amplification. The vocal style of the "crooner" popular singers, such as Frank Sinatra, Bing Crosby, or Perry Como, was based on having to sing in large music halls with either no amplification or very bad amplification systems. This meant that singers had to learn to sing with a loud voice that would project to the back of the hall. Studies by anthropologists have shown that, naturally enough, we use a soft voice in speaking within an "intimate" distance – that is, when we speak to someone very close to us in space – and a loud voice in speaking across longer social or formal spaces, such as when we are speaking to a large audience. Now that audio amplification systems for sound recording or for concert performances are of very high quality, a singer can whisper as if into the ear of a lover and be heard by hundreds or even thousands of people as singing very intimately to them. Of course, the old group of singers retained their earlier style, even when the technology allowed a completely different use of sound technology.

As we have shown above, this same process has occurred with the telephone. First, before the telephone, the telegraph was a very limited ICT and messages had to be extremely brief and succinct – "telegraphic" is often used to describe this type of "telegram language." When voice transmission became possible with the telephone, it was already influenced by "telegram language," and the norm of clarity and brevity was continued because the technology was quite poor in its ability to transmit the full sound range of the human voice. Telephoners stood the risk of sounding rude with their shouting.

Thus norms of politeness were introduced to mitigate this rudeness – say "hello," say "goodbye," and the like. Wherever the telephone first developed widespread usage in business, principally in North America, England, and parts of Europe, these "norms" which were required by the low level of technology became standard, conventionalized business practice, much like the QWERTY keyboard has become the standard layout for keys.

Our telephones now are very sophisticated and mobile. We can speak in easy, conversational voices in almost any physical setting to people all over the world. Nevertheless, we see people shouting into their telephones and following the C-B-S rules as if it were the original Bell telephone they were using. Ironically, it is in the places where telephones first developed that telephone use is most conservative and conventional. In rapidly developing countries where telephones are relatively new, people have been able to "leapfrog" over the period of bad technology and in many cases are bringing the new telephone technology straight into existing social practices without having to adopt the C-B-S style.

In figure 2.1 we illustrate how there has been a constant restructuring of our technologies and of our styles of communication. First, the crude technology of the telephone transformed the ways in which we communicated because it was difficult to get messages across low-quality transmissions. This required clear, brief, and often loud styles of communicating. This C-B-S style then became thought of as the *typical* business communication and was enshrined as the *right way to communicate* in all business settings. Again and again, each new form of technology has taken the old style and reshaped it into a mix of old and new to produce a "new" style, which has then been taken as the norm for successful communication. As we will argue below, throughout the world, many people have not come to the telephone through the old, low-quality technologies that have produced this history of the telephone, but have first been introduced to contemporary, high-quality instruments working across high-speed and high-quality lines and satellite transmissions. There is no need for them to alter their traditional communication styles, as the quality of the technology makes it possible to simply speak conversationally.

Client or Colleague?

Successful professional communication in international settings depends on mastering the technologies of communication which we have at our disposal. New ICT have the possibility of opening many new ways of communication but also carry with them a load of conventional uses. We still

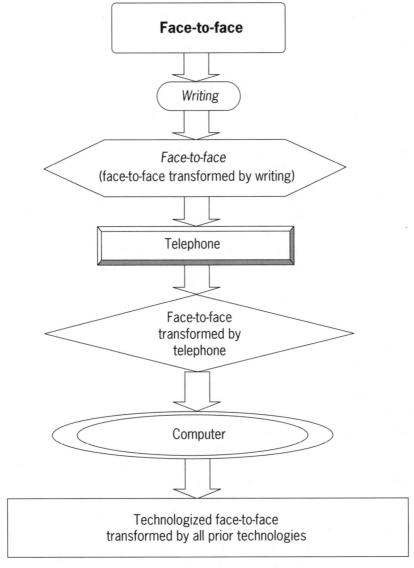

Figure 2.1 Technological transformation of communicative style

teach the C–B–S style of communication in business textbooks as if it were international law, when the new ICT has made these conventional ideas about communicating as awkward and out of date as the QWERTY keyboard. This means that one of the first areas we need to re-examine in international communication is the use of ICT. We need to learn how we can exploit the resources of this technology to improve communication on the one hand, and to learn what we need to discard in conventional communicative styles which had their basis in the old, low-level technologies on the other hand.

Even if we approach this question from a completely different direction, we find we come to the same conclusion: all telephone calls are not the same. Not even all business telephone calls are the same. In a series of studies, one of the authors (R. Scollon) found that the so-called C-B-S style was only used in what he called "client calls." For example, in Ron Scollon's study of telephone calls in the Hong Kong offices of an international bank, a European bank officer used the C-B-S style when he was talking to one of his clients, but when he was talking to a colleague in another bank – still a business call – they developed a very different structure for their telephone call, which went against everything said in business and international communication handbooks. Ron Scollon decided that a basic distinction needed to be made between at least two types of business telephone calls, what he called client calls and what he called colleague calls. These two types of calls were constituted through very different activities which produced contrasting structures.

To summarize this work, client calls proceed much as the practical textbooks tell us they do. Immediately after the initial channel has been set up through such means as the ring of the telephone, the answerer saying "hello," and the identification sequences, the reason for calling is introduced. Analysts have called this the "anchor point." This is the point right at the beginning of the call but just following after opening up the channel and identifying the speakers. This is where the topic is expected within the classical C-B-S telephone style. In a client call, that is, when the caller and the answerer are in client–provider service roles, the client call then proceeds directly through the business at hand and concludes with no unrelated deviations from the purpose for calling.

In stark contrast to such client calls, in the colleague call the significant business dealt with at the anchor point is *not* the caller's reason for calling. When the caller and the person called get to this anchor point, they do not begin to talk about the purpose of the call, they focus on establishing their personal relationship. This is where they chat about visiting relatives and other incidental topics. Only after a period of such nonutilitarian chat do they come to the reason for the call in an almost offhand manner. Following completion of the reason for the call, they then return to such non-purposive talk as trying, and most often failing, to arrange to have lunch together.

What shows up most clearly as a contrast between these two types of telephone calls is that in the client telephone call the social identities of the participants are taken to be entirely instrumental and utilitarian. In the client call, one calls to transact business; there is no further social relationship to be pursued. On the other hand, in the colleague business telephone call, the social identities of the participants are socially foregrounded as the main point of the call; the business which is transacted is backgrounded. The call serves to constitute and to legitimate the social network within which the participants identify themselves. It is important for us to emphasize that "colleague" calls are also business telephone calls. We believe our data shows that as much business is conducted among "colleagues" who have regular business and personal relationships as between strangers in the strictly client relationship. In fact, many calls are a mixture of these two types. One calls a "colleague," or someone one knows and has a good relationship with, for the purpose of conducting business with him or her. None of these calls follows the advice and rules given in standard business textbooks on telephone communication.

Without going into a lot of detail about that research project, one other point should be brought up, and this has to do with closings of telephone calls. If we think of the business call as the client call, there is really no reason at all to pay attention to the end of the conversation. Once the business is done, the callers have no reason to talk to each other again and can simply hang up. This is certainly the impression one gets from a review of the standard textbooks on business and international communication.

Nevertheless, the telephone call in business is compounded of both utilitarian and social needs. The telephone call is a social activity that reflects the social practice of paying attention to the social relationships between the callers, whether this is as clients or customers or as old friends or colleagues. If we assume that nearly every business telephone call has consequences for the future relationship between the callers, then the closing of the telephone call is extremely important. We know this when somebody says, "I don't know what happened; he just hung up on me." This suggests that the person saying this feels he or she has been rudely treated. The close of any social interaction is the time and place where we tell each other both how we have felt about the interaction we are finishing and also what our expectations are for the next conversation. How we say goodbye on the telephone tells the other how we expect to continue our relationship in the next meeting.

In our research we have found that closings of telephone calls are as important as the openings. They follow a particular and regular pattern. First the callers bring their "topic" to a close. This can include many kinds of comments, but normally this will be a summary of the main points or agreements made. Then they bring their relationship to a close. This usually means that they say thanks to each other. Finally, they bring the telephone channel to a close. This is almost always with the word "goodbye." In the same way as the colleague telephone call opens up with an extended period of time when the callers talk about personal matters, it closes with a return to such personal matters. Most often this is a formulaic discussion of meeting to have lunch or to have a drink. It is interesting that in most of our data, the callers never actually make a firm agreement for a time and place to have lunch. "Having lunch" seems to be more a formula for saying, "I have found this chat with you enjoyable and would enjoy doing it again sometime such as over lunch." It seems to be focusing more strongly on the relationship than on the utilitarian topic.

From this research we can see that, in the first place, the standard textbook formulas for how to make a successful telephone call are really based on an outmoded and conventionalized set of practices that have more to do with the low level of early telephone technology than with anything that comes out of business or communicative necessity. We use the C–B–S style for the same reason we use the QWERTY keyboard; it's conventional and that's "our" habit. This is not really how telephone conversations work in our contemporary world.

In the second place, we have now shown that even within rather conventional settings – business telephone calls in a banking office – there is no single way of making a telephone call. We have only analyzed two different types of calls, the client call and the colleague call. Surely readers will be able to describe many different types of calls that depart from the model of the business communication textbook. What is important for professional communication in international settings is to know that *there is no one standard way of making a telephone call*. There is no standard of efficiency or of politeness. The only way we can really know what is the best way to speak on the telephone is to study our own practices and those of others to see what we actually do and what effects this has on others with whom we are doing business.

How to Study Actual Practices

As we have described in chapter 1, the authors conducted a research project over several years in which we compared business communication practices among three primary sites – Hong Kong, Beijing, and Jyväskylä, Finland.

We also included, of course, surveys of "normal" business practice in North America and Europe as a background against which to reflect this research. Our goals in this research project were not to directly analyze what people did so much as to analyze what people thought about what the business people from the other sites did. That is, we did not want to make an objective analysis from our own point of view but an analysis of the participants' subjective views of each other. Our purpose in doing this was to try to discover how, for example, Finnish business people responded to the communicative practices of Hong Kongers and of people from Beijing. Then, in turn, we wanted to know how the people in the other sites responded to the comments on their own practices. This model of CDP exchanges has been described briefly in chapter 1 and will be developed further in chapter 6 and in the appendices.

As part of this research project, we studied three telephone calls made by one Hong Kong professional in different business contexts. These three calls differ in internal structure and in the use of "face strategies" because of the differences in perceived social relations and situations. That is to say, callers treated each other with different levels of politeness which were not absolute (the same in all telephone calls), depending on how they saw the particular telephone call. Much as we have just said above, we cannot in practice assume that there is simply one way to make a telephone call, but we have to look into each separate situation to see what people do and how others respond to it.

Following, and repeated in appendix 2, are three telephone calls made by an IBM networking representative in his office. These calls were recorded by the representative as part of his professional Communication Display Portfolio (CDP). That is, the first thing we need to notice is that this IBM representative included these telephone calls in his portfolio because he felt they represented his best practices. Of course, the names of participants have been changed to protect their confidentiality. The three calls were originally in Cantonese. They are transcribed and translated by the authors. The following conventions have been used in presenting the transcription:

01   The number before each line indicates the turn taken by the caller (only the caller's speech was recorded).

italics   Words in the conversation in *italics* were said in English by the participant in the original.

_____   A long dash represents indecipherable speech.

Telephone Call 1

Eric is an IBM networking representative making an inquiry call to a retailer asking about the price of a product.

01   Hello, may I ask, is this CEC?
02   Yes, excuse me. I have something that I want to just *check check*. Do you have ____ ?
03   I need one with BMC on one side and UTP on the other.
04    $1100 each? Wow, that's so expensive, so . . .
05   Oh, oh, wow, that's very expensive. Do you have anything less expensive?
06   No? I really need BMC to transfer . . .
07   Yes, yes.
08   Have to use ____ ?
09   OK, then. That's alright. Well, thank you anyway. *OK?* Oh, *bye-bye*.

Eric is a customer. He did not identify himself at all throughout the conversation. He spoke at a very fast rate and used an exaggerated exclamation: "Wow." He did not make much use of politeness strategies in his call. In other words, this telephone call departs from the basic principles of politeness and of self-identification normally given in business textbooks.

Telephone Call 2

Eric is an IBM networking representative calling his client.

01   Hello, good morning. May I ask if Frank is there?
02   Oh, he is at a meeting. I'm with IBM networking. My name is Eric Fung. Do you know when he will finish the meeting?
03   Oh, OK. My number is 91308894.
04   Eric Fung.
05   Yes, ah. Is Tim there?
06   Has gone to the branch office. Then, then, maybe, can I bother you to ask him to return my call?
07   OK, thank you. Thanks! *Bye-bye*.

In this second call, Eric identified himself at the second turn. He used an appropriate opening remark to ask for the person being called. He repeated the information given to him by the other party (lines 02 and 06). In the closing, he thanked the other party twice and said "Bye-bye" to close the conversation. In this case, Eric is conducting the sort of call most often described and what in our research we have called a client call.

Telephone Call 3

Eric is an IBM networking representative making a call to a customer for after-sale service.

01 Good morning. May I speak to Carrie?
02 Hello, Carrie.
03 This is Eric from IBM networking.
04 I'm calling to *confirm* with you. You connected your computer yesterday, and are now running *World One Image*, right?
05 Then this afternoon about three o'clock, we, Tom, William and I will go to your place, then . . .

06 Oh, *OK*, OK, OK. We hope we can fix it this afternoon. In *worse case*, if we can't finish it, we will bring all the stuff back and ask our *overseas expert* to fix it. Actually, *for your information*, I *sent* a *fax* yesterday to make inquiry. He asked me for *return code*, and things like that, because I didn't copy it down last time. But they said it is *unlikely* that the *system* has *problem*. It's most likely the *configuration* has some problem, so . . .
07 Yeah, we hope that is the problem.
08 Yes, yes. We also found something. We'll go to your place to try some *scenario* first.
09 OK, we'll see you in a while.
10 OK. Thank you. *Bye!*

This call followed the standard structure of a business call. Eric used a polite greeting phrase to open the channel. When Carrie answered the phone, he immediately identified himself and stated the purpose of his call. Then he explained the procedure of their visit and what he was going to do to help the client. The telephone conversation is more elaborate.

All three of these are business calls, but they differ in the degree of business contact. In the first call, there is no established business contact. It is an initial business call, or what we might call a one-time only call. It is brief, and sounds a bit "rude." The second call is to an established business contact, a client. It is more polite. The third one is to a client who has already bought their service. This is a potential long-term business contact.

These three calls differ in the opening, the self-identification, and the elaboration of details. With a one-time-only call, the caller did not identify himself. He used "Hello" and "May I ask" to open the channel. With an established business contact, the caller used "Hello," "Good morning," and then "May I ask" to open the conversation. He then stated his name and company to identify himself. The caller switched between the two codes of Cantonese, which is the local language in Hong Kong, and English, which was the official language in the colonial days until 1997. All three calls ended with "OK," "Thanks," and "Bye" as the closing remarks.

We were able to obtain two sets of views on these three telephone calls. Our Hong Kong focus group participants commented that the first call sounded a little rude and that the use of informal exclamation expressions sounded quite unprofessional in conducting a business call. The second and third calls seem quite standard business calls. Nevertheless, the focus group participants showed understanding of this difference, because there are different types of business relationship involved. In the first call, the caller is a customer calling a retailer for a price quote. In the second and third calls, the caller is speaking to customers.

The caller himself gave the same explanation for his different treatments of the three calls: the difference in the type of business relationship. He said he felt he had to be careful with his customers. Offending customers might result in the loss of revenue. On the other hand, when he himself was the customer, he did not feel any need to concern himself about whether he sounded rude or polite. He said he did not have to show much courtesy. Another reason he gave is that, in the first call, he was checking a price quote for a computer part, which just involved a small amount of money, a few thousand (Hong Kong) dollars (equivalent to a few hundred US dollars). To him, that was a very minor matter. When calling his customers, on the other hand, he was selling a whole computer network, which involved a huge amount of money ("a few hundred thousand or a few million dollars"). He commented that this revenue-generating politeness was the basic principle for the use of face strategies when making business calls.

From this we conclude that in addition to the ICT or technology used in telephone calls, and in addition to the situation of being a client, a customer, or a colleague, the actual amount of business or the importance of the business is another significant factor to take into consideration in producing the structure of a telephone call. We cannot say to what extent this utilitarian approach is due to the high levels of stress in Hong Kong society. Perhaps it is because of the fast-paced and crowded business environment that business people do not have time to attend to the niceties of every business contact. Company personnel are concerned mostly with those business contacts that are part of a continuous relationship. Thus they use different business styles when dealing with long-term and short-term clients. That is why Eric showed such a difference in his attitude when making these business calls. What is important is not what causes these differences in style. What is important to realize is that many factors enter into shaping the structure of a telephone call – technology, differences in the situation or the relationship, or differences in the financial or other significance of the event.

Our Beijing focus group participants reacted differently to these three business calls. They said these calls were too "business-oriented." They felt they lacked "personal feeling," because the caller went straight into talking about business. That is, they did not like the *deductive* nature of this telephone call. They felt the pace was too fast and that the conversation was uncomfortably brief and abrupt. They commented that the fast speed and direct topic introduction gave the impression of a cold, "business-is-business" call. Although they themselves sometimes receive these no-nonsense calls, they do not appreciate them. To these people, who are mostly in the same business, the caller sounds busy, indifferent. They said that he "didn't care whether the other party was listening or not," "didn't try to get the attention of the other side," and "didn't have any emotion." They concluded that this was the Hong Kong style, which represented a busy, modern society that lacked interpersonal interaction and close relationship. Business is the ultimate goal, the be-all-and-end-all, of such a society, in their view.

The respondents in Beijing also showed a strong reaction to code-mixing between Cantonese and English in these calls, but they thought it was acceptable for Hong Kong people to use mixed codes among themselves for historical reasons. That is, Hong Kong was a British colony for 150 years and returned to China only in 1997. Nevertheless, it would have been considered annoying and unacceptable for these Hong Kong Chinese to use mixed codes in speaking to Mainland Chinese, because it might indicate a feeling of superiority over the local Chinese and create distance in interpersonal relationships. Beijing focus group participants thus made a distinction between the behavior in an inside (among Hong Kong Chinese) relationship and an outside (between Hong Kong and Mainland Chinese) relationship.

The crucial point in the focus group discussions is that telephone practices are associated with sociohistorical developments and cultural practices.

Some practices may be acceptable in one society, but offending in another. People also allow situational variation in their telephone manners and adjust their linguistic and politeness strategies in telephone calls in accordance with business contacts and social relationships. These variations can be caused by business volume, types of business contacts, types of interpersonal relationship, and closeness of the personal relationship.

Cultural Differences

There are not only situational and relational differences but also cultural differences in how to make telephone calls. Telephone calls, like any kind of verbal interaction, are governed by cultural norms of language use within a given society. Some phrases and expressions are natural in telephone conversation in one language, but are expressed in different ways in another language. It is rare that direct translation of certain set phrases and expressions from one language into another without cultural adjustment is seen as appropriate telephone manners.

One of the authors (Pan) has consulted with an American telecommunications company, monitoring the professionalism and politeness of their sales representatives. The training manager of the telecommunications company was trying to get their Chinese-speaking sales representatives to use markers of politeness such as the equivalents of English "Please" and "Thank you" in making their sales pitches. The sales representatives were rated on a scale of 0 to 3 on whether they used these politeness markers at every possible point in the conversation where it would be appropriate in American English. They got 3 points if they did this in a "natural" manner.

On the first day of the monitoring, 6 calls made by three sales representatives were monitored and all rated 0 points. On the second day, 6 calls made by three other sales representatives were monitored, 4 calls rating 0, and 2 calls getting 1 point. On the third day, 7 calls made by 4 sales representatives were monitored, 3 calls rating 0 points, 2 calls scoring 1 point, and 2 calls getting 2 points. All the sales representatives monitored during that week failed in their performance evaluation. The irony in all this is that most of them succeeded in signing up their customers for the company's service. That is, they were awarded 0 points when their performance was entirely effective in terms of actual sales. The evaluation of "performance" was based not on sales but on an aspect of language.

In many languages, including Chinese, it is not customary to use expressions like "please" and "thank you" in daily conversation. These terms are used mostly on very formal occasions. In conversations politeness is indicated by prosodic factors such as tone of voice, intonation, or rate of speech, with appropriate pauses and other discursive features. In fact, to use politeness expressions such as "please" in informal situations sounds quite ironic, sarcastic, or like a put-down. This is much like when a mother might tell a child, "Clean up your room *if you please!*"

It was obvious that the telephone sales representatives were very resentful of the manager's explicit instructions. The calls that were monitored were very polite by Chinese standards and resulted in signing up customers for service. Yet by the manager's rating scale they received 0 points.

As we have shown in our study of the history of the C–B–S style in telephone and business conversations, the use of such general courteous phrases as "Please" and "Thank you" has been historically thought to be good manners on the telephone in American society. But in Chinese society, in which the telephone was not available to common people till the 1990s, telephone conversation style is similar to face-to-face interaction, with an emphasis on close personal relationship and the use of positive politeness strategies. In Chinese face-to-face interaction, the use of "Please" and "Thank you" enlarges, instead of closing, the social distance between the participants. When used excessively in sales talk, it sounds fishy and gives the feeling of setting up a trap to get customers to buy the service. In other words, these "politeness" formulas have a largely negative effect. That is why Chinese sales representatives refrain from the frequent use of these formal phrases when making sales calls. But they did occasionally use a polite phrase at the closing. The training manager operating out of an American English standard insisted that employees follow the instructions and use the expressions at every possible chance. In the guise of "professionalism," employees were being pressured into speaking in ways that seemed unnatural. "That's too much!" protested one woman sales representative. "Mark me down if you like."

Sales representatives were also asked to identify themselves as soon as they answered the phone. But many of them refused to do it or just reluctantly gave their last names. The practice of immediate identification is the standard telephone practice in America, but foreign to Chinese. As our data shows, identification of the caller and callee in Chinese language environments is rather uncommon. Chinese sales representatives might feel it is awkward to adopt this new practice in making their calls. Some of them openly resisted it. One sales representative got a full mark in every other item in the evaluation, but failed every time in the item that says: "Give your name." When the training manager asked her repeatedly to identify herself immediately, she refused to do it. In the eyes of the training manager, she was not motivated to improve her performance. However, she was a successful sales representative and helpful to her customers. Even the training manager had to acknowledge that she did very well in all areas and could be a model sales representative "if only she could identify herself at the very beginning of the phone call." Examples such as these show that there is a conflict between the two cultural practices in telephone manners.

Other Sociocultural Conditions

We noted at the beginning of this chapter that Bateman and Sigband (1989) made it quite clear that the telephone should be answered by giving your name. We have just seen that at least one cultural group feels this is an unusual and undesirable practice. Other researchers have noted considerable variation across different sociocultural environments. For example, Dutch and Swedish telephone callers are reported in the literature as always giving their own names upon answering whether in business or in personal circumstances. This is also common practice in Finland. On the other hand, in some cases, no such identifications are given. Some researchers have argued that the relevant dimension is one of "high trust" and "low trust." In "low-trust" environments such as Los Angeles, these researchers argue, self-identifications can be either dangerous in giving out information about one's whereabouts or at the very least opening oneself to nuisance telephone calls.

While there is certainly a significant difference between personal telephone calls to the home and telephone calls received in a business or other office setting, as we have seen above, frequently practices from one sociocultural setting carry over into another one. We can see, then, that there is at least the possibility of misinterpretation. If "low-trust" answering is indicated by not giving one's name, then not giving one's name signals to the receiver a "low-trust" situation. It is quite likely that this intuition is what was motivating the trainers in the "cultural" example we have just given. The "Chinese" practice of not giving an identification is *heard as* signaling "low trust" to the potential customer, not as signaling Chinese social behavior.

Of course, to make certain we do not leave the reader with the suggestion that "low trust" is the only situation in which the use of no identifying name is used, we should clarify this. That is, we should not immediately get the impression that Chinese do not trust each other when they answer the telephone. This would be the mistake of taking a sign as having the same meaning in all situations, which is never the case.

Another situation in which nonidentification takes place is between intimates. People who know each other very well will count on voice recognition when they call to show how well they know the other person. Perhaps we have all been offended at one time or another by having to identify ourselves to a very close friend or family member because they have not made an immediate identification based just on the sound of our voice. In other words, voice-only identification without giving one's name is used in two very different environments: (1) those of close intimacy between the callers and (2) those that researchers have called "low-trust" situations. Our point is that we cannot know *from the signal itself* which situation we are involved in, but we are likely to draw conclusions in any event. These conclusions might be quite wrong.

Summary

We began this chapter by arguing that the C-B-S style of clarity, brevity, and sincerity advocated by textbooks in business communication at least in part grew out of early telephone technology and may no longer be necessary or appropriate with contemporary technology. Not only is telephone communication even at a distance virtually effortless in terms of instruments and connections, but also supporting information can easily be transmitted visually by means of caller ID systems, e-mail attachments, and fax. The emphasis on clarity and brevity in telephone communication may be outliving its usefulness. The frequency, duration, and function as well as the cost of telephone calls are undergoing transformation. Thus, common-sense assumptions which underlie textbook advice may no longer be reliable guides.

Besides differences arising from technological development, we described situational and relational differences which favor inductive or deductive modes of introducing the caller's topic. A European bank officer in Hong Kong, for example, used the prescribed C-B-S style with a deductive approach in addressing clients but a friendlier, inductive approach in making business calls to colleagues. That is, the C-B-S style was associated with instrumental, utilitarian relationships with clients, while business calls to colleagues foregrounded social relationships while backgrounding the business transacted. In distinguishing between calls to clients and calls to colleagues, we argued that not only is there no standard way of making a telephone call, but it is necessary to go beyond textbook prescriptions for opening calls and introducing topics to look at how calls are ended.

Since there is no standard of efficiency or of politeness, we suggest our method for finding out what people actually do when making phone calls and how these practices are evaluated by people in different communities. We presented three phone calls recorded by a participant in our research project. These calls were made by the same IBM networking representative to different business associates for different purposes. The calls differed in opening and self-identification formulas, as well as elaboration of details and degree of politeness, according to the degree of business contact and projected future relationship with the person called.

We ended the chapter by introducing cultural differences in making and evaluating phone calls. What was considered appropriate practice in Hong Kong and conformed with textbook advice was judged to be curt and impersonal by comparable business associates in Beijing. Chinese-speaking sales representatives in the United States were unwilling to conform to their American trainer's dictums of polite speech, and the trainer persisted in demanding compliance in spite of the success of the callers in selling to Chinese-speaking clients. We thus showed that there are at least four factors contributing to differences in making telephone calls: technology, situation, type of relationship, and cultural practice.

What we have presented in this chapter also illustrates the four perspectives of our research in professional communication. We began with the members' generalizations found in the "commonsense" guidelines of textbooks in business communication. With this we contrasted objective records of telephone conversations in the form of audiotape recordings made of a bank officer and sales representatives. The recordings formed the basis of individual case studies and contrastive studies of interpretations of the same phone calls by participants in different communities.

To take just one practice, that of identifying the caller by name, the contrastive data provided by our research and consultation calls into question the commonsense view that callers as well as answerers should identify themselves by name. In our objective data we found that the same caller identified himself in some calls but not in others, and that sales representatives who did not identify themselves were responded to differently by recipients and monitors of their calls. The same behavior of answering the phone without identifying oneself can be considered appropriate for responding to an intimate or inappropriate as displaying lack of trust.

These conflicting interpretations, we argue, can only be resolved by observing and consulting with the people with whom one needs to engage in professional communication. There is no global standard to which we can resort in dealing with people from different countries or cultural backgrounds.

3

The Resumé:
A Corporate "Trojan Horse"

Getting a Job

WASHINGTON – A new and dangerous computer virus dubbed "Killer Resume" is spreading through e-mail systems using the Microsoft Outlook program, the FBI said Friday night. . . .
The text of the message reads:
"To Director of Sales/Marketing,
Attached is my resume with a list of references contained within. Please feel free to call or e-mail me if you have any further questions regarding my experience. I am looking forward to hearing from you.
Sincerely,
Janet Simons." (Ho 2000)

As we were writing this chapter, this story appeared in the *Washington Post*. Computer viruses are one of the rapidly growing contemporary concerns of both individuals and organizations. The ancient walled city of Troy was impossible to penetrate, but the enemy was able to get inside and destroy the city by offering up the gift of an enormous horse which had hidden inside it the soldiers who would jump out and begin the destruction of Troy's defenses. Computer viruses are like the Trojan horse because they arrive in the form of messages or software that we want to receive and so we unknowingly also accept the viruses hidden within.

The "Killer Resume" virus is interesting to us in this book because it could only work if resumés were considered desirable in the first place. If you did not want to receive someone's resumé, you would never open the file, but just throw it away like any other junk mail. The virus can only work because the resumé in business is like the gift of the Trojan horse. It is something we take so much for granted that we can hardly imagine business operating without receiving resumés from strangers.

This story indicates very clearly how much the resumé, or biodata as it is called in some cases, has become a fixture in our lives. In this chapter we will work our way through many of the contradictions in the business literature on resumés to show how you can make an effective presentation of your own abilities through the best use of the resumé in making portfolio exchanges. Like the Trojan horse, the resumé may have one appearance – entry to new job opportunities – but have hidden within it many dangers both for the walled city of the corporation or other organization and for the person who lies waiting within.

Historical Perspective

The daughter of two of the authors (Scollon and Scollon) asked whether or not we had been taught in high school to write resumés, as she had. Like many of our readers, she accepts the resumé as an inevitable part of contemporary life. Yet it is only within our lifetimes that the resumé, or curriculum vitae as it is still called outside of North America, has become institutionalized, first within academia and then spreading to business and the professions. The *Oxford English Dictionary*, for example, gives the early 1960s as the first attested use of "resumé" and the late 1930s for "curriculum vitae." One thing we should note here is that the word "resumé" itself has undergone a change in recent years. Once it was always written with an accent on the final letter "é" ("resumé"). Now more often than not, the word is written without the accent in American English, though "resumé" is still acceptable in North America and is the standard form in British English. Of course we also mean to include in our discussion of resumés all of the other forms that go by somewhat different names such as the CV ("curriculum vitae") or the "biodata" or "bio statement."

We surmise that the mobility that resulted after the end of World War II disrupted earlier forms of job placement through contacts provided by family and friends. At the same time military practices of maintaining dossiers of personnel were easily transposed into requiring job applicants to keep a resumé or summary of their relevant educational and job-related experience. In our own experience the resumé has most often followed personal contact with someone looking for prospective employees and been used to satisfy institutional requirements.

In earlier times the real curriculum vitae, the record of the course of a life, was known by potential employers in stable communities, or could be vouched for by people they could trust. Even today in a small country like Finland people within academic or business communities can rely on personal contacts to make judgments about people they do not know personally. It is not so different from the days in imperial China when official appointments were made on the basis of examination results mediated by contacts made with business cards. According to fictional accounts, officials would judge a name card according to whether the name represented a person whose family was known. Exam results might then be manipulated accordingly. In this, of course, we are not saying that the Finns are like the Chinese or, even worse, that they are old-fashioned. Rather we are reminded by these examples that placement in contemporary organizations does not operate so differently, in spite of the commonsense acceptance of the importance of the resumé. A professor at an American law school estimates that the chances of getting a job by submitting an application and resumé without prior personal contact are about one in a hundred.

Although in many circles the resumé functions as a supplement to face-to-face contact, in international settings the document assumes more importance when distance intervenes in personal contacts and job interviews may be held by telephone. Although international settings highlight the importance of these documents, because they function differently from place to place, it is necessary to personally investigate how the resumé one submits might be interpreted by the distant people who evaluate it.

Speaking and Writing: Conversations and Documents

Telephone calls are actions; resumés are documents. This is the first thing we have to take into consideration when we think of resumés in professional communication in international settings. In the course of our ordinary lives, both in and out of the businesses or organizations of our professional work world, we spend much more time talking and listening to others than we do in writing or reading what others have written. This simply means that from the time we are children we have a lot more practice in spoken communication than we have in written communication. It also means that in speaking we integrate our practices and habits from our past, from our childhood, from conversations with our friends and families, and from the whole of our lives, both personal and professional, but we have to specifically learn how to produce a resumé.

Nobody starts to write resumés when they are two or three years old by watching the grownups around them doing this; but this is how we first learn to have a conversation or to use the telephone. What this means for us in this book is that none of us has intuitions about what would be a good or a bad resumé which are *based on the form of the resumé alone*. To put this another way, resumés are much more the products of our professional worlds than are telephone calls. There is nothing really "natural" about writing or reading a resumé.

In today's business world, your resumé following the business card is almost always the first formal representation of yourself you make to another business contact. Of course there are many contacts which are made through face-to-face introductions and you are judged by your appearance, which includes how you are dressed, how you act in relationship to others, and how you speak. Also, it is fair to say that the business card is probably the first really significant document in putting together a professional appearance because these are exchanged within the first encounter. Nevertheless, the resumé is in most cases the document which is used to open up the first possibility of a longer-term relationship, as in applying for a position and in international settings, the resumé is the primary way people get to know new business associates or evaluate them for advancement in position.

Most of the sources we have reviewed express the common belief that resumés have great impact in getting job interviews, in actual hiring, and in obtaining the salaries one desires. In fact, because of its importance in the hiring process, resumé writing has become a business and a profession itself. In the United States, there are professional resumé writers for people seeking employment or higher salaries. There is even an association called the Professional Association of Resumé Writing. This shows that the market and demand for resumé writing in the contemporary business world is not only large, but also quite stable. Things are not likely to change in the immediate future.

But we are still faced with a problem in preparing resumés for professionals working in international settings. Even within the narrow circles of business in North America, how to write a resumé and what to include in it remain controversial issues. A professional resumé writer admits that:

> the employment resume – its style, organization and content – has long been a topic of considerable discussion and debate. Like religion and politics this is a subject fraught with controversy. It is one of those topics where there are many "experts" who will provide you with considerable "professional" advice and counsel as long as you are willing to listen. (Beatty 1995:1)

Not only is this an issue in the resumé writing business, it is also a problem in how the person that a resumé represents is perceived by others, especially across the cultural boundaries in international business settings. Here we begin by discussing the three main variables in resumé writing given by the experts:

- *length*. Should it be long or short?
- *type*. Should it be chronological or functional?
- *presentation*. Should it include "personal" information or be "strictly professional"?

As we will see, this last problem may well be the most significant in dealing across international or cultural boundaries.

After we discuss the rather complex and usually contradictory "rules" for resumé writing given by experts, we will look at what we have learned in our own research project. As in the experts' advice, there is a lot of contradiction between what people in our research project *said* (members' generalizations or conventional wisdom) and what they actually *did* (objective or neutral observations). What is important to know, however, is that whatever you do, your resumé will be a major source by which others will make personal and professional evaluations of you and your capacity to work in future positions.

Finally, we will outline ways in which this tremendous amount of conflict and contradiction can be resolved in your favor through the exchanges of portfolios like the ones we are recommending in this book.

No "Standard" Resumé

In preparing for this chapter we went to many bookstores in our home area, Washington, DC, to see what would be available to anyone just going into a large, North American national chain bookstore. We found that there is always a section of career development in which there are hundreds of books on how to write a resumé. As this field is now becoming highly specialized, books are available which are designed for different types of job seekers and levels of employment. There are books for (US) Federal resumés, for professional resumés, and for entry-level resumés, just to name a few. These books, written by professional resumé writers, attempt to help the reader prepare a good or "powerful" resumé to impress the potential employer, to get job interviews, and eventually to get hired. Most of the books give a detailed list of "dos" and "don'ts" in writing a resumé. Some books provide detailed analysis of bad resumés and suggestions for good ones.

Two basic types of resumé are suggested in the many popular books: *chronological* and *functional*. A chronological resumé is one that lists the person's employment history according to the dates. The most recent employment is given first and then one works backward to the first job. This is usually thought to be a more traditional form of resumé writing. A functional resumé is one that groups skills and qualities under headings that constitute important functions in a particular kind of job. Of course, there are some variations of these two types. Some books classify resumés as the work history resumé, the focused resumé, or the competency cluster resumé.

The content of the resumé is organized into several components. The most common categories for a *chronological* resumé are as follows:

- heading
- objective
- professional experience
- education.

For a *functional* resumé, the most common categories are as follows:

- heading
- qualification summary
- major accomplishments
- work history
- education.

There are different views, however, about what you should do and what you should not do in writing a resumé. For example, Tepper in his *Power Resumes* (1998:136–7) suggests ten power resumé ingredients:

1. Avoid functional resume
2. Avoid objectives
3. Do not give your age, marital status or graduation dates
4. Give specific accomplishments, not duties and responsibilities. Stress value-added
5. Write in clear, concise terms. Use active verbs
6. Tailor the resume to the company
7. Use a summary at the beginning of the resume
8. Limit the resume to 2 pages
9. Do not put in salary requirements or references
10. If you have space, insert extracurricular activities

Tepper's ingredients for a "power resumé" boil down to the characteristics we described in chapter 2 of the C-B-S style: clarity, brevity, and sincerity. It is not surprising to find these characteristics in a book which overall adopts this North American business-style set of values for communication. As we will see below, however, these values are not entirely accepted across the boundaries of different international or cultural settings.

But not only that, Tepper's advice is contradicted in another book (Provenzano 2000) on resumé writing designed for the North American business market. There the author favors a format that combines features of a chronological and of a functional resumé and suggests putting a profile in the beginning of the resumé. We would like to note that this book is intended for executive resumés and says that a two-page resumé is really not enough to include all relevant information for an executive position. In other words, it is not simply a matter of using the C-B-S style, but it is also important to consider one's own position and the position for which one is applying.

Resumé writing, like any other cultural or social practice, is ever-changing. The books on how to write a resumé represent the generalization of the practice of resumé writing at a certain time, in a certain cultural environment. The point we would like to make here is that there are a lot of contradictions in the views of what is a good resumé in these various books teaching people how to write one. Different books seem to say different things since they all have a different focus and emphasize different aspects of the resumé or of the type of position. While these are valuable suggestions for resumé writing, we believe that in the international setting, such advice can cause some confusion and difficulty for the reader. There is really no one-size-fits-all format for resumé writing, because different fields have different conventions in writing resumés: professional (accountant, lawyer, tax expert, computer technician), teaching, and academic. There are also different levels of career: entry-level, mid-level management, high-level management, and executive.

Word-Processing Resumé Wizards

In the midst of these contradictory opinions and advice about resumé writing, word-processing technology has begun to standardize the writing of a resumé. The last several generations of word-processing software now include resumé wizards to help the user write resumés, and such wizards are also found on websites. The style, format, organization, and content of a resumé are programmed into a set of well-defined questions and check points. The user can simply choose the style and format he or she likes and then click the headings for the organization of content. A resumé is then well laid out. All the user needs to do is to add the information in the box prompted by the program.

The wizard included with Microsoft's Word®, for example, provides the format for four types of resumé:

- entry-level
- chronological
- functional
- professional.

These four types of resumé can be set up in three design styles, which are called:

- professional
- contemporary
- elegant.

Each type of resumé included within this wizard has similar headings. The main difference is in the order in which the headings are arranged. The headings include the following, taken from the "professional" resumé:

- name and address
- summary of qualifications
- education
- professional experience
- patents and publications
- additional professional activities
- professional memberships
- languages
- community activities
- references
- objective
- extracurricular activities
- accreditations
- hobbies
- interests and activities
- volunteer experience
- security clearance
- civil service grades
- awards received.

For the chronological, functional, and entry-level resumé in this resumé wizard, there is just a slight change in the terminology. For example, "work experience" is given instead of "professional experience" for a chronological resumé, and "employment" for a functional resumé. These headings constitute the elements to be included in a resumé. All the elements are suggested for each of the four types of resumé. The main difference between the different types of resumé is the order of these headings. The wizard intends to give a comprehensive format and formula for resumé writing so as to make it easy to write one. But what the wizard does not tell the user is the criteria for choosing the type. Which type of resumé is appropriate for what field remains a problem which the user must figure out. Also, since all the elements are present in four types of resumés, we may well ask: is there really any need to try to make a fine distinction among different types of resumés?

Handling Contradictory Advice

Our interest in this book lies with professional communication in international settings. In the case of the telephone calls we wrote about in chapter 2, we said there was a particular set of values – the C–B–S style – that have come to be the dominant ones that are stated in textbooks on business telephone calls. Nevertheless, we found that even within the same cultural or business environment there were different types of telephone calls with quite different features. The telephone call with a client is not the same as the call with a business colleague.

Now in considering resumés, we find that before we even come to the question of what people actually do, we have found an enormous amount of contradiction in the "expert" sources on how to prepare a resumé. This is partly because, as we said at the beginning, the resumé is a document that has no function outside of organizational, institutional, or business circles. You don't send a resumé to a friend. Children don't play at making resumés. Resumés are very *institutional* documents in their nature, and so reflect the great amount of variety among institutions, situations, positions, and people on the one hand, and on the other are often very different in nature from what we would ordinarily do if we were left to our own intuitions.

To clarify what we mean by this latter point, most people are quite modest in dealing with new situations or with people they do not know well. We are taught as children in most societies not to brag about ourselves and our accomplishments. In most societies it is felt that it is more polite to let others discover our qualities rather than just boldly telling others how great we are. Of course this varies from group to group and what seems modest in one group might seem boastful in another. Nevertheless, it is very rare in human societies to have a place or a time where the whole purpose is to make the strongest possible statement of our own qualities. From this point of view, our intuitions go completely against the idea of writing a resumé.

It is no wonder that this type of document is full of contradictions, because these are based on the contradiction of trying to boast about our own accomplishments on paper while at the same time trying to be polite and modest people in normal face-to-face interactions.

Our approach to trying to understand these contradictions was to conduct the project "Professional Communication Across Cultures," as we have described in chapter 1. We thought that we could never resolve the many contradictions involved in deciding what would be the best or most appropriate resumé ourselves. Instead we asked professionals in the three sites to exchange their resumés and to see how the others responded to them. In the section which follows, we will first describe the resumés and their exchanges. Then we will discuss how the focus groups in the three sites, Hong Kong, Beijing, and Finland, responded to the differences in the resumés which were exchanged. We hope that in doing this we can do two things. First, we want to show that it is very difficult to know *from what people say* (members' generalizations/conventional wisdom) about resumés how they *actually react* (neutral or objective observations) to resumés they receive. That is, it is very important to discover how people actually respond to resumés of different kinds and not to rely on expert opinions about resumés – especially when you are involved in exchanges across lines of nation or culture. Second, we want to show that when a resumé is much different from what people expect, they do draw negative conclusions about the person whose resumé it is.

One of the most important findings of interactional sociolinguistics is that people do not often pay attention to the surface level of language use. Instead, they make interpretations. That is to say, they do not just say, "Oh, he's used a functional resumé rather than a chronological resumé." They tend to say, "He's not very well qualified. He should know how to do this better."

We hope in what follows, and in the portfolio exchanges we explain in chapter 6 and in the appendices, readers will find a workable way to learn what is most effective for themselves in actual situations rather than relying on "expert" advice which in the long run will always be contradictory and difficult to use.

Case Study: The Long and Short of a Resumé

In our research we wanted to find out what people in real business environments within an international and intercultural setting felt about the preferred format, style, and organization of a resumé, as we have said. The professionals in our three sites of Hong Kong, Beijing, and Finland were asked to provide us with their resumés. Of course, we had collected a large number of resumés from other places and within other institutions as part of our own institutional work and used these resumés (confidentially) as a background against which to evaluate those we studied in our project. Some of these secondary resumés were academic, for hiring and for research, and some were related to business and governmental consultation projects.

The two resumés we used in exchanges and for our focus group discussions were from business professionals in Beijing and in Hong Kong. The Beijing professional is a tax consultant who works in a joint-venture export company. The Hong Kong professional is a computer expert working in a large international computer company. The resumés were originally in English, because it is common in resumé submission (as well as for business cards and other documents) for English to be used as one of the languages which is shared among participants from multiple national and cultural environments.

It is most interesting that we ultimately failed to obtain a resumé from a Finnish professional. Such a professional agreed to work with us on this project. One of our research team met him in Finland and two of the other research members met him and went to his presentation in Hong Kong. He was very helpful and cooperative in letting us videotape his presentation and in discussing his professional presentation and his work, including his employment history, with us, but he was, nevertheless, quite reluctant to give us his resumé.

In another consultation case involving a major Finnish company, we found that the Finnish counterparts were not only reluctant to provide resumés, they did not request any resumé from two of the authors, even though a relatively important consultation contract was involved. A colleague in Finland told us that in her university no formal written contracts had been issued. She said that interpersonal trust was the key to such institutional relationships and that it would be thought insulting to be engaged in legal documentation either of one's professional capacities or of one's legal obligations to the university. She said that on the university's part, it would be felt to be insulting to the professor to demand a contractual obligation when it was understood that anyone would be of good enough character to always meet those obligations.

When we described, to another Finnish colleague, our project and our difficulty getting a resumé, she gave us an envelope containing a kind of portfolio. She had it close at hand and did not take any time to put it together. It contained photocopies of articles she had written describing the results of a project she had undertaken, a summary of the project and the organization which supported it, a copy of an award she had won for her work on the project, signed by a prominent dignitary, a copy of a notification that she had been admitted to a prestigious society, and a brochure for an organization for which she served as president. There was no resumé. Instead there were letters of congratulations and offers to collaborate, and at the top of the pile a letter of reference with the salutation "TO WHOM IT MAY CONCERN." This letter was in effect a one-page resumé listing her major accomplishments. By providing us with this portfolio she could inform us of her abilities without seeming to brag, as it was other people praising her accomplishments.

This particular "cultural" view appears to be supported by another colleague who works in a rather significant diplomatic position for the Finnish government. As it happens, she is a member of a family the name of which is very well known in Finland for its connections with high-level government. Because of this, she is often very embarrassed on being introduced, as she does not like to say her family name or to have other people know her high-level connections. She feels it is already very offensive to be saying her name to other people because this could so easily be thought to be bragging of her power and connections.

We should point out that this reticence regarding *personal* achievements is not applied to national or Finnish achievements. Within our study as well as in other contacts with colleagues in Finland we have found them quite ready to speak about the importance of various Finnish contributions to the world. What is important is that while Finns, at least within our study, showed a great deal of collective pride, they were very hesitant to display personal or individual pride in the form of resumés.

We do not want to make too much of these cultural considerations because we also know that many people in Finland have come to feel such practices are a bit outmoded and do not themselves feel it is necessary to be so reticent in order to be "Finnish." University students are taught in Finland as in other countries how to prepare resumés. What we want the reader to notice here is that, as we said above, there is a contradiction between "normal" social behavior and what is required in preparing a resumé. Most of us do not mind putting our accomplishments into the written document, but would find it difficult to speak very boastfully about them. Perhaps these few Finnish people we have consulted are at an extreme, but for them the resumé itself is a violation of normal patterns of politeness, and so they have avoided making one at all.

This is the first thing we learned, then: the act of making and sending a resumé may already be considered by some people an affront to normal human dignity. This is not really so hard to understand if we remember that for most of us this would be true *outside of professional or business circles.* Imagine a young person making a date with another. They like each other and have hopes that this date will lead to an extended relationship. Can we imagine that they would exchange resumés to present their best qualities to each other? We think this would be a very strange exchange. The resumé is a document restricted to particular institutional situations and, from our attempts to get a resumé from our Finnish participant, we learned that for him the professional relationship was in many ways like our personal relationships. We think we could say that he wasn't making such a clear distinction between personal and professional as we tend to make in North American business environments.

Now we will turn to looking at the two resumés which were exchanged in our project. The resumé which was prepared by the professional in Beijing, "Linda Chen" (a pseudonym), is a quite standard two-page resumé, in chronological format. It lists the history of employment, and has three components of "professional experience," "education," and "other experience." Personal information such as gender, age, and marital status is not listed. Linda Chen's resumé is given in appendix 2, with the main identifiers changed for the sake of confidentiality.

The resumé from the Hong Kong professional, "Eric Fung" (a pseudonym), has eight pages with detailed information. It is also given in appendix 2 with identifiers changed. Eric Fung's resumé starts with a page of personal details of date of birth, current employer, contact information, and language abilities. The second page is a career snapshot, a brief summary of positions held and achievement awards. The third page is a summary of technical skills. The fourth, fifth, sixth, and seventh pages are the employment history, giving detailed information of his positions and responsibilities. On the last page are reference information and hobbies and other interests. The resumé is organized to give a summary of his professional experience and technical skills, then the detailed presentation of his work history.

Although these two resumés differ in length, style, and format, we consider them both to be successful. In the first case, the Beijing professional, Linda Chen, used this resumé to find herself a better position in the company, and to receive further training in the United States. This is considered highly favorable treatment within a Chinese company and reflects the high evaluation made by her superiors. The Hong Kong professional, Eric Fung, used this resumé to seek and to be hired by another international computer company in Hong Kong, which was an upward career step. In other words, both of these resumés are *good* within the original contexts in which they were used. Whatever we, the focus group participants, or the reader might want to say about them, these resumés have met the pragmatic test of achieving career advancements for the professionals who have used them *within their own particular cultural environments.*

Focus Group Reflections: Contrasting Views

As we have described in chapter 1, we conducted focus group discussions in the three sites of Finland, Hong Kong, and Beijing to get participants' comments on these resumés. Our purpose was not so much to evaluate the resumés *per se* as to use the participants' evaluation of the given resumés, to learn their subjective views of the other sites and the views of their own practices. The two resumés can be seen as the opener of the discussion. In the discussion participants gave their opinions about what they thought would be appropriate information to be included in a resumé, as well as what is not appropriate practice. While the resumés they were considering were written in English, the discussion within the focus groups was in the local language. That is, the Hong Kong focus group spoke in Cantonese, the Beijing focus group spoke in Putonghua (Mandarin), and the Finnish focus group spoke in Finnish.

Hong Kong focus group discussion

Hong Kong focus group participants showed rather different views on what a good resumé should include. They also had different views on the format a resumé should follow. Most of them agreed that the ideal length for a resumé would be two to three pages. They felt that a long resumé would reduce the applicant's chances of a job interview, because the resumé reviewer would not have the time to go through a long resumé. They said that a resumé, like a telephone call, should aim for clarity and brevity.

There is a contradiction, however, between what they claim to be the right practices and what they actually do. While the Hong Kong professional's resumé is eight pages long, the Beijing professional's resumé is two pages. In spite of this, and in spite of the fact that they said that an ideal resumé should be brief – two or three pages – the focus group participants thought that the Beijing resumé was too simple and too brief. There was not enough information to judge the person, they said. They also thought that the Beijing resumé focused only on Linda Chen's business experience and did not include other relevant information to give the reader a better idea of what kind of person she is.

Personal information is an important consideration to which we will return below. It was first brought up in the reactions of the Hong Kong focus group to Linda Chen's resumé, which, they felt, did not include personal information.

The writer of the Hong Kong resumé, Eric Fung, was present at the Hong Kong focus group discussion. He gave the following explanation for the eight-page length of his resumé. He said that it was a general resumé – one which covered all aspects of his career life. The first three pages, he said, contained all the necessary information which prospective employers would want to know. The following five pages gave further details of each advancement in his career path in case reviewers wanted to know more. He felt that if the writer was really keen about a particular position, he would most likely tailor the resumé according to particular job requirements.

Focus group participants in Hong Kong also commented that the functional resumé is the preferred format nowadays – within the Hong Kong environment, of course. They felt that resumés do not have to be presented in chronological order; instead achievements and awards should be highlighted in the resumé and presented first (after personal details). Many companies are very "achievement-based" and would like to see the applicant's achievements right at the beginning of the resumé, because employers are interested not so much in the nature of previous positions as in the achievements in a particular post. The participants commented that the trend now is how to "sell" oneself. That is, the resumé is fitting within a marketing model. So a resumé should focus on what the applicant has achieved in each position, not how many years he or she has worked in a company. In their comments, then, Hong Kong focus group participants stressed the importance of "selling oneself" by giving the main achievements at the beginning of a resumé.

In our review of standard expertise on resumé writing we found that many books in the United States argue against the idea of putting a photo in the resumé. They say that this is because it will provide a bias toward judging the applicant by his or her appearance, not abilities and achievements. But in Hong Kong, the focus group said that another important aspect of "selling oneself" is to provide a photo. In some fields such as sales and technical support departments, employers would like to see what prospective employees look like, they commented, because the person doing sales needs to have a presentable image. They are aware that this is not common practice in places outside of Hong Kong, but they would prefer applicants to provide a photo so that they can see whether or not the applicant is suitable for the position. Many books published in the United States advise applicants not to include personal information such as sex, age, date of birth, and marital status in a resumé. Of course, this is because of legal restrictions. Still, most of the Hong Kong focus group participants thought that personal information should be included to give the employer an idea of what kind of a person they are hiring.

Neither focus group members in Hong Kong nor the experts on resumé writing we surveyed at the outset make any mention of the legal questions surrounding providing personal information in resumés. Within the United States many aspects of personal information are actually prohibited in employment or interview circumstances. This is based on legal concerns to provide equality of access and employment so that job candidates will not be discriminated against on the basis of sex, age, race, or any of the other formally and legally defined categories. We cannot say whether or not the sources in the United States are simply assuming knowledge of this legal history or if they might not have simply taken on as *common sense* what was initially produced as legal requirements. In any event, it is clear that there is within North American practice as well as within other western countries a general prohibition against using personal information in the process of hiring, at least in overt and explicit documented forms. As a result, this information is considered improper for resumés or any other official documents involved in the hiring or evaluation processes of businesses and governmental or other institutions.

The authors have been involved over the years in many hiring processes both in academic worlds and in those of business and government. It is clear that employers and other evaluators *really do want* this personal information, even if and when it is illegal. That is to say, personal information is always considered very valuable in assessing a person's likelihood to be a productive employee. The trick is getting or giving personal information when it is proscribed by legal constraints. One of the current methods for doing this is for candidates to include in their resumés the URL of their personal homepage. With the click of a mouse the employer may find out what the person does for recreation, may see photos of the children and of the candidate himself or herself, and may get a great deal of other very personal information that is prohibited in the formal documents of the job application process. Employers also judiciously use e-mail and telephones to glean information from acquaintances who know the candidate.

There is a contradiction, then, between the kind of knowledge people have of each other on a personal basis and the kind people have formally within the restrictions of institutional, organizational, and legal requirements. As we have noted above, the Finnish participants simply did not provide *any* personal *or* professional information about themselves. The Hong Kong focus group participants (and the Chinese ones as well, as we will see) felt it was important to provide as much professional *and* personal information as possible. We believe that in the long run, this conflict between personal and professional information is the most significant aspect of self-presentation in professional communication in international settings. This is a question to which we will return again below.

Having said this, then, it is ironic that this personal information is not included in either the Hong Kong or Beijing resumés except for the few comments at the end of Eric Fung's (Hong Kong) resumé about his personal hobbies and other interests. In Hong Kong, focus group members disagreed as to whether hobbies and extracurricular activities needed to be included as part of a resumé. Those who favored inclusion argued that it would give a more balanced profile of the individual. Those who were opposed said that for a technical position, at least, extracurricular information would not be considered – what really counts, they said, is the person's working experience and qualifications.

In summary, one important observation should be made from the Hong Kong focus group discussion:

The views of what a resumé should be like differ even among members of the same cultural group.

The participants' comments on the length, format, and content of the two resumés vary. There are internal contradictions among the group and there are serious contradictions between what they said a resumé should contain and what they actually do.

Beijing focus group discussion

Within the Beijing focus group, unlike the Hong Kong group, participants showed a general consensus of what a resumé should be like. They agreed that a good resumé should be:

1 *brief* – no more than two pages
2 *stylistically focused* – a summary paragraph outlining the applicant's major achievements and abilities
3 *job-focused* – job-related with a category of "objectives"
4 *personal* – detailed personal information.

Much of their discussion was centered on these points and then, of course, how they felt about the deviations from these standard practices which they have seen and which they saw in the two resumés they were considering.

Concerning the length of a resumé, they agreed that if it is too long, the potential employer will be overloaded and will easily disregard a long resumé like the Hong Kong one. They felt that a one-page resumé is sufficient to outline the professional experience and to summarize the applicant's achievements. A long resumé, on the other hand, gives the reader an impression that the applicant doesn't know what he or she is doing and doesn't have a purpose and focus in his or her job pursuit. This would have a very negative impact on the applicant's chances of success. From this point of view, they thought that the Beijing resumé, Linda Chen's, was the right length while the Hong Kong one was awfully long. They did not think highly of the Hong Kong resumé simply because it was too long.

Though the focus group participants in Beijing did not use the words "functional resumé," their comments showed that they prefer to see a functional resumé with an emphasis on achievements. They said that the summary of achievements should be the first thing to put in a resumé, highlighting important points, awards and training for each job, certificates, etc. Nevertheless, both the Hong Kong and Beijing resumés followed the format of the chronological resumé. The focus group participants attached some negative value to this chronological format. They thought a chronological listing of employment history is like writing an archive, and not at all interesting. The focus group participants believed this archive writing style is typically Chinese, because in Mainland China, many people have been accustomed to filling out personal archive forms for political dossiers and giving a list of employment dates for their work units. They are not used to putting what they have accomplished in a position into such records, because those evaluations are thought to be for their superiors to write. We have found that many Chinese include letters from their supervisors in applications. In this, of course, the "traditional" Chinese practice is somewhat like that of the Finns in our study who hesitated to put forward their own personal accomplishments.

The negative evaluation the Beijing focus group participants made of this chronological "archive" format is that listing employment history is "questionable." This is because the applicant seems to "take note of everything." They did not believe anyone could remember the details such as years, job titles, and company names for an entire career. In other words, they cast doubt on the applicant's character in that they thought such a detailed record must be falsified. They also thought the applicant might be too young, in other words, not experienced enough in his or her field, to come up with any achievements to list. During the planned economy era (1950s to 1980s), the official archive in China was an effective means for the government to tightly control its people and society. On the other hand, it suggests repression and surveillance from the government. Its influence on the form of a resumé thus triggers negative evaluation from the focus group participants.

As an aside we might comment that this matter of exact chronology and archival details might have many resonances with other social questions. In the United States, where such resumé keeping has been in effect for quite a few years since the 1960s or so, even a person in his or her sixties might have been keeping such a resumé for an entire career. Each item has been added to the preceding one over a career of forty years – that is, since about the 1950s or 1960s when such resumés started to become more widely used, and so the resumé is really, in a sense, the chronicle of a person's career. Even though one might have very little recall of any of the exact details, a glance at the cumulative resumé will bring these details back into focus. So for such a person, there is no difficulty in having and maintaining such a record. Even though we are all aware that each resumé is a selection among these details, any of the particular details has actually been documented for this entire span of years.

In contrast to this, an international colleague whose career has developed under very different circumstances will have a very different career history – most of it either undocumented or, in some cases, not willingly documented. We do not mean to single out China here at all because this would also apply to our colleagues in Europe and in many other parts of the world. One might have significant periods in one's life where such documentation would be associated with repressive governments or with war-related activities which for many reasons the candidate would prefer not to document in a resumé. One of the authors first developed his own detailed list of employment right down to the exact dates and locations as well as residences at that time as part of receiving a security clearance in the US Army.

The point we want to make here is that whatever participants in these focus groups have to say and whatever the expert books on resumés have to say, behind the scenes, so to speak, there are many reasons – both good and bad ones – why a person might prefer a very short resumé which is simply to the point of the job at hand. And from that point of view the person might consider the idea of a long and detailed resumé to be a somewhat dangerous or repressive intrusion into matters, whether religious or political, that he or she is not ready to make available to a future employer. This is particularly the case now, as employers are making such massive and intrusive invasions into the privacy of the lives of their employees.

To return to the comments of the Beijing focus group, the issue of having a focus is another point they commented on over and again. They all thought that a resumé should be job-related and have an objective related to the job desired. If not, they felt it would lack focus. Lacking a focus would create a serious problem in presenting oneself, because, as one person put it: "We are in a fast-growing society. It would be very difficult to go around if you don't have a focus. It must be you that is to be blamed." Therefore, when a resumé doesn't show a focus, they said, it implies the writer is "not logical" and "has problems." These negative comments were made about the Hong Kong resumé writer, Eric Fung.

Personal information was regarded as an important component in a resumé for the Beijing focus group, as we have said. They insisted that gender, date of birth, and a home telephone number should be given first. The focus group participants said that the first thing they want to know when viewing a resumé is the gender of the applicant. Of course this provides a strong contrast with employment practices in much of the western world, and also with formal party ideology in China, where it is argued that there should be no discrimination based on gender. It should be noted that Chinese names are not often easily identified for gender and so the name alone is not often a very good indication of the person's gender. Western employers may be equally concerned with gender but in most cases this information may be apparent from the given name, as they are in the two resumés provided, though the Beijing participants apparently could not read this, being unfamiliar with western names.

Here we should note, as we will take up next in chapter 4 when we write about presentations, that there is a divergence between what this Beijing focus group described as "cultural" behavior for "Chinese" and what they said was their own or preferred behavior. In other words, while they said it was "Chinese" to write long, detailed, archival lists, they also said that they (as contemporary Chinese) did not do this. In this we found that there was sometimes a clear distinction drawn between "Chinese" behavior and "our" (contemporary Chinese) behavior. From this point of view, we think it is always of the utmost importance to distinguish between what people say when they are telling you about "cultural" or normative behavior – what we *should* or *did* do at some time in the past – and what we *do* do now in the present. As we shall see, there is even a lot of divergence between what people do in the present and what they say they do, but this is again divergent from past or "traditional" or "cultural" behavior. In many cases it is important for people to tell foreigners what is expected or "cultural," even when they fully realize that it is not their own practice. Successful communication depends crucially on making sure we do not mistake norms for actual practice.

Finland focus group discussion

The Finnish focus group had only the two resumés from Hong Kong and Beijing to see, as we have said above. They were not surprised at the absence of a Finnish resumé, and put forth various possible reasons, an apparently obvious one being that the person asked to put together a professional communication portfolio was already employed and had no need for a printed resumé. One woman said it was not customary to teach graduates how to prepare resumés, but that they were just starting to do this at the university. Perhaps this reflects the common assumption we have mentioned above that a Finnish participant just would not submit to this process.

The general impression shared among the Finnish focus group participants was that Eric Fung's (Hong Kong) resumé was too "heavy" and lengthy. They said that there was a lot of information in it. For some, this was considered "good" while others preferred the Beijing resumé (Linda Chen's), which gave a quick overall picture of the applicant.

What Is a Good Resumé?

From the actual successful resumés we have considered and from the focus group discussions in our project, we can conclude that resumé writing is never a standardized practice across cultural boundaries and across professional fields, although the resumé is an accepted way of presenting a person in these environments. We noted, for example, that none of the focus groups said that they would not use a resumé. Even the Finnish group did not say this, in spite of the fact that the Finnish participant had not provided a resumé. The problem remains: how does one write a resumé and what should be included in it? Opinions on these questions vary a great deal. There are many factors to consider in producing a resumé and there are many ways to write one. Even where the focus groups acknowledged this, it was clear that they had certain characteristics in mind, and when a resumé departed from these characteristics, they felt it reflected negatively on the person who was presented in it.

The three characteristics which were commented on again and again are:

1 length
2 focus
3 personal information.

There seemed to be much agreement among the three focus groups that a resumé should be brief. That is, we could say that it should be framed in the C-B-S style we discussed in chapter 2 on telephone conversations. As with the conversations we examined, however, there is a lot of divergence from this ideal of C-B-S style and the actual resumés. We cannot stress too much the fact that the long resumé, which was generally thought to be "too heavy" or "too long," was a successful resumé in practice. The ideal of brevity is frequently expressed, but this departure did not bring about a negative result in terms of employment. Nevertheless, it is important to notice that it *did* produce a negative evaluation in the context of a focus group.

Perhaps the most important characteristic is personal information. Here we found the greatest contradictions. Both the Beijing and Hong Kong focus groups felt it was important to have personal details. Neither of the resumés they were examining actually had included such personal details and yet both had been successful. As we have noted, the Finnish case was the extreme in offering *neither* personal *nor* professional details, because no resumé at all was offered. We also noted that in North America and perhaps most of Western Europe, only professional details are considered relevant and even legal.

Personal or Professional?

We are writing this book just because throughout the world there are many contradictions in professional communication, particularly when this communication is in international settings. Imagine, for example, a Finnish paper products manufacturer and a Hong Kong electronics company working together on a project. From our research we would expect the Hong Kong partners in this project to provide quite long resumés as a way of introducing themselves. These resumés would contain professional and personal details as a way of establishing the relationships. On the other hand, we would expect the Finnish partners not to provide resumés at all. In fact, we can expect that they would do very little, either in writing or in speaking, to show their own individual abilities, connections, or experiences. They might well speak very positively of their company, its position in world paper production, and the quality of their products. But individually, we would expect them to say almost nothing. How are these two partners in the project to get to know each other and to come to establish personal and professional relationships that will make the project run smoothly?

The contradictions that arise often have to do with the fact that we are institutional or organizational people, and at the same time we remain humans and maintain constant use of human knowledge, or what we have called here personal information. What this means is that even if we might be very careful in job application processes to eliminate all reference to this human or personal knowledge, as soon as we are on the job, it is personal knowledge that takes over as the main way we get through our days. The colleagues who hid the flowers from our friend's husband would not have done so had they seen on her resumé that she had been married only once. Whether or not they knew anything about her marital status, their natural unconscious reaction was to jump to some conclusion and act accordingly.

In research done on counseling interviews, Erickson and Shultz (1982) defined what they called "gatekeeping situations." These are situations like the job interview in which access to an institution (or advancement to a higher position) depends on passing through a "gateway" of close evaluation. As they point out, most such gateways are very tightly constrained by legal and institutional rules and processes. The resumé is one of the major gatekeeping devices. If you have the right ticket – such as a properly prepared resumé – you get through the gate. If there is something wrong with your ticket, you do not get through.

For our purposes here, the most interesting part of the work of Erickson and Shultz is their focus on what they call "co-membership." They found that the most favorable thing that can happen for a person who arrives at a job interview or some other gateway for evaluation is for the gatekeeper to discover something in common with him or her. If the employer is a postage stamp collector and the applicant is also a philatelist, that interview will go better than if they do not share that interest in stamp collection. In other words, the most important thing working in favor of a person is personal information or what we have called human knowledge. As legislation in North America and elsewhere has also acknowledged, such human knowledge is also the strongest factor working against a person if the gatekeeper and the person hold negative opinions about personal aspects of the other.

We believe that the participants in our focus group were showing a good understanding of these principles in their interest in seeing personal information reflected on the resumé. We also know that this is the reason such information is prohibited in most North American and Western European resumés.

Portfolio Exchanges: Professional *and* Personal

Our strategy in this book is to help professionals who are communicating in international settings to develop a method for bringing into their relationships with other professionals *both* professional *and* personal knowledge and information. We have shown that the advice of the expert books on resumés (and other aspects of professional communication) are likely to be difficult or misleading for two reasons: First, they cannot possibly include the amount of complexity that is evident in the day-to-day world of international communication and so are forced to present just a few fixed formulas. As we have shown in this chapter, the C-B-S style formula is mostly the stated preferred one, but in real cases it is not the one actually followed. Second, these formulas cannot take into consideration the many complexities of professional expectations and of legal requirements across different groups or jurisdictions. We believe that the only successful (and in many places the only legal) way of building *both* professional *and* personal knowledge into international business relationships is for the participants on whom this information has a direct impact to exchange it voluntarily among themselves.

This is the essence of the professional Communication Display Portfolio (CDP) exchange. Not only do participants in the exchange send resumés (and other professional communications) back and forth. This is normal practice and it is subject to the problems we have already noted. They exchange their responses to these communications in a guided environment. That is, with the CDP you can not only send your best resumé, you can also see how your counterparts in the other company or country react to it. This gives you the opportunity for reflecting on that and revising the way you have presented yourself. As we will show in chapter 6, with the examples in the appendices, such a portfolio exchange can be an effective tool for bringing into your contacts in international settings both professional and personal information that will give you the basis for successful and continuing business relationships.

The Long and the Short of Getting a Job

We began this chapter by pointing out that the resumé, though a seeming fixture in our lives, has only recently become considered necessary for getting a job. Our fathers never had to puzzle over how to write a resumé. They landed jobs through personal contacts, whether with strangers or with acquaintances. We ourselves were never instructed in writing a CV. We merely followed the model of our professor. "Resumé" was not a household word until we started teaching and researching professional communication.

Because we have a long history of spoken communication before we ever think of looking for a job, we tend to overlook the importance of face-to-face contact in hiring and assigning employees. It is much easier to specify how to write a resumé than to detail the process of making personal contact, especially across boundaries of nations, regions, ethnic groups, professions, gender, or generation. Nevertheless there is no general agreement on the basic variables of length, type, or professional presentation, though experts seem to agree on a basic C-B-S style. We argue that these recommendations grow out of a particular cultural climate, that of North America in the late twentieth century, and they are not generally found outside of this environment.

In spite of the controversy among experts and the considerable variation both within and across cultural groups, and despite change across time, the resumé is a major source of professional evaluation. Conflicts arise because of the tension between being taught to be modest in face-to-face contact and being expected to do what amounts to bragging in writing a resumé. This conflict was brought home in our research project by Finnish participants who did not provide a resumé even though they were otherwise very helpful and cooperative.

We have shown that there is a divergence between members' generalizations about what should be done or what is traditionally done and what members of particular professional groups actually do in evaluating job applicants. Moreover, there is a negative response to resumés that fail to meet the expectations of evaluators, whatever they say they look for in a resumé. These practices lead us to recommend a CDP exchange as a way of finding out what people whom one is likely to encounter in their professional dealings do in actual situations.

We have illustrated a range of guidelines by experts for preparing and standards of evaluation of different types of resumés encountered in our focus groups, and set these readings in sociohistorical context. For example, the chronological resumé was frowned on, though used by participants in our project. Focus group discussion revealed that the year-by-year archiving of activities resembled too closely the dossiers kept in China during the Cultural Revolution for people in Beijing to be comfortable with a form of presentation that reminded them of that archiving. Yet the reasons given for preferring functional resumés resembled textbook advice.

Differences of opinion arose around the presentation of personal mixed with professional information. Perhaps because of the institutional nature of dossiers kept by work units, the Beijing participants insisted on personal information such as gender and age, in spite of their expressed preference for clear, concise resumés. They preferred narratives or descriptions of goals and achievements to simple lists of experience.

In evaluating a resumé, the factors of length, focus, and personal information were recurring criteria. Although the long resumé we presented as a neutral, objective artifact effectively achieved its goal, it was invariably judged negatively. There was also consensus that information should be focused on the job being applied for. As with length and focus, there was no agreement between what was done and what was prescribed, but there was greater disagreement regarding the inclusion of personal details.

In distinguishing between personal and professional information, we make reference to an earlier distinction between human knowledge and institutional knowledge. Personal, human knowledge is based on our experience as members of involuntary discourse systems such as national origin, when we were born and into what class or ethnic group, our gender and position among siblings, and the like. This early and largely involuntary and nonconscious knowledge affects our voluntary, goal-oriented institutional knowledge.

These two kinds of knowledge, largely nonconscious gained by involuntary association on the one hand, and mostly conscious and voluntarily obtained on the other, infiltrate each other, surfacing as contradictions in focus group discussions. Americans may be unaware of the onerous task of archiving official information borne by Chinese, who may in turn be unaware of the legal restrictions in western countries on the presentation of personal information such as gender or marital status.

In order to bring to bear both personal and professional information across international boundaries, we recommend the exchange of CDPs. Not only is professional information sent back and forth in the form of resumés, but also personal reactions to these documents are made available to both senders and recipients, providing the basis for successful job searches and long-term relationships.

4

The Presentation: From Dale Carnegie to Ananova the Avatar

Human Face to Cyberface

The *Washington Post* carried a story about "Ananova," the "news droid," as we began to write this chapter on presentations. Ananova is a computer-constructed newsreader, or what computer scientists call an "agent" or "avatar," according to the *Post*: "She's a mass of sophisticated speech-recognition software and computing power designed to put a human face – and personality – on our interactions with machines" (Farhi 2000). This computer simulation of a human face to "read" the news has been constructed because, according to Farhi, "People would rather interact with people – even ones that are only vaguely human – than with silicon and cold type" (Farhi 2000).

More than sixty years ago, Dale Carnegie's book *How to Win Friends and Influence People* (1937) signaled the arrival of the "American friendly" style of interpersonal behavior, which has come to dominate the world of business and organizational communication. Now, six decades later the 1998 Windows 98® PowerPoint® Wizard includes a "Carnegie Coach," which advises users on how to make successful presentations using this presentation software package. The advice given is straight out of the 1937 Carnegie book:

Make a positive first impression:
* Establish eye–contact.
* Display poised, confident body language.
* Be relaxed.
* Be well groomed.

This advice to "establish eye-contact" is encapsulated within a presentation technology which virtually guarantees that our audience's *eyes will be elsewhere – glued to the screen* upon which our PowerPoint® slides are being projected.

There is a growing tension between the rapidly developing technologies of presentation, which are now a *must* in professional presentations, and the person of the presenter. The technologies presuppose or even demand certain ways of presenting while, at the same time, human beings continue to prefer human face-to-face contact – apparently even if it is just simulated by a computer image.

When we began our research into intercultural communication over two decades ago, our main concern was in coming to understand how people from different cultural or social groups could communicate successfully with each other in face-to-face situations. Now we can see that it is more often that the relationship between people is being mediated by some presentation technology, or in the case of Ananova, the avatar, the person is being replaced by a computer-generated image of a person.

Contemporary Presentation Style

On an airplane from California to Washington, DC, we read, in a magazine intended for business people traveling by air, the title "Winning presentations blend great technology with skill and preparation." The summary paragraph under the title says:

> Successful business presentations require a combination of top-notch hardware, sophisticated software and finely honed presentation skills. All the companies featured in this month's special section offer tools that can help road warriors become more efficient and more effective. (United Airline flight magazine, March 2000)

It has become essential in professional presentation in international settings to use the most up-to-date technologies of presentation. The use of these technologies is viewed as having a universally positive impact on the audience and their reception of the presenter. This is true not only in North America, but also internationally in places as far removed from each other as East Asia, South America, and northern Europe. The use of technologies in business and professional presentations is considered a form of professionalism in itself. In our own lecturing experience in Hong Kong, Finland, or the UK we have found lecture halls are now equipped with a computer, VCR, CD player, overhead projector, and projector screen as a basic minimum for presentations. At our university in Hong Kong, a trainer

assigned to assist faculty in developing their presentation skills and to famil-
iarize them with the newly installed equipment was very enthusiastic about
all this technology. He said that, of course, you would be using some presentation software on one screen with the outline of your talk. On another
screen you would want slides or, better, video clips. You would, no doubt,
be using the visualizer to project physical objects for demonstration and you
would, naturally, also be giving your lecture to link these together. He went
on to say this would probably be somewhat boring to the students, who
are expecting higher levels of technology, so that you should also play a
CD of your favorite music to back up this presentation and make it more
"interesting."

Perhaps now this same technological team is designing avatar-professor
lookalikes to spare real but boring people the effort of getting down to the
lecture hall on time to run all this technology. Perhaps avatar-students could
be programmed to ask interesting questions during the question period at
the end of the lecture as well.

Not only business people and professors but politicians have trouble integrating technology with Dale Carnegie-style warmth and sincerity. Shortly
before Hong Kong was returned to Chinese sovereignty in 1997, the new
chief executive Tung Chee-hwa was criticized by the press for his inability
to make eye contact while reading his speech, which was posted next to the
television camera. A photograph showing his eyes focused upward has the
caption "Taxing task . . . Tung Chee-hwa had trouble making eye contact."
Tung was said to have had training in oral presentation by American professionals in the Dale Carnegie tradition.

In our contemporary world the great cultural and personal diversity of
presentation styles is rapidly being restructured through the use of standardized presentation technology. As we found in our research covering
Finland, Hong Kong, and Beijing, while each of these sites once had a differing face-to-face communication style, now they are tending to converge
in their use of technologies for presentation and new problems are developing, having to do less with cultural difference than with the contradictions that come from trying to maintain interactivity between the presenter
and the audience and the use of complex technologies. With the globalization of business and trade, the preferred presentational style tends to be
standardized on the basis of the old Dale Carnegie style of eye contact, confident body language, and "relaxed and warm" interpersonal style so often
associated with "western" or "American" interpersonal style. Yet in the
heartland of Dale Carnegie influence, an anthropologist reports on the
difficulty of maintaining the warm style demanded by his face-to-face
audience without excluding the audience who viewed him only through

technology. He felt glued to the floor, in view of the camera but unable to move freely toward the people seated in the room. The point we are making here is that good presentation is not a matter of conforming to an existing style but of reconciling conflicting demands, whether we are Finnish or Chinese, French or American.

The Dale Carnegie World of Oral Presentation

The authors made a review of many widely available sources on presentations within the business or organizational environment. The summary below shows that many of the features first outlined by Carnegie are still considered major features of any successful business presentation. It is particularly important to notice the emphasis given to nonverbal communication through eye contact with the audience:

1 *Delivery*
    (a)   Anyone giving a presentation must be aware of the added dimension a message acquires as a result of eye contact, gesture, posture, and conversational tone of voice.
    (b)   Establish eye contact with each member of the audience before starting a presentation, and maintain eye contact 90 to 100 percent of the time. Eye contact shows the speaker's confidence and enthusiasm.
    (c)   Have an "open" facial expression, smile and be emotional, excited and enthusiastic, entertaining, and eager.
    (d)   Use appropriate gestures and other body movements.
    (e)   Use gesture to add power to the presentation.
    (f)   Use body movement such as walking forward toward the audience to emphasize a key point.
    (g)   Place your feet 8 to 10 inches apart and keep your feet pointed toward your audience.
    (h)   Have natural and relaxed movement.
    (i)   Speak in a clear, strong, and distinct voice, and use full vocal range.
2 *Research and evidence*
    (a)   The speaker must both know what he or she is talking about and know where facts fit best in the presentation.
3 *Organization*
    (a)   Different presentations must be well organized in different ways.

4   *Audience*
    (a)   Decision makers: the decision-making power held by those who hear a presentation means that the customary role of speaker and audience in the public speaking situation will be reversed.
    (b)   Size: the speaker should organize and prepare the presentation as it would be in speaking to a large group.
5   *Length*
    (a)   Even though the standard presentation may not cover as broad a topic as a speech, it will probably take longer to deliver.
6   *Visual aids*
    (a)   OHTs (overhead transparencies)
    (b)   Videotapes
    (c)   PowerPoint®
    (d)   Audiotapes
7   *Handling questions*
    (a)   A presentation may be interrupted by questions at any time as the listeners are in positions of power, whereas a public speaker would almost never find such a practice desirable.
8   *Team presentations*
    (a)   It would be wise to use more than one speaker in a presentation.
    (b)   If several topics are covered, an expert may be required for each.
    (c)   Because a presentation may be rather long, a team approach will give it variety.
    (d)   The team approach gets more people involved in the preparation of the presentation.

In this tradition of presentation, the ability to interact with the audience is emphasized and highlighted. The speaker is expected to be the center of attention throughout. He or she is told to employ, in addition to verbal communication skills, features of nonverbal communication such as eye gaze, gesture, and body movement to convince the audience. That is why detailed guidelines are given in these textbooks about how to place your feet, how to make gestures, how to move your body, and where to look. This reflects the norms of people in face-to-face communication, where there is a direct interaction between two human beings with one as the speaker and the other as the listener. This traditional presentation style could be diagrammed as in figure 4.1.

Here the relationship is direct and face to face. In this model there is no "mediation" between the presenter and the audience. The effectiveness of the presentation depends on the presenter's ability to directly engage with the audience through eye contact, gesture, and his or her own personal style.

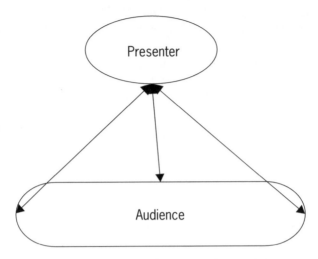

Figure 4.1   The "Dale Carnegie" model

In the years since the late 1930s, of course, various visual aids have come to play an important role in our ideas about presentations, as shown in a variety of expert sources on making presentations. In the summary above we have seen that visual aids of some kind are normally listed as integral aspects of presentations. The use of visual aids is believed to have various advantages in delivering a powerful presentation because "when visuals are used, 1) retention and learning are increased; 2) meeting or class effectiveness is increased; and 3) the image of the speaker is enhanced" (Kupsh and Graves 1993: 6–7). The introduction of technology in giving presentations has also opened the door to a variety of computer-generated visuals. Visual aids have become an important part of presentations.

Popular readings on how to give presentations all include the use of visual aids as an essential ingredient. The advantages of using visual aids cited in popular readings can be summarized as follows:

1   Visuals clarify your ideas.
2   Visuals keep you on track.
3   Visuals break down language barriers.
4   Visuals add interest and variety.
5   Visuals build confidence.
6   Visuals simplify complex material.
7   Visuals shorten the length of a presentation, making the time more productive.

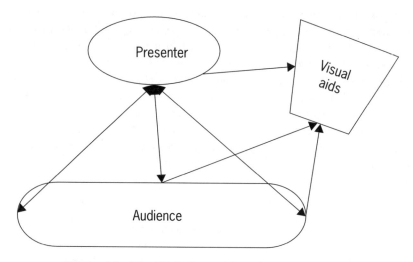

Figure 4.2 The "Dale Carnegie" model with visual aids

8   The audience will stay alert and remember much more about your presentation.
9   You become much better organized.
10   You are perceived as being professional.

But while the importance of visual aids is highlighted in these popular readings on presentation, interaction with the audience has not lessened in importance but is still emphasized. Almost all sections on visual aids are followed by a section on how to use visual aids in an interactive manner, such as this:

• Be sure to talk to the audience, not to the visual.
• Project your voice and increase the volume of your voice when using the visual.
• Face the audience, not the visual.
• Never read visuals to your audience or repeat word for word what's on the visual.
• Don't look at the visual while explaining what's on the visual to your audience.
• Make eye contact and gesture.
• Establish rapport with the audience.

This model is still the original basic Dale Carnegie model, but with visual aids introduced. This could be diagrammed as in figure 4.2.

This model, which introduces visual aids, already shows the complexity of following the original dictum of always maintaining eye contact with your audience. As these books suggest, even when using visuals, it is important to speak to the audience, not to the visuals. Nevertheless, no matter what the presenter does, there is a tendency for the presenter to have to compete with his or her own visuals for the attention of the audience. A presenter can work very hard on delivery and the preparation of visual aids, but it is difficult to control where the audience will focus attention. No matter how confident and enthusiastic a presenter may be, the visual aids may be more compelling. How can you maintain eye contact when all eyes are on the visuals?

Technology-Based Presentations

The use of visual aids poses a new question or problem for the study of oral presentation. The traditional presentation style, the "Dale Carnegie" or "American" one, is speaker-centered. As we have seen, textbooks on business communication and professional presentation emphasize that the speaker should use an interactive style, with adequate eye contact, gestures, and body movement to engage the audience. The traditional study of oral presentation in intercultural communication is also based on face-to-face interaction, with the speaker as the center. Verbal and nonverbal elements of linguistic expression, tone of voice, contextualization cues, eye gaze, gesturing, and body movements are considered crucial in face-to-face interaction and presentation. With the introduction of new technologies, there came a new element that calls for our attention in intercultural communication.

Technology-based presentations have introduced a new semiotic basis which is a strong departure from the speaker-centered presentations. There are competing focal points in a technology-based presentation. This is not only true for the audience: at any particular moment, they must work out whether to pay attention to the speaker or to his or her visuals. But it is also true for the presenter in a technology-based presentation that his or her focus tends to be on the operation of the technology – computer or projector, screen, and slides. Sometimes this includes pushing the presenter physically to stand by the projector screen or the overhead projector. He or she is no longer the physical center of focus within the room. The audience's eyes tend to focus on the screen and slides. The presenter then takes up the role of a technician who is running the show. There is competition for eye gaze on the part of the presenter as well.

The operation of visuals also constrains the movements of the speaker. In the earlier Carnegie style, the presenter could move about the podium or stage making broad movements and gestures to maintain the focus and interest of the audience. With presentation technologies, the presenter cannot easily move around during the presentation. He or she has to stand by the machine to operate the technology and point at the slides. Often there is also a change in lighting when using some technologies, such as computer presentation software like PowerPoint®. The dim light makes it easier for the audience to see what is on the screen. On the other hand, it changes the atmosphere of the presentation and may also make it difficult for the presenter to see either his or her notes or the audience. To some extent, the presenter disappears from the main stage, taking up the role of a voice-over narrator.

On the positive side, the use of technology makes it possible to include a lot of information in one presentation. In a single slide, a presenter can put symbols, pictures, charts, and texts. He or she can bring colors and sound effects into the presentation. For example, in one case in our research, a Hong Kong computer sales representative filled his slides with text in small fonts and colorful charts. These busy slides, however, competed with the presenter himself for the audience's attention. The audience had to spend more time processing the information presented on the busy slides, and thus was not able to focus on the presenter. The busy slides also forced the speaker to run through the presentation rather quickly to voice the information contained in these crowded slides. Perhaps this could simply be said to be ineffective use of the technology, but we have seen many such presentations, including several from presenters in medical research who have been commended widely for the quality of their presentations. In these cases, it is interesting to note that what one remembers is the slides, images, and graphics, not the presenter or even his or her main point.

The use of technology in oral presentations has not only introduced a new mode of communication in international settings, but also a new problem in intercultural communication. The conflict between the use of technology and the speaker as a person is an issue that has not been touched in studies of intercultural communication. As the research we will discuss below shows, the introduction of presentation technology in oral presentations leads to new problems for communication in international settings. We have tried to capture this restructuring of the presentation brought about by new presentation technologies in the diagram in figure 4.3. In this model it might be that the relationship between the presenter and the audience is really secondary to that between the technology and the audience, and that the presenter is in a somewhat peripheral role as the technician who makes this relationship happen.

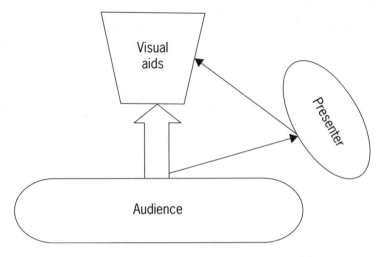

Figure 4.3   Presentation with voice–over model

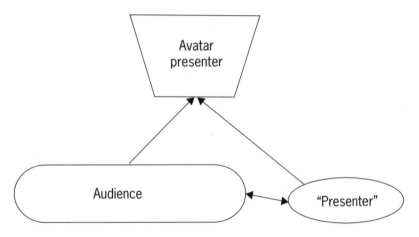

Figure 4.4   The Avatar model

Naturally, it is only a short step from this model to the complete replace-ment of the presenter by a computer-based "agent" or "avatar," as our opening example suggests. To reunify the focal point of the presentation, the "presenter" has to be placed in the center of the visual field. To do this, and to simultaneously retain the use of information technology, perhaps it will be found necessary to use an avatar as part of the visual display, as in figure 4.4.

Other Complexities

Many sources on public speaking emphasize the importance of analyzing your audience as an essential aspect of preparing any presentation. We would agree that this is an important aspect of any public or group presentation. Having said that, however, it is important to realize that this is not the only consideration in making an effective presentation. One of the criticisms Chinese sources on public speaking make of "western" concepts of presentation is that they are too narrowly focused on the relationship between the speaker and the audience, as if that is the only thing that the speaker (or the audience) needs to be concerned about. The basic model is that of the conversation between two independent and equal parties, as we have said about the original Carnegie model of presentations.

One basic textbook on public speaking in China (Li and Zou 1997) outlines quite an elaborate set of considerations, to which we have also added a few. To begin with, there is the relationship we have mentioned between the speaker and the audience. To this Li and Zou add the relationship of the speaker to his or her material. A person speaking about a subject which he or she has just encountered or just prepared will speak in a very different way and with a different kind of authority from someone who is speaking about something he or she has known for years or about which he or she is an expert. We can understand this from the difference in confidence and control we have when we are speaking about our own private experience and when talking about a highly technical subject we have just come to master.

At the same time, this same source tells us, we must consider the relationship between the audience and the material of the presentation. Again, the audience will respond differently to material which is quite new to them and to material they know a lot about, and the speaker must take these different audience-to-presentation relationships into consideration.

We could diagram this set of relationships as in figure 4.5. In other words, one relationship between the speaker and the audience is mediated *through* the material of the presentation but another one is quite independent of the material. This is what somebody would mean if she said, "George is a great person, but I think he was in over his head in trying to make a presentation on the current situation in Hong Kong. He's really a specialist in Northern Europe." The person is saying that her relationship with George is quite good *outside of the situation of the presentation*, but as far as the presentation is concerned, George doesn't really handle the material well. Of course, we might also hear someone say, "I don't like George much, but I have to admit

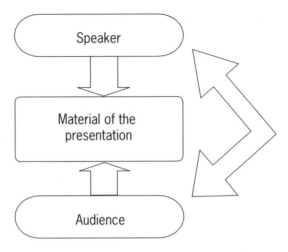

Figure 4.5   The double relationship model

that his presentation on the financial situation in the European Community was brilliant."

Again, Li and Zou make this picture more complex by pointing out that there are also relationships among the audience members that must be taken into consideration. Speaking as a stranger to a group of people who know each other very well, as one might as an invited after-dinner speaker to a business association, is very different from speaking to a public group who are all strangers to each other. The audience dynamics are very different and can work for or against the presentation of the speaker.

On the other side of the podium, there are often relationships among speakers sharing the same platform for an event and between them and the organizers of the occasion. If you are making a presentation in a group, the roles of each presenter must be clearly signaled – who is the leader of the group, who is the technical person, who is in sales, and so forth. And when your presentation or your group's presentation is sponsored by the organizers it carries a very different importance from when you are, perhaps, simply being allowed to present your views.

In one consultation project in which one of the authors was involved, the management had made the formal invitation to conduct a management training project, but this was only after they had been forced into this position by the organization's bargaining unit. The relationships between management and the bargaining unit were hostile and at the beginning, as outside consultants who had been hired by management, our group of con-

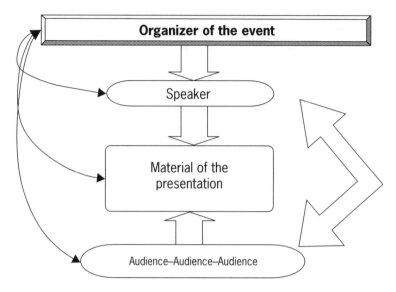

Figure 4.6 The multiple relationships model

sultants was viewed as *being on the side* of management. At first we received a very hostile reception from members of the bargaining unit. We were able to overcome this in the course of a two-day training session, but the relationships between management and the bargaining unit and our position as hired consultants of management were stronger than any presentation of our materials could be during the first several hours of the training session.

A more complex model would look like figure 4.6. It is likely that in each different situation, cultural group, or even corporation or organization these relationships will be very different. One major Finnish company with which we have had a consultation contract prided itself on having a very "flat" organizational structure. Our presentations for this company were influenced very little by senior corporate management and there was quite wide-open discussion among members of the audience, between the audience and the presenters, and among all three groups – presenters, audience, and management. In the case mentioned just above, however, there was a great deal of hushed discussion among the audience of bargaining unit members, another flurry of hushed discussion among members of the management, and very little discussion between us presenters and either of these groups. Our presence at first was limited strictly to our presentations from the podium.

If we combine these complexities with the ones we introduced earlier having to do with the use of presentation technologies, we can see that there is now a very complex situation in presentations in international settings. Presentations represent probably the most prominent aspect of impression-making in professional settings. Unlike resumés, which are seen by limited numbers of people, presentations put one in the center of attention. As we have said in chapter 1, our research shows that participants have very contradictory views about what should be the correct or most effective strategies for communication in international settings. Now we will turn to that research and show how participants made presentations and how they reacted to them.

The Faces of World English

In a study of both international and local television newsreaders in Hong Kong broadcasts, we analyzed three broadly different styles: *objective*, *emphatic*, and *evaluative*. The one we used to characterize Chinese presenters, whether speaking Putonghua in China or Cantonese in Hong Kong, we might call objective. In presenting the news, these readers used little facial expression or variety of intonation, speaking with steady volume in the same narrow pitch range. As we will see below, this *objective* style of presenting the news is much like the style used by both the Beijing Chinese and the Finnish presenters in our research project "Professional Communication Across Cultures."

In contrast to this *objective* style, presenters who read the news in English, whether Anglo, Chinese, or Indian, used what we call an *emphatic* style. In this style the presenters emphasize important words and phrases with increased pitch or volume, head nods, and raised eyebrows. We could represent this type of reading using **boldface type** for emphasized syllables, though, of course this emphasis might be done not only with pitch and volume, but, as we have said also with head nods and raised eyebrows:

Doctors in New **York** today have re**vealed** . . .

Here the emphasis follows normal English sentence intonation patterns. The overall effect is to heighten the listener's involvement in the news, but it remains nevertheless objective. We might have called this *objective emphatic*.

The third style we call *evaluative*. This was found in some American newsreaders, such as Connie Chung, and in other female presenters in both

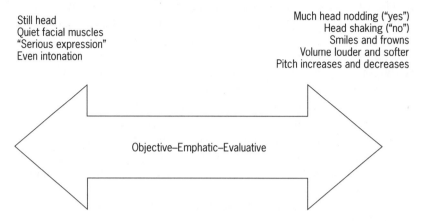

Still head
Quiet facial muscles
"Serious expression"
Even intonation

Much head nodding ("yes")
Head shaking ("no")
Smiles and frowns
Volume louder and softer
Pitch increases and decreases

Objective–Emphatic–Evaluative

Figure 4.7   Presentation faces

Japanese and Korean news broadcasts who were probably educated in North America and who spoke with American (rather than British) accents. In addition to emphasizing main points, like the presenters did with the *objective emphatic* style, these readers showed their attitude toward what they were reading by raising their eyebrows frequently, smiling and nodding or frowning and shaking their head to show approval or disapproval of the statements they were making.

We found that there was a continuum among some 50 presenters whose delivery we analyzed, with American males falling between the emphatic British or Hong Kong style and the evaluative style of American female reporters. The difference between emphatic and evaluative delivery is that the former makes it easier for listeners to process the text being read so that they can interpret it themselves, while the latter makes visible and audible what the person reading feels about what he or she is reporting.

Of course there may be variation in style depending on how serious the story is judged to be. The same person may use an objective style for reading news and an emphatic style for reporting sports. As there is variation from place to place for presenters reading the same stories, as well as situational or topical variation within the same station, a person moving from one city to another might find that there were different expectations.

For our purposes here, we bring up this research to highlight the fact that in any presentation, a presenter must place himself or herself somewhere in this *objective–emphatic–evaluative* range. This continuum of facial/head expression can be diagrammed as in figure 4.7.

The two ends of this continuum are mutually exclusive. A presenter cannot *simultaneously* give an *objective* presentation and an *evaluative* one, even when this is simply a matter of reading the main news on television. That is, it is impossible to be nodding and shaking your head *and* to be holding it quite still. It is impossible to smile and frown *while keeping your face still*. Even more than the newsreader or presenter, the business presenter is caught between these two extremes. If he or she gives an *emphatic to evaluative* presentation, the audience will most likely be very moved by the presentation and feel a high sense of involvement. But the audience cannot *at the same time* feel a sense that the materials were presented *objectively*. In contrast, a presenter who gives a very *objective* presentation might be thought to be cold or uninvolving.

Ananova, the *avatar* or *agent* computer-simulated newsreader we mentioned at the beginning of this chapter, can be analyzed as giving an *emphatic to evaluative* reading of the news. It is not surprising to us that this position has been chosen by the programmers. In our research we found that this was the dominant style of the American-style anchor person. As we will see below, even though the presenters in our research project diverged from this style in their own presentations, they did seem to hold it up as their international ideal style. Now we will turn to that research and show how the participants made presentations and how they reacted to them.

Presentations in Three Cultures

We videotaped one presentation given by a professional from each of the three sites: Hong Kong, Beijing, and Finland. Each presentation used some kind of visual aids or other presentation technology. The three videotaped presentations were then sent to each of the other three sites for focus group discussion and to elicit feedback and comments on the current presentation style. Focus group participants in each site evaluated these three presentations, including the one given by the person from their own cultural group.

The Hong Kong presentation

The Hong Kong presentation was a promotional talk about a computer software package. The talk was given by two presenters, using PowerPoint® to deliver the presentation in English. During the presentation, the two presenters stood side by side. One, holding a microphone in his hand, was the main speaker. He stood by the screen and looked at and talked to it during most of his presentation time, speaking quickly, almost nonstop. He also used a lot of hand gesturing and body movement. His hands were nearly always in motion and, in addition, he continually moved his body from left to right. The other presenter held his hands in his pockets and moved his body from left to right in synchrony with the first. At one point in the middle of their presentation there was a technical difficulty with the microphone. The two speakers stood in position waiting for the technician to take care of the problem.

This presentation was quite well received in terms of the use of technology and in terms of what focus group members referred to as "professionalism." Focus group members in all three sites commented that the two presenters were well dressed and had a good, professional appearance. They said that they appeared to be smart, professional, and knowledgeable. The use of PowerPoint® was taken to be a sign of modern, advanced technology and was commented on as quite impressive.

But even though the focus group participants spoke highly of these presenters in terms of their "knowledge" and their "professionalism," in terms of their presentation style they were evaluated very negatively. The main problems with their presentation were said to be:

- no interaction with the audience
- lack of eye contact – they looked at the screen most of the time
- lack of attention-catching skill
- boring because of the flat tone in which the main presenter spoke
- excessive hand gesturing and body movement
- speaking too fast; the presentation was too rushed with too much information
- lack of problem-solving skill; no jokes or apologies when there was a technical problem
- presentation not coherent, not well organized, not easy to follow.

Focus group members in Hong Kong, Beijing, and Finland all made similar comments regarding the Hong Kong presenters' style. The problems pinpointed were related to the use of verbal and nonverbal cues in the interaction. The presenter obviously failed to maintain eye contact with the audience because he was busy looking at and pointing at the screen. He moved his body constantly and used a lot of hand gesturing, but indiscriminately, which the focus group participants found very confusing and distracting. They felt that the presenter had used so much hand movement to "calm the nerves" rather than as an aid in emphasizing a point. All agreed that his hand movements were overdone, not used to guide the presentation or to draw the audience's attention, but only to make the speaker himself feel comfortable.

The use of technology in presentation makes it easy to include a lot of information on one slide. But since the information is densely packed, the presenter may become rather busy running through each slide. In the Hong Kong presentation there was no interval or break in the presentation. The focus group participants found the fast speed very unprofessional and disturbing. They said this in spite of otherwise saying that he was "very professional." Many participants said that it was difficult to follow the presentation because of the presenter's fast speaking speed. While this could easily be said to be because he was speaking in English and this was a second language for him as well as for the people in the focus group, one Beijing focus group participant commented that the presenter rushed through his presentation because, as he said, "He is not knowledgeable enough. This is his problem. He is not very clear himself, so he is scared that if he speaks slower, his audience may start to ask questions." This focus group in Beijing believed that a good presenter should speak at a slower pace and make himself or herself clear so that the audience could follow. They set the highest priority on the clarity of the presentation, not on the amount of information conveyed, and they suggested that it was a lack of professionalism not to recognize this.

The focus group members in Beijing also thought that the two speakers did not handle the unexpected technical problem of microphone failure well. They felt that the speaker should have made an apology, made a few jokes, or reiterated the flow of the presentation for the audience rather than just standing there, hitting the microphone. When the technical problem was resolved, he should have tried to recapture the audience's attention by raising his voice, and rephrasing what he had said earlier.

The net result of all this is that the presenter was perceived as nervous, not knowledgeable, and inexperienced by the focus group participants. The presentation was said to be "cold" because of the lack of interaction with the audience.

What is important to remember in the comments made by this focus group is that they are quite contradictory. On the one hand they said that the presenters were very professional and the group were very impressed with the presenters' use of technology for presentation. In contradiction to this the group said the presenters were unprofessional in their failure to deal with the technical problem and that they were nervous and unknowledgeable. This highlights one of the dangers of presentations when there are contradictions built into the situation: one might well be praised for making a great impression with the technology, but one's own personal impression can come off very much the worse by comparison. All presenters will have to evaluate whether in the long run it is the technology they are trying to sell or their own personal connections with the audience. We believe that this tension or dilemma is one that can only be resolved through the use of the Communication Display Portfolio (CDP) and other exchanges we are advocating in this book.

The Beijing presentation

The Beijing presentation was an internal training session on the company's administrative regulations regarding exports. The presenter used an overhead projector in her presentation. The talk was in Chinese, but the overhead transparencies were in English. The presenter talked at a slower pace, with pauses here and there. She did not use much hand gesturing. Occasionally she briefly pointed at the overhead transparencies to illustrate her point. She stood still by the overhead projector during the entire presentation, somewhat stiffly, and talked into the microphone.

The general observations made by the focus group participants in all sites was that she was professional, calm, and very clear about her presentation. She appeared to be "more peaceful," "nice but a bit boring," and she was said to speak "like an expert." They noted that she stated "why," "when," "who," "where" in the beginning of the presentation, which gave the impression that she knew what she was doing. Of course, we should remind the reader that these are the basic "five Ws" of the C-B-S style we introduced in chapter 1 and discussed in chapter 2 in relation to the telephone call. Focus group members commented that the Beijing presenter also used rhetorical questions in her presentation to start a point. Generally, they thought that this was a good strategy to get her point across to the audience in an interactive way.

The problems that were mentioned in the focus groups were that they noticed that she did not demonstrate great enthusiasm, interest, or confidence in her presentation. They commented that her tone of voice was flat with little or no variation in her intonation. We have said that during the presentation she stood still by the overhead projector and simply pointed at the overhead transparencies. Focus group members commented that she appeared to talk to herself, not to her audience. Her static posture blocked the view of some people in the audience. Her body language and facial expressions suggested nervousness, they said, especially at the beginning. Note that this presenter was said to be nervous because of very little movement of her body, while the Hong Kong presenter was said to be nervous for the opposite reason – too much movement of his body. Also notice in our summary of standard textbooks on successful presentations the caution, "Use appropriate gestures and other body movements." It should be clear from this that such advice is totally useless. In the first place, how is one to know what is "appropriate" in either gestures or body movements? In the second place, one group would consider lack of body movements to be evidence of nervousness while another group might focus on excessive body movements as evidence of nervousness. The point we want to make is that *there is no absolute* or *fixed* set of principles; the most effective means of presenting is doing so with feedback on the presentation from the target audience so that corrections can be made whenever and wherever misinterpretations are made.

One Finnish focus group participant commented about the Beijing presenter that, "Her speech was somewhat suffocating. She poured everything out and then she took her stuff and left so she gave the impression that she was not a bit interested in talking more about the subject." Here the speaker focuses on the speech, not the movement, but in traditional Finnish practice presenters speak without moving and without interaction with the audience. The speaker, a younger woman, associated the Beijing presenter's style with the old-fashioned Finnish style younger Finns are trying to overcome. As an example of this older Finnish value of nonverbal stillness, when lecturing to a Finnish audience one of the authors drew the comment from an older woman that there were too many hand gestures. The woman, a professor, said that they had been trained not to move their hands.

The Hong Kong focus group participants attributed the stiffness of the Beijing presenter to cultural practice in Mainland China, because, they said, Mainland Chinese are taught not to move their bodies while giving a public speech. Once again, we see that the same actions can be interpreted in very different ways by different social or cultural groups.

The focus group participants in all of the three sites thought that the Beijing presenter needed to be more interactive, engaging the audience by talking to them and asking them questions. But they were aware that there are differences in types of presentations. Since this was a presentation on legal regulations, there was, they thought, no need to make a sales pitch or to be persuasive. From that point of view, they said, it is acceptable to aim at clarity and brevity. Interestingly enough, the Beijing focus group participants thought that she should have used more advanced technology such as PowerPoint®, not overhead transparencies, in her presentation.

The Finnish presentation

The Finnish presentation was a paper delivered at a conference on technologies in Asia. The presenter used an overhead projector with transparencies made with PowerPoint® to demonstrate his points. Both the talk and overhead projector transparencies (OHTs) were in English. The OHTs were nicely made with their company logo at the bottom of each slide. The presenter appeared to be very formal and well dressed. He stood motionless behind a podium and read from his paper. He rarely lifted his eyes from the paper to look at the audience.

The focus group participants liked the well-designed, high-quality OHTs prepared by the Finnish presenter. But the presentation was evaluated quite negatively in both the Beijing and Hong Kong sites. The main problem again was the lack of interaction with the audience, which came down to the following issues:

- no eye contact
- flat tone of voice, no variation in intonation
- reading from his paper
- no body movement or hand gesturing.

These verbal and nonverbal cues were perceived as important ingredients for an interactive presentation. When these ingredients are missing from a presentation, our research suggests, a presenter is received quite negatively. One extreme negative comment made by one of the Beijing focus group members was that the presenter was "either junior (very nervous) or senior (paper written by others)." The general impression was that the presentation was boring, not lively or attractive.

The Hong Kong focus group members made a distinction between different types of presentations. They thought that this presentation would be acceptable for this kind of setting, because it was a technical conference. For technical presentations, they said, the content is more important than the way the information is delivered. For marketing presentations, on the other hand, they felt that style is more important. In order to make a selling point, a sales representative needs to be interactive and engaged with the audience.

Not surprisingly, the Finnish focus group participants had a different impression of this Finnish man's presentation. They commented that it was appropriate for a Finnish man to be serious and stand still while giving a presentation. This is because the Finns are reticent and serious in face-to-face interaction. In contrast, they expected the Beijing and Hong Kong presenters to be more interactive. On the whole, they prefer to see more dialog and interaction between the audience and the presenter in a professional presentation – that is, they prefer what they see as a non-Finnish style in presentations. In other words, it is acceptable for Finns not to be interactive, because that is part of their cultural practice and behavioral norm, but for global corporate practice they felt that it is essential to be interactive.

Competing Themes in the Focus Group Reflections

To summarize the focus group discussions, there were two competing and contradictory themes in their evaluation of oral presentations. One was appreciation for the use of technologies, the other was the desire for more interaction.

Participants in Finland and Hong Kong highly praised the use of presentation technologies in oral presentations. For them, it was "the more the better." Participants in Beijing also made explicit their desire for the use of PowerPoint® in presentations. They all appreciated the use of visual aids and high tech in professional presentations. But at the same time the focus group participants in all three sites expressed a strong desire for a more interactive presentation.

The Hong Kong presenters used a PowerPoint® presentation, and they were evaluated positively for that; at the same time they were evaluated quite negatively as presenters. The Beijing Chinese woman used OHT slides in her presentation, speaking in a slower manner, occasionally looking at the audience. She was viewed as doing a better job in her presentation. The Finnish man also used OHT slides in his presentation. But he read from his paper and looked very serious. He received negative comments from the participants in Hong Kong and Beijing. All focus group members preferred to see a face-to-face interaction style, with a slower pace, sufficient eye contact, just enough hand gesturing to make the point, and an engaging tone and intonation (not just mechanical reading).

What is so important about these comments is that it never occurred to the participants in this study that the use of visual aids may interfere with interaction in oral presentations. Even while expressing very contradictory evaluations, they did not themselves comment on these contradictions or on the source of the contradiction – the conflict between the "interactive" or Carnegie-style presentation and the use of high-tech presentation technologies.

In this contradictory situation, the presenter assumes multiple roles and handles several tasks at the same time. It is much more demanding on the part of the presenter to keep eye contact with the audience while at the same time operating the visuals with efficiency. There is also a competition between the visuals and the speaker for eye focus from the audience.

When this conflict occurs, how is the presenter being evaluated and judged if he or she fails to deliver an interactive presentation? As in other intercultural settings, when misunderstanding or a problem occurs in communication, the participants tend to negatively value or judge the other party. In oral presentations, when there is a conflict between the general assumption that the presenter is aiming at an interactive presentation and the use of technologies, the speaker/presenter is judged in negative terms. That is, the conflict which is built into this situation is unconsciously held against the presenter even when the materials of the presentation may be praised at the same time.

Focus group participants evaluated the presenter as boring, nervous, inexperienced, incompetent, not knowledgeable, or not confident when there was a conflict between the technology and the "interactivity" of the presenter. Participants questioned the competence and knowledge of the presenter, especially when there was a technical problem. As we can see from the presentations given by the two Hong Kong professionals, the focus group participants reacted strongly to the way they handled the situation. To some extent, the presenters were viewed as incompetent because there was a technical problem, even though it was not of their own making. They were not judged by their knowledge of the subject matter, but by how they operated the technologies. In addition to this, for the Beijing focus group participants, the technical problem incurred a loss of face as well.

We began to see the formation of a global technological ideal for post-modern presentation, one which raises problems with the modern Dale Carnegie approach. Participants expressed a Cargo Cult-like belief in the Anglo-American style of presentation, saying that because Americans were successful they themselves would also be successful if they adopted the same style. The economic success of Hong Kong and Finland is seen as evidence for this belief. However, as we have seen, the presenters from Hong Kong and Finland had trouble bringing off the Dale Carnegie ideal. Their success must be a result of other factors. To approximate the interactive style pre-ferred by Americans would require a transformation of traditional semiotic systems. Furthermore, the combination of the interactive style with high-tech presentational aids is inherently contradictory and even Americans have trouble managing the contradiction. Should we continue to uphold an ideal that is no longer functional in this context even in the country where it originated?

Conflict Between Assumptions and Practice

We believe the negative feedback from the focus group participants is the result of the conflict between the standardized world-wide business practice which maintains a focus on face-to-face interaction, with the speaker as the center of interaction, and a newly and rapidly developing standard of the use of presentation technologies. We now face a new challenge in intercultural communication: the center has shifted, to some extent, to the mediational means of presentation software and other technologies. In the increased use of presentation technologies there is a decentering of the human presenter and an increased focus on the technology itself. The interactional mode is no longer a one-dimensional mode of face-to-face, speaker–listener communication. There are multiple modalities in the oral presentation and in other modes of communication. This poses a question of how we can deal with multimodality of discourses in intercultural communication. We are especially concerned with how successful presentations can be made in international settings when there is massive cultural difference in the assumptions about what might be a good presentation to begin with, and now there is the additional complexity of the contradictions brought about through the expanding emphasis on presentation technologies.

As we saw in the case of the telephone, when a new technology of communication is introduced into a society, it often comes with a dilemma created by the conflict between our assumptions and actual practices. This is because the use of a new technology has an immediate effect on the practice, but it takes time for us to change our assumptions about what the appropriate way of doing things is. Like the QWERTY phenomenon we discussed in chapter 2, a technological development might occur for one reason but then be continued even over generations because it has become social practice within a community. The C-B-S style of business communication has been established pretty much world-wide for business communication, and we have also seen established the Carnegie style of face-to-face interaction with its emphasis on eye contact and "warm" interpersonal contact. These have become the assumptions and beliefs that are fixed cultural norms established over a long period of social practice. Into this picture we have introduced presentation technologies that are in direct competition with these cultural/social practices for face-to-face presentation. The gap between old practices and new conditions is creating a problem in communication, especially across cultural boundaries, which may well take years of reorientation before we develop new, better-adjusted practices.

Summary of Contrastive Commentary

Here we summarize comments from the three-culture project as well as additional focus groups held among students and business professionals in Hong Kong. The ideal was professional people so familiar with their content that they could speak directly to the audience, holding their attention by their lively style as well as their interesting content supplemented by visual aids. For Hong Kong focus group participants who viewed a variety of presentations, those who most closely approached this ideal were foreign trainers and a Hong Kong professional woman educated in Britain.

In viewing presentations from movies, Hong Kong participants judged Chinese behavior as inappropriate and Hollywood portrayals as natural. That is, Hong Kong movies portrayed Chinese business people as rigidly authoritarian. Admittedly both were exaggerated for dramatic effect, but both were based on behavior that has been supported by interactional socio-linguistic research, as we argue in chapter 5. While participants agree on what is preferred behavior and interactional style, they tend to judge most Hong Kong professionals as not embodying the ideal. The American style portrayed in Hollywood movies seems to have been naturalized in the sense that it is accepted uncritically by the generation of Hong Kong working women in their thirties, though the student generation finds it strange if somewhat attractive. Men seem to have a double standard, tolerating or even enjoying the interactive style in foreigners but disapproving of Chinese, including overseas Chinese, who use it.

As far as interaction with the audience is concerned, most of our partici-pants expected it in a speaker though most would find it difficult to meet this ideal in their own presentation. Thus there is a discrepancy between what they express as the norm or ideal and what they do. What people from China do is held to be aberrant, even though it may not be as different from non-Chinese, e.g. Finnish, presenters' behavior as they themselves would like to think. In short, they have been socialized or colonized to accept the norms propagated by the international media.

In sum, the general belief among all three groups was that a professional presentation in an international setting should be interactive. In this all three groups express the Carnegie standard set in America over sixty years ago. This is true in spite of their equally strong valuation of highly technologi-cal presentations which inevitably contradict the interactive qualities they say they wish to see in a presentation.

Language Issue

In this discussion we have bypassed the issue of language. While English is in common use in professional communication in international settings, there is no agreement on whose English should be taught to or used by speakers of other languages. Apart from nonverbal aspects of presentation style, the presenters shown in our focus group discussions were evaluated on a standard of exuberant American English with much tonal variation in pitch. The Finnish speaker may have been perceived by the Chinese in Beijing as a European whose style should have matched more closely the American ideal. He himself was aware that he would be criticized for the flat intonation characteristic of Finnish speakers. People from societies such as Hong Kong, Finland, and Beijing, where new technologies are widely available and adopted, may be compensating for their lack of fluency and intelligibility in English by capitalizing on the use of new information and communication technologies. Likewise, Americans brought up on Carnegie-style interaction may be resisting these technologies because they are afraid to lose their advantage.

Intercultural Communication Issue?

As we have seen, the use of technologies in oral presentations has introduced a new dilemma in intercultural communication. Here an interaction is not so much between person and person as between an audience and a media production. Now the center has shifted to the mediational means of PowerPoint®, OHTs, and other technologies. The use of visual aids and technologies limits the body movement and eye focus of the presenter. The presenter either looks at the screen of the computer or looks at the slides. Sometimes he or she talks to the screen. In meetings of scientists it is common for presenters to have their backs to the audience. However, our assumptions and expectations of oral presentation remain the same, influenced by the standardized practices of face-to-face interaction. The audience still expects to see an oral presentation as interactive and engaging. The worst outcome of this conflict between expectations and practice is the audience's negative evaluation of the presenter, particularly in a cross-cultural setting.

The paradox of oral presentation styles implies that the conflict between belief and practice is true not only in professional presentations, but also in other areas where face-to-face communication was the norm of interaction. Now there are new technologies and new ways to communicate and to present oneself, such as e-mail, the Internet, websites, and presentation software packages such as PowerPoint®. The communication mode has shifted from one dimension to multidimensional or multimedia presentations. In the age of the information superhighway and the use of high technologies in our daily life, how do we study the interaction between speakers and technological tools? How do we investigate intercultural differences in the reaction to the use of these tools? What effect do technological tools have on intercultural communication?

Telephone communication changed, to a great extent, traditional patterns of face-to-face interaction, and the assumptions we have about how we should interact with each other. Later, certain standardized criteria were established, as we have said in chapter 2, about what the appropriate telephone manner is and how we should open and close a telephone conversation. As we have seen, textbooks teach business people how to make business phone calls, though what these textbooks teach and what people actually do is widely divergent. People have developed unconscious expectations and assumptions about what the appropriate way to conduct telephone conversations is. Now with mobile phones intruding on face-to-face conversation, there is wide variance in assumptions about the place of the person whose phone rings in the middle of a conversation. The introduction of e-mail has also affected traditional patterns of face-to-face communication. For instance, the Finns are perceived as very private people, who are quiet and who do not like to interact verbally with others, but e-mail has introduced a form of interaction among the Finns which seems to be compatible with traditional communication patterns. Many Finns apparently love to communicate with others using e-mail. Finland is now the country in the world with the most PCs and the highest use of the Internet. Many prefer making business decisions through e-mail discussion rather than in face-to-face meetings. In addition, Nokia, a Finnish company, is at the time of writing the world leader in mobile telephone technology. These contradictions are very indicative of the times in which we live, where old patterns of communication are being overturned almost daily. That is why we argue in this book that no experts can put forward any really reliable principles of communication. What we *can* put forward is a strategy for *learning about communication as we communicate*. This is the only way we can come to be certain that what we are learning is relevant to the situations in which we find ourselves communicating.

5

The Meeting: Action or Ratification?

This Isn't a Meeting; It's a Party

An American professional woman who was unable to get childcare on the day of a meeting had to take her three-year-old daughter along. She carefully instructed the child in the seriousness of the need to behave well and remain quiet while the meeting was going on, and all went quite well for a while. At one juncture, however, as the discussion of a particular topic broke out into multiple side conversations and a lot of joking and laughing, her daughter piped up, "Mommy, this isn't a meeting; it's a party!"

Even very young children have begun to develop ideas about what kinds of behavior are expected in different situations. In chapter 2 we saw that children already know how to carry on play "conversations" on the telephone before they have any idea that there should actually be another person speaking at the other end of the line. Maybe the daughter of this woman did not yet have much of an idea of what a meeting should be, but she did know what a party was like and from her childish point of view, all that conversation and laughing seemed like a party.

It is easy to dismiss such simple and direct perceptions as just the thoughts of children. On the other hand, in preparing for writing this chapter we did a search on the Internet for the topic "business meeting" and were surprised to find that among the most frequent items selected by our search engine was "luxury hotel." As we all know, many business meetings do take place within situations that most children would not be able to distinguish from parties, dinners, casual chats, or even late-night entertainment. Once again, as we have noted throughout this book, the professional literature on business meetings tends to focus quite narrowly on a very few types of business meetings and to set aside the almost limitless ways in which people in business, government, and other organizations meet each other to accomplish their business.

Real business meetings take place in conference rooms, of course, but also in corridors, at the water cooler and office coffee machines, on the metro or subway on the way to or from offices, in airport lounges, at lunches, or in coffee shops. We might have forgotten now that the world famous insurance company Lloyd's of London began in 1689, when Edward Lloyd began insuring shipments on the high seas, out of a back room of his coffee shop in London. Burgess (1984) comments that, "Insurance companies, merchant banks and The Stock Exchange of England all had their beginnings in the coffee houses of London" (Burgess 1984:75). We even know of a person who took up smoking because he felt that in the health-conscious world of late twentieth-century America, many important decisions were being made during smoking breaks taken outside of the office and only smokers were actively involved in the process. We also know a Chinese journalist who quit smoking but resumed the habit because she felt she could not adequately do her job without joining others in smoking.

Whether we meet on smoking breaks, in coffee shops, in luxury hotel conference rooms, or in our business partner's office, the basic question raised by our friend's daughter is the first we have to deal with in professional communication in international settings: what is a meeting? We need to come to an understanding of what a meeting is, where meetings take place, who the participants are, how the agenda or agendas are set, what the mood or tone of meetings is, when and where decisions are made and implemented, and how meetings fit into the overall culture of the organization and business framework in which we are working. We know of people who have agreed to have a meeting on a particular topic, traveled thousands of miles to meet, spent quite a few hours together in sight-seeing, elaborate banquets, and other forms of apparently social activity, and then parted. On one side we have heard, "We had a great and very productive meeting. We think things will go very well from now on." On the other side we have heard, "It was extremely frustrating to go so far and then never be able to actually get down to having a meeting. It looks like we'll never be able to come to any agreement."

In this chapter we have to admit to the impossibility of covering even in very broad strokes everything that might be useful to consider about meetings in an international setting. One reason for this is quite simple: in our own research project from which most of our materials are drawn we found it extremely difficult to get participants to provide direct exchanges with each other on meetings. We found this was so for two reasons, both of which make our task here rather complex. First of all, we found it was hard to pin down what we or anybody else meant by a "meeting." What for one was a casual dinner was an important business meeting for another. We didn't know for sure whether we should include chance encounters in the corridor or airport as meetings or whether on the other hand we should restrict our attention to much more formal, planned meetings within conference rooms with specific agendas. When we felt that it would be good to follow the second path, we found – not to our surprise, of course – that such meetings are most often felt to be highly confidential matters which participants did not feel they could easily share with others who were not already legitimate participants.

On the one hand meetings come in so many varieties that it is hard to know what to document in a Communication Display Portfolio (CDP); on the other hand formal meetings, which are easier to identify, are much more difficult to document for reasons of confidentiality. It is like what someone once said about the difference between rock identification in geology and bird identification in ornithology. Birds are very hard to actually see in their natural habitat, but if seen clearly they are highly distinctive and easy to identify. Rocks are very easy to see and examine carefully and can be easily removed, at least in pieces, for identification in the laboratory, but they are so complex in structure that it is very difficult to be certain just what rock has been identified. In what follows below, we will try to make a few observations which we hope will be useful about "bird-like" meetings – fleeting encounters and casual meetings – but most of what we will analyze will be more like the rocks of geology. We will focus on several well-documented studies of actual meetings and their structures, from which we can compare meetings across cultural groups. As we will see, while we can focus fairly clearly on these, our conclusions will have to be somewhat tentative because of the enormous human complexity of such events as formal business meetings.

As we will argue below, what happens in reality is that organizational decision making takes place both within formal business meetings and in pre- and post-meeting events and activities. We will recommend various strategies by which we can use other, less sensitive and confidential materials in focus groups and CDP exchanges to uncover deeper ideas about what makes for successful meetings of all kinds in international settings.

A Functional Approach to Business Meetings: Cultural Variations

We believe that the most important point to consider is this: what is the function of a meeting?

There is a danger of falling into structural descriptions of meetings, as often happens in standard textbooks on meetings. One finds instructions on how to set agendas and many other matters that have to do with the structural properties of the meeting, but the most important concern when we begin to work across the boundaries of our own commonsense ideas is that we might all make an agenda, but what is its purpose? We may have an appointed chair for a meeting, but what is the role of that chair? Is this person a primary decision maker, perhaps *the* primary decision maker, or is he or she working in a facilitative role to encourage a group decision-making process? Two meetings might appear very similar in structure but function very differently if we make just these two different assumptions about the role and function of the chair.

In international settings, the business meeting is an inevitable activity of any organization or company. In the complex organizations which we find most commonly in international settings, company policies and decisions are made through a consultative and feedback process which normally involves meetings; business and sales negotiations are done to a large extent through meetings. Virtually never are sales or other arrangements made simply through selections from catalogues, for example.

At the same time the meeting can be a place for group members to air their own views regarding the issues of their concern. It can also be a place for group members to develop group cohesion and build team spirit. There are, however, many subtle and important factors involved in a meeting. The social positions and relationships among participants are negotiated or ratified in a meeting. The function of a business meeting thus always goes beyond a mere business deal. In many cases the "central" business task is really only a carrier of these more important interpersonal or interorganizational relationships.

While the procedures and structures of meetings may follow a similar pattern across different international settings – meeting together, topic or agenda opening, discussion, decision making, and topic or meeting closing – there are many variations in practice behind this obvious meeting procedure. Assumptions about how to conduct and how to behave in a meeting differ from one cultural group to another and even from one corporate or organizational group to another. In companies such as advertising agencies or entertainment producers, the gulf between the "creatives" and the "management" can be as great as any gulf we might encounter flying halfway around the world to do business in a totally foreign culture and in a different language.

Questions such as who has the right to open a topic, when to close a topic, how much a meeting participant can or should talk depending on his or her status or level of expertise, or when not to talk are all open to analysis and cannot be taken for granted. Assumptions about business meetings are related to cultural values and practices from outside the context of the meeting as well. For example, in some societies or organizations, information is viewed as being of primary importance, whereas in others social relationship takes precedence. This might be true throughout the society but also has an important impact on how a meeting is run. Whether rank or expertise has the deciding power in a meeting affects the way decisions are made as well.

We began in chapter 1 with the comment that in Brazil meetings may appear to others to be quite chaotic, with "everyone speaking at once." In what follows now, we will turn to studies of American, Japanese, and Chinese business meetings to illustrate the complexities we can find in what simply appears to be a meeting, and the different meeting practices in these three cultural groups. First we will look at a study in which American and Japanese business meeting practices were analyzed. Then we will examine several research projects which look at the conduct of meetings in China. Following that we will present a study of a negotiation between an American researcher and a Japanese media company, which shows how participants in the same situation can have quite divergent views of what is actually happening as the situation develops.

Our purpose in looking at these three different types of research is not to emphasize the exotic nature of Japanese or Chinese business or cultural practices. In fact, our purpose is just the opposite. As we have found in the CDP exchanges that we have done, our first impression of how others do things differently is often a surprise. We feel that others are really very different from ourselves and we feel, if we are sympathetic, that we might want to adjust what we do to make communication with them more successful. On second thought, however, we begin to see that our own practice is not really so very different – it's just that we haven't seen very clearly what our own practice is. The comparative perspective often tells us more about ourselves than about the others we are examining.

For example, when we see below that in Chinese business meetings little decision making is done within the meeting proper but that the *real* work gets done outside of the meeting, both before and after, we might think of this as exotic practice. Our own business textbooks tell us how important the business meeting really is in arriving at decisions. This is our normative or members' generalization view of such meetings. Still, don't we all know of cases where the head of a department will consult with key figures before coming to the meeting, to be certain that they will support him or her, and then after the meeting check around again with them to insure they will carry out his or her decisions? As we will argue, this is "normal" Chinese practice and not often explicitly discussed in western business textbooks, but we believe it is, in fact, very characteristic of western business and organizational practice as well.

We hope that in the research which follows we can see new ways to conceptualize the practices of meetings, both so that we can be readier to interpret what others are doing and also so that we can come to analyze our own activities and practices.

American Business Meetings

This first project gives us rather interesting insights into American business meeting practices from the point of view of a Japanese researcher, for whom the normative style put forward in American (and other western) business books is the "strange" practice and for whom Japanese practice seems the more commonsensical way to do things.

In chapter 2 we noted that the C-B-S style (clarity-brevity-sincerity) seems to have arisen in American business style at least in part because of the poor initial technological quality of the telephone. From there, of course, it spread throughout business environments to become the dominant speaking style. Yamada (1992) carefully compared two business meetings. One of these was in an American bank and the other in a Japanese bank – both meetings taking place in the US. She compared them speaking-turn by speaking-turn from the beginning to the end of the meeting and found that the American practice of favoring C-B-S style in business is reflected in how Americans conduct a business meeting and their view of it. For them, a meeting is a decision-making process during which an agenda is followed and specific decisions should be made (sincerity). The meeting was taken to be a place for talking about business only, not a place to develop personal relationships or to talk about nonbusiness matters (brevity). The meeting followed a formal structure in the form of an agenda, and topics were predetermined and predesignated (clarity). Yamada found that each participant was responsible for certain items on the agenda, and had the right to give his or her opinion related to the issue on the table. The participants could negotiate their positions throughout the meeting. All decisions were made through discussions and final, deciding votes.

The main differences between the American and the Japanese bank business meetings could be summarized as follows:

- *role of information.* The Americans tended to set apart business from personal relationships. In their view, a business meeting is task-oriented and targeted at resolving specific problems. Thus information is regarded as more important than interpersonal relationships in the business meeting. The participants focused on information related to the items on the agenda, and were actively engaged in the talk. It was noted that, "for Americans, because interaction is intrinsically problematic, and talk resolves such problematicity, 'talking it out' accomplishes this; decisions are reachable through talk" (Yamada 1992:55).

- *function of the meeting*. Because of the high value placed on talk, meeting participants talked to negotiate their positions, to reach agreement, and to make decisions. The meeting thus had a concrete purpose and specific tasks to resolve. In order to achieve the goal of the meeting, an agenda was set up to include items for discussion, allot speaking time to each item, and guarantee the distribution of talk to all participants. Through rounds in the agenda, the meeting participants distributed talk to each and every individual. Such talk distribution, of course, assumes that each individual wants to talk, and that each participant has something to report on individually. So by virtue of the agenda, the meeting participants knew in advance specifically "who" was going to talk about "what."

- *agenda*. The organization of the meeting through an agenda was consonant with broader American management practices, in which "American managers are trained for specific responsibilities" (Harris and Morgan 1987:389); thus, Yamada found that they held to a code of a "division of labor." The preassignment of talk also helped set each American individual apart in the group. The agenda setting reflected, Yamada felt, the American values of independence and individuality.

- *topic assignment*. With regard to topic management in the American meeting, there was a clear sense of topic ownership by the participants. Each participant independently raised and concluded his or her own topics. Each reported on relevant issues according to a predefined agenda for the meeting. Topics were organized in such a way that one whose future outcome was best known was talked about first; a topic whose future outcome was least known was talked about later. This contributed to a sense of clarity as the meeting progressed. Further, as participants owned their topics and were granted the right to deliver information and express their ideas, there was a sense of sincerity.

However, the participants had to position themselves and their topic openings with respect to the other team members. They did so by using certain traffic signals or discourse markers for interactional positioning, e.g. "alright," "uhm," "and," "so," and "OK," to check on their right to open topics. Such positioning shows the American bank officers' respect for other individuals in the group; the participants could open their own topics, but they had to make sure that their right to do so was ratified by other meeting members.

In sum, topic management in the American bank meeting used the following strategies:
– Each speaker opened his or her own topic.
– The agenda organized topics in a linear order from best-known outcomes to least-known ones.
– Speakers used discourse markers with an optional filled pause to negotiate opportunities for topic opening.

Japanese Business Meetings

In contrast to the Americans Yamada studied, she noted that in Japanese society talk is in general viewed as untrustworthy. She argues that this negative view of talk led the Japanese to use linguistic strategies that would de-emphasize the significance of talk in the business meeting. So the business meeting operated along very different lines. In the Japanese bank meeting, the "big" question appeared to be more a determination of the company philosophy than individualized, task-oriented decision making.

Yamada further points out that because Japanese do not view talk as a decision-making tool, the purpose of interaction for Japanese is to enjoy each other's company. Thus the Japanese business meeting placed significance on "nontask sounding" talk; that is, small talk. Small talk had the function of building personal relationships and developing feelings of trustworthiness among participants. To the participants in the Japanese meeting, building personal relationships through sounding as if they were not on task was at the heart of the matter. Yamada notes that trustworthy business relations are established on the basis of personal relationships. Therefore Japanese partake in much talk which seems off task, small talk during the business meeting, to build personal but yet "professional". relationships. Another researcher, who interviewed Japanese sales personnel, reports that one pharmaceutical salesman spends less than ten minutes out of every hour discussing business, the rest of his calls at hospitals being devoted to chatting with doctors about their hobbies and current affairs. Sincerity for these business people is more a matter of building relationships of trust than of sincerely transmitting information or negotiating sales.

Of course this made the Japanese negotiation process almost painfully long and complicated from an American point of view. Americans tend to see such practices as unbusinesslike, particularly within a formal business setting, though as we all know, it is common practice to engage in this sort of relationship building outside of the situation of the formal business meeting. On the other hand, these practices do serve the goals of Japanese business, as they support the Japanese business person's primary need to establish personal ties within work settings such as the business meeting.

Here it is important for us to inject a note within this discussion of Yamada's research. What is strikingly different between the American bank meeting and the Japanese bank meeting is something about the structure and function of formal meetings. It is not a difference between Americans and Japanese in a broader, cultural, or social sense. In other words, it is equally important for Americans in business settings to establish social relationships with their colleagues. What is different is that for Japanese in Yamada's research this was done *within the confines of the meeting itself* but for the Americans in her study the meeting itself was dominated by information and the C-B-S style. Relationship building was taken to be something which would be done elsewhere. The differences, then, are not cultural in a broad sense, but in the much more specific sense of the assumed function of the business meeting.

Yamada also noted that since Japanese emphasize teamwork, boundaries between individuals were blurred. Meeting participants did not rely on a "contract" in the form of a predetermined agenda to distribute talk to each individual. Rather, they depended on established personal ties to draw the focus away from the negatively viewed talk that might divide them. The absence of an agenda in the Japanese meeting meant that the particular talk of each member was locally determined. That is, the distribution of talk among the meeting participants was open-ended; it occurred on-site, during the meeting.

Topic management in the Japanese business meeting was naturally very different from that in an American meeting because of the difference in the function of the meeting. In the Japanese meeting, each officer did not single-handedly report on a topic. Each Japanese participant was not singularly assigned to a task. Because many participants were involved in consensus decision making, the kind of individual rounds evidenced in the American meeting did not occur. The conversational structure in the Japanese meeting appeared much looser, as any participant could raise and contribute to a topic, topics were not verbally concluded, and any participant could bring up the next topic. To an American, such a conversational structure as that of the Japanese meeting would sound "chatty"; it would not carry a businesslike tone.

Yamada argues that because Japanese view talk as untrustworthy, and to open up a new topic initiates talk, it is not in the best interest of any Japanese interactant to open a topic. That is, it might be considered a kind of insincerity to become too attached to any topic. When the opportunity to open topics was available to everyone, this distributed the burden of talk to all, and no one was singled out to shoulder the responsibility of engaging in negatively viewed talk. This lack of topic ownership creates an ideal situation for Japanese to meet their expectation for nonconfrontational interaction.

In the Japanese meeting, topics for discussion were organized in a circular manner. That is, participants could hop back and forth among topics, returning to a previous one that had already been determined as nonconfrontational, or dropping one that appeared to be threatening. They had the benefit of reopening topics freely. Circular topic organization promoted nonconfrontational interactions, as it allowed for a nonspecified ordering of topics; participants had the option to open topics in any order. In this sense, topics were not owned by individuals. They were collectively operated and delivered. This open-ended movement among topics is facilitated by having no formal agenda and no topical ownership.

This close comparative analysis of two business meetings provides a view of a suitable fit between cultural expectations and the necessities of business activities. The Japanese style of decision making allows nonthreatening discussion of topics and collective movement toward agreement without singling out any particular speaker as the topic leader. Of course this requires more space and time for personal relations. Americans, because of their assumption of a C-B-S style for business meetings, are often frustrated in negotiating with Japanese because of these significant differences in assumptions about the function of business meetings. As we will see in the research of Nakano below, Japanese are equally frustrated with the American drive to establish clear topics and to come to a decision on each point in sequence before moving on to the next topic. This appears to the Japanese participants to be excessively focused on information at the expense of establishing good interpersonal relationships.

Chinese Business Meetings

We have seen that there are rather important differences between Japanese and American business meetings, but at the same time, as we have said above, these shouldn't be thought of as broad cultural differences. What is truly different is where and when certain important functions are carried out. All business and organizational activities depend on establishing good social relationships as well as on exchanging good and clear information. What is different, we have seen, is that Japanese put the function of establishing good social relationships *within the boundaries of the meeting itself* whereas the Americans focus the meeting on exchanging information and arriving at a decision and work at establishing good social relationships else-where in different kinds of social interactions. This is the role of casual encounters, lunches, and other such social events. While Yamada's study compared two meetings, one Japanese and one American, Pan compared Chinese meetings in governmental organizations and banks with interaction in other settings. Our other source on Chinese meetings, Gu (in press), generalizes on the basis of the analysis of many different meetings.

Before turning to the analysis of Chinese business meetings, then, it is important to make a few brief comments, based on Pan's research, to set the Chinese business meeting within the broader context of other events in Chinese society, which is perhaps more of a mystery to westerners than is Japanese society. Many paradoxical statements are made about Chinese society. This is partly because authors are not being clear about just *which* Chinese society they are talking about. It is common, unfortunately, to mix up quotations from ancient classics, observations made about overseas Chinese immigrants in the UK or North America, and observations made in Taiwan and in Mainland China. This makes as much sense as trying to describe what "the English" are like by quoting Chaucer and mixing obser-vations made in London, Capetown, and Peoria, Illinois. Here the research we report on from Pan is based on comparative studies of three different situations within the southern Chinese city of Guangzhou (Canton). While this allows less comparative latitude throughout Chinese society, we must remember that it would be very difficult to generalize meaningfully about what is approximately one fourth of the world's population. We prefer to be narrow in our scope but to be relatively confident that the statements we make are based solidly on research.

We present Pan's contrastive analysis in order to set business meetings within a broader framework of contemporary Chinese society, where social encounters among strangers are very different from those among insiders, and lines are clearly drawn between Chinese and outsiders. Since an out-sider is unlikely to have a place within a Chinese power structure, a narrow focus on business meetings would provide few clues as to how to behave. This will become evident when we come to Gu's analysis of the distribu-tion of power in meetings and the places in which foreigners might have a role. Pan's research also makes clear that power is important in the alloca-tion of speaking-turns whether at a family dinner or at a business meeting, but it is the sources of power that differ.

Pan studied three different kinds of situations – formal business meet-ings, family dinners, and service encounters; that is, situations in which cus-tomers or clients are served by clerks or other sales personnel in a public environment. Without going into an extensive analysis of this research, what is important for us in order to understand the Chinese business meeting is that social relationships and power operate differently in these three situations. That is, in what we say below about business meetings we mean only to focus on those meetings and not to generalize any characteristics about Chinese which would apply throughout all other situations.

In Pan's research, a family dinner comes closest to what we think of as traditional Chinese society. Most important in this is that the conversation at a dinner table is controlled by seniority and gender. That is, older people have more privileges and general control over the conversation, including introducing their topics, than younger people, and men have greater privileges than women in these family conversations. To put it most succinctly, the conversation will be dominated and controlled by the oldest male participant. He will either introduce topics or legitimate topics introduced by others. In this way it is age and gender which predominate in these private and personal social interactions.

Service encounters in present-day China are with two kinds of services: state-run and commercial. In state-run service encounters such as at the post office, one comes to think the customer is always wrong or at least a nuisance. The person who is providing the "service" is a state employee. The wages are the same whether or not the service is provided to the "customer" and so social relationships are "outside" relationships. That is, service providers do the absolute minimum that they must do, and the customer expects little else from them.

In commercial service encounters such as at a privately owned fashion boutique things are very different. Here the customer is wooed with praise, friendship, and warm family-like greetings. Personal and kinship terms such as "aunt" are used to formulate a kind of pseudo-relationship with the customer. Thus in service encounters of this kind, customers are treated as being in an "inside" relationship with the service provider or sales clerk.

Pan concludes from this that for the service encounter what is most crucial is establishing the social relationships of "outsider" or "insider." It is in these sorts of relationships that we see what is most often thought of as the "Chinese" or even "Asian" social relationships. Although this is not Yamada's analysis, we could say that in the Japanese bank meeting, one of the major goals is to produce warm "inside" relationships among the participants. That is, the goal is to come to feel that they are all part of the same group. Pan's research shows that such "inside" relationships support rather than undermine the traditional and almost Confucian male and age domination within the family, and they are artificially produced in the private-sector service encounter for the sake of encouraging business.

Chinese business meetings, unlike either the family dinner or the service encounter, operate on an official power hierarchy. That is, it is the official (governmental or quasi-governmental) status or the status within the business hierarchy which dominates activities in the meeting *per se*, as well as the activities before and after the meeting. For Chinese, a meeting is not just a fixed time and place to meet, but comprises a series of pre-meeting and post-meeting activities. These have the function of balancing different powers among participants and organizations, and reaching agreement among the different parties concerned. Most of the time, these activities are more important than the actual meeting itself.

Gu's research on Chinese meetings was conducted in Beijing, and while at first glance this might be questioned in comparison with Pan's research in Guangzhou, the situations studied were very similar and both authors argue that the central organizing dimension is official power and status. Gu's research shows that there are three kinds of power in current Chinese society governing the operation of an official meeting. They are leadership, administrative, and expertise power. Each of these forms comes from a different source. Leadership power (*lingdao quan*), power to make policy, is the legitimate power of the ruling party, secured by the latest version of the Chinese constitution. This power is exercised through the control of national policy making, that is, those policies that are believed to best protect the interests of the ruling party and the people.

Administrative power (*xingzheng quan*) is the power to govern. That is, administrative power is subordinate to leadership power because it is seen as the power to carry out the policies set by leadership power. It is exercised through decision making or what we might better call implementation. Decisions that are made to solve specific problems – social, economic, educational, diplomatic, military, etc. – fall under the rubric of administrative power. The policies made by the leadership power serve as guidelines or principles under which problem-solving solutions are considered. These two kinds of power are the traditional forms in contemporary China.

Now a new dimension is being added to China's power arena. This is the power of expertise. Because rapid modernization of China in this period has been set as a priority of leadership power, but also because most leaders and administrators of the older generation do not have expertise in new technologies, those who do have this knowledge or expertise are coming to exercise a kind of power which it is essential for leaders and administrators to recognize as part of carrying out their own forms of power. Thus the power of expertise is a personal one due to the possession of special knowledge. This is in almost all cases achieved through education in new technologies. Expertise power is one of the forms of power both recognized and legitimated for foreigners within Chinese business and governmental contexts.

Leadership power

These three forms of power – leadership, administrative, and expert – are displayed in different domains and have different functions in meeting activities. Gu's work shows that leadership power is exercised most in pre-meeting activities and then again in the conclusion of the meeting. Pre-meeting activities which are discussed by Gu include:

- initiation of a meeting
- fixing an agenda
- deciding on the participants attending the meeting
- deciding on meeting site
- meeting notification
- seating arrangement.

The *initiation of a meeting* comes from a person with leadership power, who will consult his or her superior and equals for a second opinion. If someone does not have leadership power, he or she is not in a position to initiate a meeting. About the only means of "calling a meeting" in this case would be to discuss with someone with leadership power the need for a meeting, which would then be called by that other person.

Agenda fixing is a more sensitive issue. Deciding what is to be on the agenda, and what is to be left out, is a form of control. Some issues require prior negotiation behind the scenes before they are placed on the agenda. As we look below at how meetings are conducted we will see that the primary function is to ratify or legitimate a decision which has already largely been established before the meeting. Thus it seems that establishing the agenda is already a significant portion of the process of making a decision.

The *decision about participants* is also carefully considered. Participation must include all who hold leadership power. Failure to invite those with leadership power means serious disregard of the leadership, and the decisions reached at the end of the meeting are likely to be null and void. Put another way, participation by those who hold leadership power is already a major source of ratification of the decision which will "be made" in the meeting.

The *meeting site* and *notification* are also sensitive to leadership power. The meeting site must favor the person who is highest in leadership power. The higher a person is in the rank hierarchy, the better the meeting site he or she is thought to deserve. Both convenience for the highest-ranking person and the actual physical circumstances are considerations in preparing the meeting site. The notification of the meeting must come from a person of equal rank. A high-ranking official should be notified by the personnel who can represent the organization in question or by a person of the same rank. Lower-ranking participants are invited or notified by people of their own lower status.

Seating arrangements are by no means trivial. These are also made on the basis of leadership power, and are perhaps most rank-sensitive when the occasion is most formal. There are powerful seats and subordinate seats. Powerful seats are represented by the formula: up, front, first, and central. Subordinate seats are those which are lower, in back, occupied later, or in sideways positions. Participants should take up seats according to their rank. That is to say, the highest-ranking person will be seated in an elevated position, in front of others when there are rows, in the middle when there is a circular arrangement or a line, and this person will be the first person to go to his or her seat and to sit down. Others follow in order of rank.

During the meeting proper, leadership power determines the participants' speaking rights and speaking-turns. The higher a participant is in rank, the more he or she is free to take turns and to enjoy longer turns. However, taking into consideration Pan's research below, we would want to say that often this right of the highest-ranking person is exercised by that person being silent while others speak to open up discussion of secondary or minor points. In any event, as we will discuss below, both the opening and the closing of a meeting are highly power-sensitive. The highest-ranking person will invariably declare the meeting open and then make the closing moves as well.

Administrative and expertise power

The other two forms of power – administrative and expertise – only play a small role in pre-meeting activities and the meeting proper. But they do have a strong role in the post-meeting implementation. This is often a continuation of the meeting, which occurs often in the same place, but after the meeting is formally concluded. In Gu's analysis, which is supported by Pan's research and many observations we have made at meetings throughout China, post-meeting action consists of six main activities taking place before the participants' departure and immediately after the meeting. They are:

- discussion of implementation of actions and decisions
- further private and individualized discussions

- minor follow-up meetings, small groups
- off-agenda items or impossible items
- interpersonal *guanxi* (connections) development
- entertaining at meals.

These post-meeting activities can be as important as the meeting proper, in that without them the decisions reached during the meeting may not be effectively carried out. The meeting proper is a form of power display, while the post-meeting activities are the implementation procedures within which actual courses of action are negotiated and constructed. It should be apparent that in these post-meeting activities administrative power and expertise power can be called upon to direct and shape the policies and decisions made in the earlier stages of this process. In actual examples, we have seen "implementations" of policies and decisions which turn almost 180° from the decisions and policies set up by leadership power.

The sequence of activities and the roles of the different forms of power are shown in figure 5.1. Obviously, there is much variation in this sketch. Our main point is to simply suggest that the meeting itself, at the center of this diagram, is really just one in a sequence of activities and that it would be very difficult to understand the activities of participants in a meeting without seeing it within this longer stream of power relationships.

To summarize Gu's analysis of the roles of these three forms of power, each has a preferred situation for use. We are now in a position to offer advice based on this analysis:

- If your power is not official (that is, if it is not leadership power), the most effective way to work is to influence preplanning through expertise.
- If that is not possible, then focus on post-meeting implementation through expertise and administrative power.

Understanding how the power is structured and when to use what kind of power is of primary importance in having an effective meeting in the Chinese context.

Of course, as we have said above, this analysis of the "Chinese" meeting structure and function is based on Gu's study of official meetings in Beijing, the nation's capital. Nevertheless, there is much here which would be recognizable to officials and business people throughout the world.

Pan's study of Chinese government official meetings and company business meetings, as we have mentioned above, indicates a close correlation between rank hierarchy and speaking patterns in a meeting. As Gu's research suggests, in the Chinese context, a meeting is a formal and official

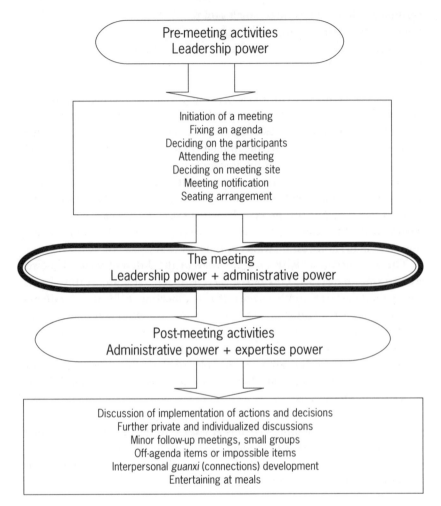

Figure 5.1   Power in Chinese meetings

procedure to ratify existing power relationships and hierarchical positions. Linguistically, speaking rights and linguistic features in the speech of each participant are correlated with his or her rank position in relation to others. When and how much to speak is also related to the rank position a speaker occupies. To a large extent, the meeting flows topically according to the distribution of power among the participants.

The flow of the meeting or the topic opening and closing follows a certain pattern that is correlated to rank hierarchy. The meeting does not open until the person who is highest in rank (person 1) starts the meeting, usually by introducing the main topic to be discussed. After a brief introduction, which can often amount simply to saying, "Mr X would like to say Y," the highest-ranking person then passes the floor to "Mr X," who is, of course, the person that comes second in rank (person 2).

From this point forward the meeting can appear to be much like meetings described elsewhere; for example, by Yamada for the American meeting of bank officials. Person 2 opens, and a period of discussion among the participants follows. During this, participants in lower-ranking positions give their opinions on the issue under discussion. They will very often be quite free in raising questions, objections, difficult points, and the like. During this portion of the discussion, person 1 stays out of the discussion most of the time and takes up the role of an observer. Of course, all of the participants will be monitoring this person for indirect signals of his or her approval or disapproval of points being made. In practice, these signals, such as the sound of a cough, an eye gaze, or a nod, can seem absolutely opaque to foreign observers.

Then, after a period of discussion, person 1 takes the floor again and makes it clear what his or her view of the topic is. This is very likely to have been known by the participants, but whether it is known or not, this is taken as the signal to close the topic for all of them. Person 2 at this point will express his or her support for the view of person 1. The other participants then join in to show their support as well. It would be quite surprising to find anyone who would take a dissenting view now that the one with leadership power has expressed his or her position.

Then person 2 summarizes and confirms the group's agreement. Person 1 finalizes the decision, usually by saying how happy he or she is that agreement has been reached, and the topic is closed. In all of this, person 1 is not the most voluble person by any means. He or she can seem quite removed from all this discussion. Nevertheless, person 1 speaks at the critical moment, such as to settle a conflict or close the topic.

The meeting/topic opening and closing flow shows a circular pattern correlated to rank, as shown in figure 5.2. Speaking-turns are thus allocated according to the rank hierarchy. The meeting participants follow this pattern in taking up their turns to speak. They enter the discussion and speak at the right moment. If a participant picks up a turn that is not allocated to his or her position, it is regarded as inappropriate.

Not only are speaking-turns allocated on the basis of the participants' ranks, but so is the amount of speaking time. After person 1 opens the topic, persons 2 and 3 then occupy most of the speaking time. These two participants can give lengthy presentations and even present opposing views of

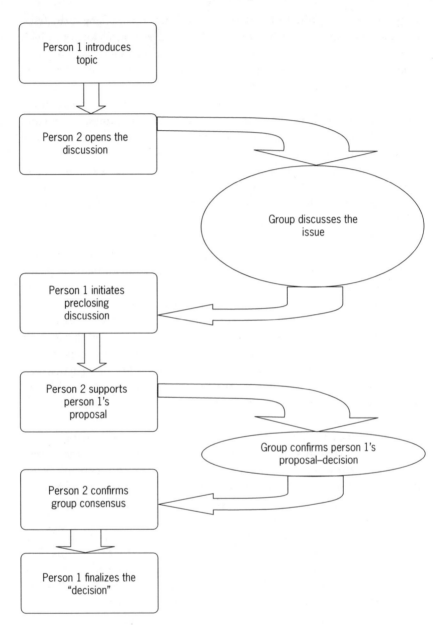

Figure 5.2   Power flow in Chinese meetings

the issue. Other participants lower in rank normally give support to one or the other of them. Most of the discussion is between persons 2 and 3, with other participants providing supporting points to the two positions. Junior members and those lower in rank speak very little at the meeting. They usually contribute to it after those higher in rank have spoken, to give their support to a position. This practice of speaking according to one's rank is part of the participants' cultural knowledge, so that even before coming to a meeting, participants know when they can speak and how much time they can take during the meeting.

If a conflict occurs during the discussion, there is also a correlation between rank and directness in expressing opposition. Person 1 is most direct in raising objections, person 2 is a little less direct, and the others less and less direct as their rank goes down. Conflict is resolved when the person highest in rank gives his or her opinion. Participants are not expected to defend and develop their positions through argument during the meeting.

Because of the significance placed on rank hierarchy in such Chinese meetings, those lower in rank do not have the same speaking rights as those higher, and they do not have the same rights in decision making. As we have said above, in this situation, the age and gender factors which are quite important in family circles are less important than official rank. If a female participant has a rank high enough, she is in a good position to contribute to the meeting. Those senior in age, but lower in rank, do not have the same rights as those junior in age, but higher in rank. Decisions, especially important ones, are usually made by those who are in higher positions, and are made prior to or after the meeting by a group of key members. To a very large extent, a meeting proper is more a ratification procedure for policies and decisions which have already been made than a decision-making procedure. Normally those in higher ranks use the meeting to inform other members of their decisions and assign tasks to individuals. The pre-meeting and post-meeting activities are most crucial to the decision-making process through the practices of implementation.

Conflict in Perceptions of the Meeting

When people of different cultural backgrounds come into a meeting with different assumptions about the structure or the function of meetings, they inevitably encounter tremendous difficulty in comprehending what is going on. As we have shown above, meetings are run on different dimensions: while information is emphasized in one cultural environment, social relationship is the key in another. A meeting can be a place for giving opinions and talking over issues for some people; it can be a place for power display for others. People with different assumptions will rely on different expectations and analytical frames to interpret what happens and what is said in a meeting. Very often confusion occurs because participants see the meeting as a different kind of event.

For example, from an American view, the Chinese meeting would appear to be boring, with a few people in power talking all the time, but the one with the power to make decisions saying very little. The American would feel quite frustrated by the difficulty he or she might find in getting the right to speak in the first place, and then by being ignored when the summary of the decision is made at the end, particularly if he or she has spoken out against the leader's position. A Japanese participant might feel that the meeting was too oriented toward information or problem solving on the one hand and then, apparently quite pointlessly, with the resolution in favor of the most powerful person present. If a person participates in a Chinese meeting not knowing the normal practices of the power structure, he or she may offend other participants by taking the wrong seat, speaking at the wrong moment, or talking too much for his or her position. Or he or she may be talking to the wrong person. Also, he or she is likely to be very confused about the decision-making process, if he or she does not know where and when the decision is made in a Chinese meeting procedure.

The patterns we have summarized above arose in meetings among people who were all members of the same cultural group – Japanese business people within the same bank, Americans in the same bank, Chinese in the same organization. In the countless other Chinese meetings observed, there were no participants who would not have had a basic agreement about these matters of the structure and function of meetings or about rank and power in their societies. Now to close this section of the analysis we want to turn to an example in which a negotiation was carried out between a group of Japanese media producers and an American consultant, to see how these differences in baseline assumptions actually did result in very different perceptions of what was going on in the meeting.

The American business style of C-B-S may appear very abrupt to Japanese, while the Japanese style of building a trustworthy personal relationship through small talk may seem too casual and time-consuming to Americans. When people from these two cultures have a business meeting, each can be very frustrated. As an example of this, Nakano (1995) gives an interesting analysis of a negotiation meeting between an American consultant and a Japanese TV production company. The TV production company intended to hire the American to work on a program. A meeting was held between the Japanese company and the American consultant to discuss the details and to conclude a contract. Seventeen minutes were spent at the outset on small talk. The American consultant, operating with a C-B-S style, then went straight into talking about business. He opened up by trying to negotiate his consultation fee with the Japanese company. From the American consultant's point of view, this was absolutely the very first detail which would have to be ironed out before it would be possible to enter into a protracted negotiation of the substance of the joint project on which he was consulting.

The Japanese company, on the other hand, was operating within the Japanese style of building a trustworthy business relationship through establishing a personal relationship. The Japanese company's representatives did not mention how much they would offer the American consultant in the way of fees. Instead they emphasized three points which they felt were essential: (1) how they would resolve future differences between them, (2) the mutual benefit from the project for both the company and for the consultant, and (3) the company's respect for the American's expertise. Each time the American brought up the issue of payment terms, the Japanese side-tracked the topic to focus upon one of their three points. The American interpreted this evasion of his topic to mean that the Japanese did not want to accept his price, so he tried harder to negotiate by offering different options. The more he talked about the consultation fees, the more vague the Japanese became. He made several attempts and failed in each of them.

Examples such as this one show that, like the child with whom we began this chapter, participants have specific expectations about meetings. We *know* what a meeting should be and what a party should be, and when the meeting goes in a direction we don't expect, we feel frustrated in trying to interpret why. In Nakano's case, the American expected a meeting to deal with specific business issues, particularly his consultation fee, and to resolve the business aspect of the deal before getting to the substance of the consultation project. On the other hand the Japanese expected a meeting for the purpose of developing a trustworthy relationship between them and the consultant, with the assumption that the business and money matters would arise naturally once they had established a basis of trust. To the American, the Japanese meeting appeared casual and the participants even seemed evasive rather than businesslike. For the American, the formal structure of a meeting is what makes the business encounter appropriately impersonal and "businesslike"; personal relationships are reserved for family and friends or after the business is completed. For their part, the Japanese wondered whether they could really establish a relationship of trust, given the American's single-minded focus on his fee.

The C–B–S style of apparent equality and independence allowed by a predetermined agenda is fundamental not only to business meetings but to many other spheres of American communication. For example, the annual presentation of Oscar film awards in Hollywood, while referred to as a party, resembles the American bank meeting analyzed by Yamada in that speakers are delegated slots in which to speak on assigned topics, such as costumes, set design, and other aspects of film art, as part of the presentation of each award. That is, topics are distributed relatively equally according to functional role in a predetermined agenda. Each speaker is allowed a minute or two to deliver his or her introduction to the award category before announcing the nominees and presenting the award to the winner. As in the bank meeting, each speaker owns his or her topic and speaks independently in his or her field of responsibility and expertise.

In contrast, the Hong Kong film awards follow a style that is in many ways more hierarchical and based on quasi-kinship relations, though of course different from Chinese business meetings. Conversational genres resemble a party more than in the Oscar presentations. The hostesses in the 1996 awards reminisced among themselves and felt free to interrupt other speakers. In this they behaved more like the senior members at a Chinese family dinner than the officials at a meeting who say little while controlling the flow of talk. Unlike the Oscars, in which each award was presented by one person, some awards were presented by a group of actors who were shown having a conversation in which they used casual language and interrupted each other. Participants addressed each other using kin terms, such as "uncle" to show respect or "older brother" to show intimacy.

In spite of the ideal of clarity, brevity, and sincerity, divergences of opinion often result in arguments that may seem quite the opposite of the idealized standard in meetings taking place in the US, the UK, or continental Europe. Professionals from cultures that value harmony may find these conflicts shockingly uncomfortable. We have seen people wring their hands or even leave the room. This, like the other differences in expectation we have discussed, can be resolved through our method of contrastive observation, analysis, and discussion.

Meetings in Hong Kong, a Multilingual Society in Transition

Thus far we have described a few meetings that took place in one or at most two languages within fairly homogeneous companies. Even if these meetings were characteristic of, say, Japanese or American or Chinese meetings of banking personnel, there is no way of knowing how they resemble meetings taking place in this new century or in companies with international staff in societies undergoing political and economic transition. We will now turn to a company typical of many corporations in Hong Kong, where there is a history of complex language use in business, government, and education.

Like many Hong Kong corporations, company X has been undergoing a process of localization in the transition from British to Chinese sovereignty over Hong Kong. Formerly run by English expatriates, the company has recently elected a local Chinese as chief executive officer as part of a move to establish a Chinese identity. Even though they are cultivating a Chinese image in the international environment in which the company operates, the management still sees a need to prepare employees for this international milieu by "upgrading" their skills in English and other commonly used languages, including Mandarin Chinese. At the same time, during the Asian economic recession they cut back and consolidated divisions responsible for language and audiovisual materials development and training.

Monica, a Canadian from Montreal, was hired as an assistant manager in charge of language training within this new section. That is, she was hired for her expertise in training in English and French language skills. In this account we rely on her perceptions of what took place in meetings of company personnel.

The meetings described above were all recorded with special permission for the purpose of sociolinguistic analysis. When we attempted to get participants in our project on professional communication to record a meeting as part of a CDP, they either ignored the suggestion or, when pressed, said it was not possible because of considerations of confidentiality. We thus rely on generalizations based on our own observations as well as those of colleagues.

As a Canadian in her thirties, Monica expected her role to be one of arranging meetings with section heads for the purpose of planning training in language skills felt to be needed by the management. She assumed that these contacts and meetings would follow the requirements of C-B-S style and did not hesitate to discuss issues with the section heads as well as the members of her team. Her supervisor, an older Cantonese with traditional assumptions about organizational hierarchy, ran team meetings in a manner that may have resembled the manager of the Chinese bank meeting described above, with the difference that two languages – English and Cantonese – were used.

Meetings were generally restricted to a length of one hour. At first, remarks made in Cantonese were translated for Monica's benefit, but as the weeks went by these translations were judged by the manager who ran the meetings to be prolonging the meetings unnecessarily, and were cut off as the leader steered the meeting to other topics. Other team members also felt her attempts to exchange information freely to be wasting time. It is quite likely that she did not understand the complex process of decision making we outlined above.

We do not want to dwell on this one example of conflict in assumptions about the functions of meetings, but introduce it to say that the inclusion of transcriptions of meetings in a portfolio exchange is by no means a simple matter. In a typical Hong Kong company, meetings may be conducted ostensibly in English while discussions which lead to decisions take place in Cantonese. These conversations may take place in or out of formal meetings and may be inaccessible to a foreign employee.

In international settings, typical meetings are likely to include discussions in languages not understood by an employee attempting to assemble a CDP. Our experience with focus groups has been that it has been difficult to obtain adequate translations of languages we do not ourselves understand. For this reason, as well as the fact that so much decision making takes place outside of formal meetings, we suggest you might undertake a language audit, which we describe in chapter 6.

The CDP and Meetings

Meetings in all their varieties, from casual, chance ones in airports and coffee shops to formally structured ones with agendas, are a central aspect of professional communication in international settings. Here we have only discussed some of the features of meetings from the points of view of North Americans, Japanese, and Chinese in Beijing and Guangdong. We might have added other cultural groups to this mix. For example, as we mentioned at the start of chapter 1, in Brazilian meetings everybody talks all the time about whatever they like and non-Brazilians simply cannot work out how anything is decided. We related there how a Brazilian and a South African had very different interpretations of a meeting at which many people talked at once. We do not want to continue to elaborate different cultural styles for holding meetings. This is because our main concern in this book is not to go through all the research literature on various topics of international communication; instead our main goal is to show how we have been able to use the idea of CDP exchanges as a tool for communicative and cultural learning.

Unfortunately, as we have said at the outset of this chapter, even though for telephone calls, resumés, and presentations we were able to get good comparative material for exchanges, we were not able to get the participants to produce any very useful material about their own practices in meetings. What we did therefore was to make video clips of meetings from Hollywood and Hong Kong movies and to show them in focus groups in Hong Kong and Finland. As in the meeting where two people from different continents had different versions of what happened, by showing the same footage to different groups we were able to elicit what people thought about the meetings they saw. The clips were of course exaggerated, stereotypical portrayals of meetings in the United States and in China, including Hong Kong.

Reactions to Film Portrayals of Meetings

As we said in our comments about oral presentations, Hong Kong banking professionals accepted uncritically the Dale Carnegie model of presentation exemplified by North American and British speakers, but few of the Hong Kong professionals we videotaped used this style in presentation. Though they upheld the global ideal, few of them embodied it. In the case of meetings, we learned not only what people said they did or should do, but what they did, as the focus group is actually just a special kind of meeting. For one thing, we found that though the participants in the focus groups were friends and knew the convener, there was relatively little small talk. This shows the acceptance of the C-B-S style among the participants in these meetings convened to exchange points of view.

One clip showed a meeting taking place in Hong Kong around a rectangular conference table with the chair at the head. The item under discussion was where to build a factory in China, and various proposals were discussed. Finally the chair announced that because he was Chinese, the factory would be built in Yunnan, a province in southwestern China that shares borders with Burma, Thailand, and Vietnam. Students and professionals had the same reaction.

A group of Hong Kong business students found the arbitrary decision quite unreasonable. Here is a translation of a portion of the focus group discussion. Y is the convener:

Y: Let's talk about the first presentation. That part played by Lam Chi Cheung was supposed to be a meeting. Did Lam make the decision without the process of voting? It seems that he just asked everyone's opinions and then came to a conclusion.

L: Yes, they have voted.

Y: Then Lam just announced that he decided to set up the factory.

W: What I think was not so appropriate is that he asked for others' opinion, and then made the decision without any consideration of them. I think this is inappropriate.

E: Also, I feel strange that they did not discuss before they voted, on the contrary, they discussed after they had voted. I feel it very strange, I think this was not a two-way meeting, just like Lam Chi Cheung was the chairperson, and he just ordered the others to follow his instructions. Besides, I do not think everybody got the chance to voice out their opinions on that matter.

L: Also the opinions were too simple, just one sentence, without any evidence. Seems to be very strange.

R: I think a "real" meeting is not like this.

L: Need some figures to support.

W: Due to time factor.

R: All is the film's problem.

Y: I think this can help us to find the difference between the presentation in the movies and our expectations towards the real-life presentations. For example, we would expect there was a two-way discussion before the voting process took place. However, this part was neglected in the first presentation.

A group of women who worked as banking professionals also found the meeting unrealistic:

B: And we will chat a lot before the meeting is held.

J: We will not be so serious and vote immediately!

Y: I would like you to express this kind of opinion, as I want to know more about your points of view, always you would consider that just because they were movies, you would think lots of settings were due to the requirement of films. In fact I would like you to compare between real-life presentations and those constructed in movies.

J: *(Asks A, B)* Did we encounter such a situation in real life? That is, we talked a lot and expressed our opinions, and then the chairman said he wanted to do this? Did we encounter this situation in real life?

C: Even if we did, the reason should not be like this . . . *(hand gesture indicated "that" reason, i.e. "I am Chinese")*

(All participants laugh)

B: People just expressed their opinions without providing any supporting evidence.

J: In real life we would just sit over there, for example after someone expressed his opinion, then I would second. But it is different in those sections, no interaction at all, you just talked and I just talked.

B: Yes, no interaction at all, and there would be lots of challenge toward what someone said, therefore everyone would think clearly before he discussed his opinion.

J: *(laugh)* You would be damned if you said something that didn't make sense.

Y: You really would be scolded by the others?

B: Yes, in Chinese and English foul languages . . .

J: So much nonsense!

(All participants laugh)

Y: If someone voted and then said "I am a Chinese" . . .

J: No response at all immediately! How could you be the chairman and have no sense at all?

A: No, people might say nothing because he was the boss!

J: So what?

C: The boss would not fool around in his business.

A: That was a movie!

J: Movie!

A: I guess it might be common in movies but there are fewer cases in real-life presentations.

B: For example, after he said that he was Chinese, there should be more supporting evidence, for example he should describe the market in China, how the market suited the Chinese, and then vote to see if it was feasible to set up the factory in China.

J: Yes, the proposal would be very rigorous, for example in stating the relationship between cost and benefit, all would be taken into account, he just said something . . . and provided a very strange reason.

A: This was because it was a movie.

(All participants laugh)

B: No time to collect data.

A group of professionals in information systems had a similar reaction:

W: Like the first part, Lam Chi Cheung ended the meeting with a conclusion "I am a Chinese," that means there was no difference between having a meeting to discuss the issue or not, as the final conclusion was "I am a Chinese." I think this is nonsense, no such case in real life.

Y: How would your meetings be conducted?

W: Our meetings . . .

Y: In a very formal style?

W: Yes, conducted in a very formal way.

A: I feel strange that they raised an issue in the meeting but discussed the issue without any document to support it, it seems that everyone has different opinions. What is the rationale for their discussion? It seemed that people did not understand what they were discussing, they just expressed their opinion, and the last conclusion was so pointless.

Y: I am not sure how your meetings proceed. In the first part of the first tape, voting was held before the discussion of the participants, how about in your meetings?

W: To be a leader leading the discussion in a meeting, first there would be proponents and opponents of the issue being discussed, and then each of them would express their opinions. Besides, it seemed that the staff in the movie was very ignorant, they simply said "I think this, I think that . . ." without providing any proof, this would not happen in meetings of real life.

T: No time for the filmmakers to collect data!

These focus group discussions show that the participants have a view of how meetings should be run, whether or not the ones they participate in follow their prescriptive norms of using documents for support and having rational bases for discussing the pros and cons of issues. We can also see how Y, the convener of the groups, focuses the discussion. What is interesting is that while the scene from the film is stereotyped and exaggerated, it resembles in many ways the meetings analyzed by Pan. The focus group also produced real data, though it is a particular kind of meeting and may not represent what happens in real business meetings.

Finnish participants had similar comments about the meetings shown in movie clips. They commented that Finns are not so much hierarchy-oriented during the meeting. Each participant has the right and opportunity to give opinions. Decisions are made after open discussions. They also commented that Finns, perhaps because of their reticent style, often use e-mail discussion to make decisions. In this they may resemble the Chinese, who use meetings to ratify decisions made outside of formal meetings. The C-B-S style of communication is clearly the preferred norm, though it conflicts with aspects of Finnish communicative style.

In both the Hong Kong and Finnish discussions of meetings, mention was made of genres of communication that took place outside the meeting itself. In Hong Kong it was supporting documents; in Finland it was e-mail communication. Both acknowledge the important role highlighted in Gu's analysis of pre- and post-meeting decision making and implementation. Japanese researchers emphasize the importance of small talk whether it takes place in meetings, at restaurants, or on the golf course.

A Language Audit

Meetings are among the most difficult aspects of professional communication in international settings to research, because they are very sensitive events which are normally treated with high levels of confidentiality. For this same reason our professional performance in meetings is difficult to capture through the personal development mechanism of the CDP. In this case, then, we suggest it might be useful for you to do a *language audit* as one way to approach this problem.

Meetings, like the rest of the work of communication in international settings, are very complex situations in which texts and talk in many different genres are used to accomplish the overall goals. For example, a single meeting might begin with exchanges of memos and other documents which would set up and schedule the meeting. Participants might be given a sheaf of papers to study, which might include position papers, memos, product brochures, budget reports, assessments of proposals, the proposals themselves, minutes of prior meetings, and so forth. During the meeting further papers and documents might be circulated and different presenters and participants might themselves use papers, documents, overhead transparencies, slides, videos, and other visual means to present their ideas for discussion.

In addition to these texts there would also be many varieties of talk. There would be formal telephone calls to establish the agenda and scheduling. There would be casual conversation as participants in the meeting begin to gather, shifting over to formal ways of speaking as the meeting is formally convened. Even within that there might be quiet and casual asides to those sitting near one around the table.

It would be impossible to encompass all of these genres of texts and of talk that might be found within a single meeting in an ordinary organization. And, of course, as soon as we enter into the international sphere the number and complexity of these forms of communication would increase dramatically, as many of these documents and many of these conversations would take place in different languages. A recent audit of documents in a major corporation found that managers listed over 100 typical documents with which they commonly had to deal (see chapter 6). Many of these would be dealt with either within meetings or as part of preparation for or as the outcomes of meetings.

In chapter 6 we show how a language audit, including the genres and situations we have discussed in the preceding chapters, as well as dozens of other genres that may be part of the day-to-day work of the professional communicator, can be integrated into a CDP exchange. We outline the procedures for documenting with a CDP your communication as an individual, documenting with language audits the communication of organizations in which you function and are preparing to interact, and obtaining the feedback necessary for self-reflection and adjustment.

With the self-reflection made possible by the CDP and language audit exchange, you will be able to pinpoint more exactly the elements of small talk and relationship building that make a meeting seem like a party, while still being able to distinguish work from play. You may still find yourself exhausted dealing with meetings in which others seem to be enjoying themselves, but at least you will have some idea why. And if you find that decisions are being ratified but not made in meetings, you may be able to save a lot of energy that might have been spent trying to persuade people who already have their minds made up.

6

The Reflective View: Seeing Ourselves as Others See Us

Successful Professional Communication

In this chapter we have now arrived at the crucial thesis of the book:

> *Successful communication in the international workplace requires a self-reflective understanding of the processes of communication.*

We believe that the most effective way to achieve this reflective understanding is through the use of a communicative self-assessment tool such as the Communication Display Portfolio (CDP). The essential comparative element of the CDP as a self-assessment tool is the exchange of the CDP with one's counterparts from other cultures, nations, or organizations.

We developed this staff development and training tool in a collaborative project between corporate and university research sites in Hong Kong, Finland, and Beijing. The ideal CDP is a portfolio consisting of two videotapes, a group of written documents, and a language audit, which will point to other documentation that may be significant in developing a reflective analysis. The videotapes are made to display the person in two types of communications, internal and external. That is, the person undergoing self-assessment makes a recording of his or her own best practice in communication with other members of his or her group (internal) and then again in communication with someone outside of the corporate group (external: a client in a sales presentation, a seminar in a products presentation). The written documents display the person's variety of normal corporate writing (letters, faxes, e-mail, memos, promotional materials). The language audit is implicit in determining what should go into the CDP. That is, in outlining the CDP one needs to consider what kinds of language are required by the professional in his or her daily routines both within the organization and in typical situations of contact with people outside the group.

Along with the language audit, the two tapes and the written documents, the person prepares a reflective analysis. This analysis is guided by the perspectives outlined in the preceding chapters. That is to say, the person notes the extent to which his or her own practice reflects standard or normative practice, perhaps expressed as inhouse explicit or implicit performance criteria. He or she further examines this portfolio from the objective point of view using such resources as the research literature outlined in chapters 2 through 5, or, of course, may bring in further studies of relevance to his or her particular case. Finally, the portfolio is assessed in terms of the actual situations obtaining when the specific portfolio materials were made. In appendix 2 we provide three aids for the development of a CDP exchange. The first is the CDP Exchange Planner. This is a guide to planning an exchange which suggests a number of options to consider in planning such an exchange. The second is the workshop handbook for "Presenting Across Cultures." This workshop handbook is designed for two purposes: It may be used to conduct an inhouse training session for individuals who would like to engage in a CDP exchange or it may be used individually as a guide to planning a non-institutional exchange between colleagues who voluntarily wish to make such an exchange. The third contains suggestions for documentation including the language audit, which we introduced in chapter 5 and which we further discuss below. It is a way of assessing types of spoken and written language required by organizations and used by individuals. It is more comprehensive than the CDP in that it assesses more than the individual and records weaknesses as well as strengths in individual and organizational practice.

In itself the CDP is a useful portfolio for self-assessment and is much like such portfolios now widely used in self-assessment exercises. Where the CDP departs from common practice is in the comparative element of the reflection. That is, many corporate or organizational review practices involve some kind of self-assessment tool which requires the person to set out his or her personal goals and to assess the extent to which they have been achieved. What the CDP adds is the reflection together with someone from a *different* cultural (national, social, or organizational) group about the effectiveness of one's communication practices from the point of view of that other person or group. The key to this comparative element in the exchanges is that it is a mutual reflection of both parties on each other's practices.

Comparative arrangements can be made between individuals in the same corporate group, between corporate groups within the same umbrella company – for example, two regional offices could work collaboratively in producing comparative CDPs – or between groups not directly related through corporate ties. We give an example of a CDP exchange arranged through an informal network of sales representatives, language teachers, and a language and culture specialist contracted to monitor training. In this case, the exchange was between an employee of a new company and someone who worked for the leading company in the field. Teachers, trainers, and readers can make comparisons even where such collaborative arrangements are difficult or impossible. For example, while television sitcoms and movies are normally ignored for anything but entertainment purposes, they can provide rich sources of members' generalizations about normative (or stereotypical) behavior against which the CDP can be compared for effectiveness. In our training programs, for example, we have used sitcoms from Hong Kong, Korea, Japan, and the US to demonstrate different expectations for how to open a conversation, how close to stand when talking to someone else, or whether it is most appropriate to sit face to face across a table for discussions or to sit side by side.

A Language Audit

In chapter 1, we introduced four perspectives from which we approach professional communication. These are members' generalizations, the objective or neutral view, individual case histories, and contrastive studies. We then narrowed our focus to four typical situations in which communication takes place among professionals in international settings, drawing on our comparative study of professionals in information and communication technologies in three cities, as well as on the research literature. In this final chapter we summarize what we said about those four situations and show how the reader can do a more encompassing analysis both of his or her own best performance in typical situations and of the requirements of the organization within which he or she works or is preparing to work. Individual performance can be documented in a CDP. To complement this, organizational requirements in terms of genres of spoken and written communication can be specified in the form of a language audit, as we suggested at the conclusion of chapter 5.

By a *language audit*, we mean simply an analysis of internal language needs and uses for an organization. In Hong Kong, for example, it is common within the working world for all discussion to take place in Cantonese but for the documents which are the result of these discussions to be written in English. Going against the grain of this practical day-to-day reality are personnel in both governmental and corporate spheres who assume wrongly that if the documents are being disseminated in English, all the preceding discussions, meetings, and other preparations are also happening in English, and the result of this simple failure to audit the actual circumstances is that meeting time is largely wasted. With the language audit, then, the professional needs to assess the communicative patterns of the organization and within these his or her own role.

In these forms of documentation the aim is to obtain objective records of communication as well as members' generalizations. We noted in chapter 5 that it is extremely difficult to obtain objective records of meetings because of considerations of confidentiality. On the other hand, there may be an overwhelming assortment of written documents that are brought into meetings. Copies of a selection of these documents would provide objective records, while members' generalizations could be elicited by asking people how these documents should be prepared. In appendix 3 we provide a list of almost a hundred types of documents taken from an actual audit of a major corporation. This list does not include two things: (1) there is nothing here about the spoken genres that are used in meetings and elsewhere in organizational life, and (2) there is nothing here that tells us that some of these documents are normally produced in one language and some in another.

In Hong Kong, Suzanne Scollon found that the norm for organizational life was to present the majority of documents "in English" but, at the same time, virtually all of the discussion that went into their preparation was in Cantonese. Speech at interviews or meetings might be in Cantonese, with participants jotting down notes in English and discussing the items further in Cantonese as they transform them into genres of English text. This is not at all reflected in the simple listing of documents we give in appendix 3.

If we actually wanted to be a bit more thorough in developing our language audit, we would also want to take into consideration that these documents as well as the talk that accompanies them are in what linguists have called different *registers*. A register simply means a style or level of formality. Often we find that a letter to a client would be written in a very different style from a note to a junior colleague about getting together for lunch. Faxes tend to be much less formal in style and much less fussy about grammar than annual reports and product brochures. One study actually found that using very formal language in sending faxes of product prices *decreased* the acceptability and effectiveness of those faxes in conducting business.

For a language audit for meetings you would want to try to answer four questions, and you would try to answer them separately for the organizational environment and for yourself as a professional communicator. These questions are as follows:

1 What are the many forms of documents that are used commonly in meetings?
2 What are the many forms of spoken language used?
3 What different languages are normally used?
4 What style or register differences are there?

For each question you would note differences between what documents, spoken genres, languages, and registers are actually used and what members of the organization say are or should be used. For example, if you are an Australian who is bilingual in English and Italian and are engaged in an exchange with a Korean company operating in Budapest, you might find that people would say that this is fine, everything will be done in English as the international language. Nevertheless, in practice it might be that all of the initial correspondence would be in English, but many memos within the company would be produced in Korean, particularly at the higher levels of management, which would be controlled by the home company. Documents intended primarily for Hungarian middle management might be in Hungarian or bilingual in Hungarian and English. At the same time, side conversations with colleagues who are Korean would be likely to be carried on in English, but perhaps your Hungarian colleagues would know enough Italian for that to be a more convenient lingua franca.

A cousin of one of the authors recently attended a national meeting of a US government agency headed by a Chinese American of the third generation. As he had not had any occasion to write his name in Chinese since he was a child, he was horrified to find that the director was asking a colleague of Chinese ancestry how his surname was written. As this event took place in Honolulu, there were many Asians present. They began to look at each other and cringe at the thought that they might be next to be cross-examined. Though it is certainly not a requirement of the agency that employees be able to write their names using Chinese characters, they feared being shown to be ignorant in the eyes of the director.

This is perhaps a trivial form of communication that a language audit might show up. In effect you would be obtaining a third perspective through observation of individual case histories. In appendix 2 we give a rough outline of a language audit that you could do as an exchange with colleagues as part of your overall CDP. We give an example of a Chinese American who speaks Cantonese and Mandarin, two mutually unintelligible languages, but cannot write Chinese and does not control the nuances of politeness used in making sales calls to strangers. Be sure to be quite honest about your own abilities in the different languages and styles/registers. Most of us are not equally competent in our language abilities even within our own native languages. We might well have written English for years but still be quite ignorant about how to write a memo in the corporate style of a new company we have just joined, so it is important in order for this to work to be quite specific about your abilities on the one hand and the corporate or organizational requirements on the other.

With case histories of yourself as well as other individuals, you would be in a position to round out your survey with the fourth perspective of comparison and contrast. By contrasting your own behavior with that of other members of your organization as well as those with whom you exchange CDPs, you will see aspects of what you and your colleagues take for granted that other people find strange. Through discussion you will be able to reflect on what aspects of your communication may need to be modified in international settings.

Four Examples of Communicative Situations

In chapters 2 through 5, we focused on four common communicative situations in business or organizational life:

- telephone calls (chapter 2)
- resumés (chapter 3)
- presentations (chapter 4)
- meetings (chapter 5).

Our goal in those chapters was to show that there is a contradiction between the members' view of professional and international business communication and the actual practice of business communication in the international setting. That is to say, standard sources such as communication textbooks or inhouse communication or style guides put forward a set of standards or norms for communication which are most often very far removed from actual practice within businesses and other organizations. The experience of individuals is always more complex than can be captured by such standardizing sources of information.

We used these four communicative situations to illustrate that communication practices are rapidly changing in the complex environment of today's international business and organizational communication. This complexity comes from two main conflicts found in the international setting.

One of the sources of this complexity is the introduction of technologies in daily face-to-face communication and in business communication. Almost daily we are faced with the need to use new communication technologies which are not only unfamiliar, but which require us to change our communicative practices to some extent. Research has shown, for example, that the style used in faxes is very different from that used in business letters. E-mail correspondence is again very different from either business letters or faxes.

The second source of complexity is the conflict between communicative interactions at the personal level and professional communication at the institutional level. We are always both institutional or organizational members *and* private persons, and as the technologies of communication increase, the separation of personal and institutional life also becomes more complex. Further, in international settings we are faced with the need to negotiate changes of communication style not only in professional settings but also in personal relationships as well. While for our purposes in this book we have set aside the strictly personal aspects of communication, as we have seen, even *within the institutional environment* there is a constant negotiation of the personal/institutional interface from one group to another. For example, we have pointed out in chapter 3 that the Hong Kong group in our research project assumed that it was good to put personal information such as hobbies on the resumé. The Beijing group felt the resumé should reflect only professional and task-related information, though personal information such as gender was considered essential. The Finnish group resisted using the resumé at all and preferred to have professional credentials supported through quite personal third-party references.

As we have pointed out in chapter 2 in regard to the telephone and then again in chapter 4 in discussing presentation software, with the fast growth of communication technologies, business communication is no longer just a face-to-face interaction between human beings; it has become interaction with the use of mediational means – faxes, e-mail, presentation software, videos, and, of course, many forms of printed communication.

The intervention of communication technologies in face-to-face interaction has a double-edged effect on communication. First, the technology facilitates and speeds up communication. This fits well within the long-existing preference for speed and efficiency in business and organizational communication. At the same time, however, many of the new technologies constrain the communication. As we showed in chapter 2, for example, the invention of the telephone brought about a revolution in communication processes. Together with the invention of telephone technology, a new social practice of the "C-B-S" (clarity-brevity-sincerity) telephone manner was introduced into society. The practice of using the C-B-S style was developed in the first place because of the constraints of telephone technology. That is, the poor quality of the transmission coupled with the rarity of telephone lines and equipment forced users to speak quickly, loudly, and efficiently, and restricted the use of more subtle cues of voice quality that are associated with humor, irony, and affect. These very important human indicators not only of information but also of how we feel about the social relationship were difficult to produce and so a single, uniform "tone of voice" – the loud telephone voice – was adopted as standard practice.

Over the years this has become the norm for practice within the North American business world. Not only have textbooks on business communication standardized this practice, on international flights one can often pick out the traveling business people simply on the basis of the style one overhears. It is almost impossible to find a textbook treatment of business telephone calls which does not say that the caller should have his or her main point(s) in mind before calling – usually jotted down on paper by the telephone. These same books will also say that one should state this purpose or open these topics immediately and in a clear, strong voice so that the person called will know why one is making the call.

These are, of course, widely accepted business practices and in many ways these practices are good advice. It has become the business community's conventional wisdom for successful communication. Unfortunately, this common sense, or what we would call this members' generalization, presents some overly simplified statements of successful communication practices. Many situations require much more subtle communicative strategies. They require almost the opposite – indirectness, development, and subtlety or even humor – all of which go against the dictum to use the C-B-S style. However, while these standards represent an oversimplification, they are not to be discarded outright as not representing useful keys to good practice. Since they are the normative standards set out widely in international business, people are expected to either adhere to them or clarify why they do not. The point we want to make is neither that we should simply follow these normative practices nor that we should discard them. What is crucially important is to discover the expectations of our counterparts in international settings and to learn how they react to these practices.

As we have argued in the preceding chapters, there are many business situations in which standard practices may not be the most useful ones. Variations in telephone practice are a result of technological, situational, relational, and cross-cultural differences. In many societies the first developmental phase of telephone technology was by-passed. The telephone came to these societies as a more highly evolved technology. In these cases, the constraint imposed by the original inferiority of the technology in using the telephone is not strongly felt. In places such as Hong Kong or modern China, different practices have developed. The telephone entered directly into social life as a common technology that did not require significant changes in communicative practice. Thus the C-B-S style is not a significant one in such societies.

Even in normal business telephoning there are different types of telephone calls – the client call, the colleague call, and the sales call are just three examples. In each case the caller treats the call differently. Also the importance of a business deal has some impact on the caller's approach to making a phone call. But we find the treatment of variations in business communication is almost entirely neglected when members of the business community describe their practices to others. The reality is that the actual situation is normally much richer and more interesting than is commonly described in standard texts. But because it is impossible for standard texts to cover all actual situations, when variations do occur, people match their expectation against the established business practice and attach negative evaluation to these variations.

This is the same with business presentation style. The standard presentation style has been developed on the basis of North American standard practices in face-to-face interaction with an emphasis on the speaker as the center of the presentation. Of course, much of this style has developed out of the extremely influential writings and presentations of Dale Carnegie beginning in the late 1930s. In both interpersonal, face-to-face interactions and presentations to an audience, the speaker is expected to maintain eye contact with the audience, and to be engaging and interactive. The introduction of visual aids, particularly visual aids now available with computer technologies, has brought a new dimension into such oral presentations. The straightforward speaker-to-audience relationship has become a mediated speaker–technologies–audience relationship.

Unfortunately, there is a lag between the practices brought about through the use of technologies for presentations and the expectations people have of presentations. On the whole, people still expect interactivity. The presenter is left in the dilemma of how to give a technology-based but interactive presentation. The competition between technologies and the speaker as a human being poses a new challenge in today's business world. At one level, people appreciate the employment of modern technologies, which, as we found in our research, is taken as a sign of effective, advanced business communication. But at the same time, people desire a human touch in their interaction. This has brought us to the second point of the conflict between human knowledge and institutional knowledge in business communication.

We used the resumé to illustrate this point in chapter 3. The resumé is a formal written presentation of self. It exists largely for the purpose of getting entry into a position in the workplace or for advancement. In other words, it is a ticket into a new position. However, it is a ticket that is most often handed over in person after a connection has been made through some other form of contact. This form of communication presents a conflict between human nature and institutionalized practice only if it is assumed to be the sole or initial form of presentation. As human beings, we tend to interact with others on the level of personal knowledge. We want to know what kind of person the other is, whether he or she is like us or not, or what habits he or she has. But institutional practice, at least increasingly in our contemporary world, requires that a human being be judged by his or her work knowledge and professional behavior. For both legal and personal reasons, people hesitate to include personal information in their resumés. Nevertheless, the person viewing the resumé would somehow like to have an idea of the person represented by the written document. This is the constant conflict between the resumé writer and the resumé viewer. When people don't see the information they expect from the resumé, quite often, they tend to judge the resumé writer negatively. The resumé is most successful when the applicant is already known to the person evaluating it.

A business meeting is another place we find the conflict between expectations and practices, as we have discussed in chapter 5. Although the structure of a business meeting appears to be similar in different cultural settings, its function is interpreted differently by members of different cultural groups. A meeting can function to take action or to ratify the existing social relationships or power hierarchy. We showed in chapter 5 that Americans, Japanese, Mainland Chinese, and Hong Kong Chinese have specific expectations about meetings, and would act according to their own expectations in a meeting. All of these are very different from the expectations of Brazilians, as we showed in the example opening chapter 1.

For Americans, a business meeting is a business event to make decisions and exchange information. For Japanese, maintenance of interpersonal relationship is emphasized. For Chinese, power hierarchy is evidenced and the meeting process is a ratification of the power structure. For Hong Kong Chinese, a business meeting may fall anywhere on a continuum between American or British C-B-S style and Chinese official or even quasi-family discourse. While the functions of a business meeting may be similar to these for Brazilians, their conduct of a meeting seems completely chaotic from an American, Chinese, British, or Japanese point of view. Many times, of course, we are not aware that there is a conflict between our assumptions about meetings or other communicative situations and actual practices. To effectively interact in international settings, we need to have a way to find out what the expectations are about the function of business meetings, resumés, presentations, telephone calls, or any of the many other situations of communication in the minds of the people we are dealing with, and then adjust our own expectations.

Communication Display Portfolio (CDP)

As we have said above, the key to this communicative self-assessment is the tool we call the Communication Display Portfolio (CDP) for comparative self-assessment. We discussed in chapter 1 the four analytical perspectives which we believe are essential to self-reflection on business and corporate communication; that is, members' generalizations, the objective or neutral view, individual case histories, and contrastive studies. We believe that successful reflective self-assessment in communication requires all four of these perspectives to achieve the degree of flexibility needed in the international workplace. The idea of a CDP exchange is to combine these four perspectives and develop a method that can be self-reflective and help us see ourselves as others see us. It takes into account different levels of interaction in business and professional communication: cultural, professional, organizational, institutional, and personal.

In the first instance a CDP will most likely represent the standard practice or members' generalizations for the person or persons who prepare the CDP. In our experience, when people prepare a CDP they most often try their best to represent what is in their minds the "best practice." That is, they do it in what they believe is the correct way. It is interesting to us that most frequently people are quite reluctant to include actual resumés, presentation materials, or recordings of actual presentations or meetings. They make excuses that in this particular case the situation did not meet their "normal" standards. From our point of view, what we are learning in these cases is that, in fact, actual cases do depart rather significantly from normative practice and most people recognize this. Thus the CDP that is most often prepared is intended to represent what people believe they *should do* rather than what they actually do.

Then when a CDP is compared with those of members of other groups we begin to see a more objective view as well as a more individualized case history view. Most often participants will receive some comments and criticisms from the group with which they have exchanged their CDPs. Often those comments will be more practical than normative. The most common response is, "That's what I had originally, but I changed it because I thought

I should do it the right way!" That is, at the very first cut of comparison we find that actual practice is probably more effective than normative standards, and therefore one effect of the CDP exchange is to give people confidence that what they are already doing is working effectively, even when it goes against textbook or organizational standards.

Once the exchange is established, variations in actual situations can be brought out and discussed to reflect the objective approach to actual communication. The individual then can make comparisons and adjustments to adopt a communication style that best fits his or her own needs or the corporation's needs in communicating with others. This is the self-reflective phase, which aims at developing a tool flexible enough to incorporate cultural, professional, institutional, and personal aspects of dealing with others.

How to Set Up and Make CDP Exchanges

Appendix 1 gives a checklist planner for making CDP exchanges. Appendix 2 is a workshop handbook which can be used either for groups or individually in planning a CDP exchange. In what follows we will give suggestions for setting up and making CDP exchanges.

CDPs should be developed for participating individuals and then comparatively examined and critiqued by corporate members, preferably in at least three sites. Of course, in many cases only two sites will be practicable, but a three-way comparison is very much richer in insights gained. These CDPs should be made as "standard" as possible; that is, they should contain the same types of materials, but no attempt should be made to have the participants give standardized examples.

Ideally, as we stated at the beginning of the chapter, the CDP would include at least one internal communication such as a meeting and one external communication such as a sales presentation or a negotiation. These should be videotaped and all other documentation used should also be included. That is, if there is a presentation made that also includes product brochures, schedules, or other documentary materials, they should be included as part of the presentation. A *full* presentation documentation would include a videotape of the presentation, the accompanying documentation, and also the actual software, overhead transparencies, slides, or videos used. In other words, in the ideal situation the participants in the other site(s) should be able to view the entire presentation very much as it actually took place originally.

In addition to such video/documentation clusters, the CDP should include corporate documentation such as memos, e-mail, faxes, letters, product catalogs, or annual reports. Of course there is an almost limitless supply of such documents in any organizational context, and so the key is to ask the participants to select a cluster of such documents which they feel represent their best communication products.

Finally, personal documentation such as a resumé or business card should be included. In each case the purpose is not to evaluate corporate communications but personal or individual communication practices. From this point of view, corporate communications should only be included to the extent they have been produced by the individuals involved in the exchanges or are very frequently used by individuals in presenting themselves.

In the *first phase* of the project, the CDPs are prepared for local or inhouse comparison and discussion. After this, focus groups should be convened. In these groups and through interviewing, corporate members will critique their own CDP, indicating their own assessment of strengths and weaknesses. While revisions may be made at this stage, on the whole it is best not to worry much about this, as the purpose is not to make perfect CDPs but to elicit genuine commentary from one's counterparts in other organizations or cultures for self-reflection and discussion.

Once the CDPs and the self-assessments are prepared, they should be sent (or taken) to each of the other cooperating sites for comparative examination as the *second phase*. Of course it is ideal if the participants in the different sites can meet each other, but this is rarely a possibility at the opening stage of the process. In some cases, however, a human resources office (HRO) person can personally make the exchanges and facilitate the focus groups in the several sites.

Each group is then asked to critically evaluate the CDPs and self-assessments from the other (two) site(s). These evaluations and discussions should be done as focus group discussions and preferably these discussions should be videotaped. If a company HRO facilitator is present, summary notes of the discussion can be made to accompany the videotaped discussion.

Translation is likely to be an issue in most cases in the international setting. The CDPs should be prepared in whatever language would be the natural one for use in the first place. If it would be normal to produce a resumé in English, then that language should be used. If a person has resumés in two languages, both resumés (which are likely to be different from each other) should be included. The same would go for business cards and other forms of correspondence. In this process it is very important to assess the significance of the language used and so no attempt should be made to alter normal conditions at this stage.

Nevertheless, if the focus group discussion is held in a language that would not be understood by the participants in the other sites, a summary in their language(s) will need to be made. This summary should *accompany* the video of the actual discussion, as it is important for participants to begin to experience observing people speaking naturally in other languages with other styles which they are not entirely able to follow. This is a very common experience in international settings – some participants are speaking naturally in their own languages and others are guided only by translated summaries of the discussion – and should be kept as part of the CDP exchange.

In the *third phase*, the results of these focus group discussions should be returned to all sites so that participants can evaluate their own CDPs in light of the two other CDPs and self-assessments. In this phase the results of the first two phases are combined into a debriefing at each of the sites. The participants at each site then make self-assessments of their communication styles and practices and decide how to make adjustments based on these findings.

The whole process can be diagrammed as in figure 6.1. Naturally, what follows at this stage is business as usual among the participants, who are likely to form an ongoing working group. In addition to this, recommendations for communications training based on these findings can also be made for HRO use within the organization(s) involved. This provides the practical output to the cooperating corporate sites.

Possible Difficulties and Important Issues to Bear in Mind

When we suggest this self-reflective approach, we do not intend to deny the difficulties involved in the process. Like any part of professional communication in international settings, this process is by no means without setbacks and difficulties. It is not likely you will get all you have planned in every stage. Nevertheless the first thing that needs to be done is to have a well-planned procedure that addresses the following issues:

(1) *Origination.* CDP exchange can be used to address both the individual and corporate needs for cross-cultural and intercultural communication. But there are different concerns and needs for these two types of exchanges. An individual's exchange can be open-ended or address his or her specific problems and questions. In the case of corporate exchanges, there is often not as much flexiblity. This is because the corporate needs and constraints will often dictate what to do and what information is needed. The individual who does a CDP exchange *as a corporate exercise* will find that the

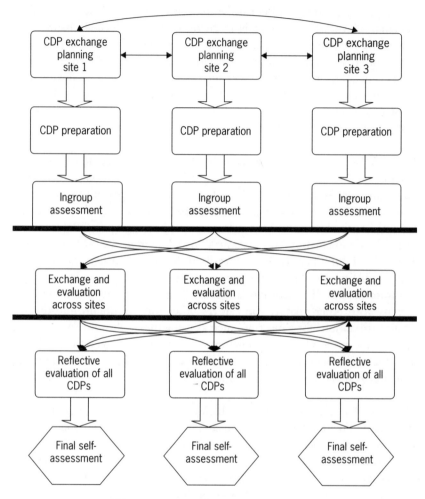

Figure 6.1 The CDP exchange process

corporate exchange will take into consideration more how to represent the corporation perhaps than how to represent himself or herself. Of course this is not a serious problem, but should be recognized at the outset in developing a CDP exchange.

(2) *Participants.* CDP exchange involves people in other sites. Cooperation among participants is crucial in the process. The first issue to consider is who is going to be involved in the project, and with whom you are going to

exchange the portfolio. This can be done in two ways. One is to utilize personal networks. The other is to go through more formal channels by contacting the personnel department in your organization, or the person in charge of cross-cultural training, to establish collaboration for the exchange project. In some environments, personal connections are more flexible and easier to get access to. But there is a limit to how much intercultural variety a personal network can cover. To go through a formal channel, of course, will probably take time and patience.

(3) *CDP items.* The next step is to decide what should be included in the portfolio and how to assemble it. This really depends on what information you want to find out from the other site and what is important in your communication activities. Are you going to include a videotape of your presentation, or a sales brochure? Do you want to emphasize corporate information or personal information? Is a resumé a "must" item in the portfolio or will a name card do? There is also the feasibility issue to consider. For instance, is it feasible to videotape a business meeting which may contain confidential information? If a meeting is a crucial aspect in your communication activity with other people, you can try other ways to obtain information about expectations for a meeting, such as using movie clips or TV shows or videotaping a role-play. Also sometimes you might need to edit the video of an actual meeting because of confidential materials or breaks in the meeting which provide no particular useful insights.

(4) *Schedule.* The procedure by which the exchanges are arranged is very important. The sequence of *when* to complete *what* is crucial in making sure that the exchange will go smoothly. Making a feasible schedule will ensure successful completion of the process. Since this schedule requires the parties concerned to exchange portfolios, it is advisable to plan ahead and give the other parties plenty of time to prepare portfolios and organize focus group discussions.

The sequence is first to prepare your own portfolio(s), then duplicate the portfolios and send them to the other sites at an agreed time. Second, agreement should be secured from the other sites about when to run the focus group discussion to review the portfolio and make comments. Third, the focus group comments are sent back to the original sites for the second round of focus group discussion to get feedback on the comments made by the other sites. The purpose of the second round of focus group discussion is to develop a self-reflective view of how others see us, and how we see ourselves. This will serve as a basis for the self-assessment and self-adjustment in the next phase. The final step is to write up a self-assessment of what you see in your way of doing things that needs to be modified or adjusted so that you will improve your communication with others. For example, you may want to rewrite your resumé to fit the expectations of the other site, or you may adjust your ways of presenting ideas at a meeting. Of course, if you decide not to change anything, you will know the reason why you don't want to change, and can know in advance what kind of reaction you will have. In this way, you adjust your expectations and will not be surprised by the feedback and reaction you receive when dealing with others.

If focus group discussions are difficult to arrange at the other sites, an alternative approach is to design a list of questions and a worksheet to get the feedback that you would like to have. For example, if you would like to know how people react to your resumé, design a questionnaire that will elicit comments on its format, style, length, and content. The questionnaire could be sent together with your resumé to have people at the other sites respond.

(5) *Cost.* It should be clear that the CDP exchange will incur some costs. First of all, the CDP consists of documents in written, printed, videotaped, and audiotaped form. There are, therefore, the costs of materials and perhaps of recording. To exchange CDPs, copies need to be produced in order to be sent to the other sites for evaluation. The reproduction costs depend on what materials are included in the CDP. For example, photo-copying is not as costly as reproducing a designed brochure. In many cases of such corporate materials, however, multiple copies will already be available. Travel is required if face-to-face meetings are thought to be necessary. Such meetings with collaborators in other sites will no doubt greatly enhance the efficiency and accuracy of the CDP preparation and exchange, but the CDP exchange can be done without these meetings if your budget does not allow you to take trips.

Another expense is the compensation for focus group participants. It is customary to either pay participants in a focus group or at a minimum to provide a small gift as a token of appreciation to people who take time out to participate.

In the research project upon which this book is based, the biggest single cost category was staffing. A research assistant is a wonderful but costly resource for carrying out the project. Our assistant was invaluable in making contacts, preparing the CDPs, running the focus group discussions, tran-scribing and translating the discussions, and doing the coding for initial analysis. It is worthwhile to have an assistant if your budget allows.

The second biggest expense in our project was overseas travel. We trav-eled from Hong Kong to Beijing twice and to Finland once to have meet-ings with our collaborators and to observe focus group discussions. Besides the meetings and focus group discussions, we learned a great deal during our travel by doing ethnographic observations and through interaction with the people in other sites. Of course when the CDP exchanges are done within the corporate environment it might well be possible to schedule exchanges in conjunction with other business travel. In cases where project teams are already meeting regularly across different international sites, the CDP exchange might be built into the agenda of such meetings.

These steps are outlined in appendix 1. While we believe such exchanges are a highly interesting and beneficial process, there are difficulties involved in each step which it is important to take into consideration. Our own experience is just a sample of unanticipated problems and ways we worked around them.

In the initial stage of making contacts, be aware that not everyone has the same agenda as you do, especially when you are dealing with people from different cultural or professional backgrounds. The ways of making commitments and meeting deadlines might be different from what you are accustomed to. In some cases, a verbal promise is seen as sufficient commitment, while in others, only a written document will serve the function. In our project, we made initial contacts through our academic colleagues in Beijing and Finland to secure collaboration (we were based in Hong Kong). We obtained agreement letters from them to collaborate in the project. The collaboration involved finding a professional in each place to put together a portfolio and to organize focus group discussions to evaluate these. Then our colleagues contacted people in the professional field to get their agreement to participate in the project. Our colleagues in Beijing and Hong Kong used their personal connections to obtain the portfolios and organize focus group discussions. They were able to call on spouses who work in the professional field to help construct portfolios and to recruit focus group participants. The Finnish researcher, on the other hand, called on a business contact established in a previous project. The focus group participants were students with previous business experience enrolled in a three-year business communication program in the researcher's university.

The difference in the Finnish and Chinese (Beijing and Hong Kong) projects' approaches tells us something about the preferred way of making business contacts in these two cultures. The Chinese researchers utilized their personal connections to establish business contacts while the Finnish researcher relied on a business connection to establish what were actually somewhat more personal contacts.

In the specific design and formatting of the CDP, we tried to achieve a certain degree of uniformity across the three sites by producing sample portfolios for middle managers that included edited video segments of a meeting, and documents such as memos, letters, brochures, faxes, posters, and flowcharts. Toward this end, the sample portfolios were produced at the Hong Kong site and presented in person to researchers from the other sites at an international conference held in Beijing. However, it was also a crucial aspect of the study that each site make its own determination of which features it considered most important to represent to the other sites. Thus some of the contents and formatting of the CDPs were not uniform across sites, and these departures are likely to represent in themselves significant aspects of sociocultural difference. One cultural difference that affected the assembly of the CDPs was that researchers in Beijing and Hong Kong called on spouses to help construct portfolios and were thus able to put together more complete portfolios than the Finnish site. Institutional placement of researchers also affected the assembling of portfolios, in that research funding provided staffing and facilities to edit videotapes and audiotapes and photocopy overhead transparencies and printed materials. We were also able to take advantage of travel opportunities and make time to coordinate the many aspects of the project. The differences among CDPs became a topic for reflection in focus groups.

CDPs were duplicated as they became assembled and sent to the other sites for focus group discussions. Even duplication, far from being straightforward, reflected cultural assumptions in the different sites. Because the Hong Kong site had research support for video reproduction, all videotapes except the one produced in Finland were edited and copied there for distribution. While the originals varied in quality, with the Finnish tape which was produced in the television studio of a university being of notably high quality, copying not only led to loss of quality, but entailed decisions about what was important, for example where to begin, which segments to include, how much context to provide. From the start, standardization was not a possibility.

In actual collection of CDP items, there was a major adjustment at almost every stage in our project. The Hong Kong professional decided to include a videotaped oral presentation, but could not find a good time to do the presentation that he intended. We contacted the personnel office in his company, only to find that since it was the Christmas holiday season we needed to wait for a long time before any oral presentation would take place in the company. So we decided to videotape an oral presentation of other professionals from the same company instead. Also, as we have said above, the Finnish professional did not provide us with a resumé. The Beijing professional gave us e-mail messages which were not included in the other CDPs. The Finland focus group discussion consisted of only one round.

We conducted the second round ourselves when we went to teach a short course; we did the discussion of the CDPs and the other focus groups with our students.

Just as we tried to maintain some uniformity in CDPs, we sought to achieve some similarity in focus groups by giving general guidelines but leaving the particulars up to the participants in each site. Different facilities made uniformity impossible, and differences in format reflect cultural assumptions about the purpose and audience of the focus groups. In Beijing and Hong Kong, the focus groups were facilitated by spouses of the individuals who prepared the CDPs. They took an active interest in eliciting comments, having a personal concern with the comments from the other sites. Focus group members were recruited among professional friends who had an easy rapport and did not hesitate to offer comments. Discussion was facilitated by sessions being conducted in the home language of the participants, Mandarin in Beijing and Cantonese in Hong Kong.

In Finland, on the other hand, the focus group was recruited among business people enrolled in a three-year university course. While the facilitator was a Finn, he was not a member of the research team. The format of the focus group staged the facilitator off-camera while the other participants lined up facing the camera, unlike the other sites in which the cameras were unobtrusive, ignored, or avoided and the participants sat around a table. In keeping with the physical arrangement, participants spoke not to each other or to the facilitator but to a presumed camera audience, in English as well as Finnish. Though our research design called for two rounds of focus groups with the same participants, this was possible only in Beijing and Hong Kong, where, as mentioned above, the facilitators had a personal stake in the project. In Hong Kong because of practical considerations the two rounds were held back to back. In addition, in Finland the authors took advantage of a summer school directed by a collaborator in the research to conduct discussions that served as quasi-focus groups.

We would like to emphasize that the goal of these focus groups was not comparative; that is, the goal was not to analyze the portfolios and the presentations and to develop research findings regarding "cultural" differences. Neither was the goal to establish the best way to approach each situation. Rather, the goal was for the participants to reflect on their own portfolios, to reflect on what others say about them. Our primary interest was in what they say and the ways in which they talk about their perceived differences.

Though we had different ways of obtaining videotaped presentations at each site, in no case were we able to get the presenter to sit down with a researcher and view and reflect on his or her presentation. From previous experience using videotapes of university classroom teaching in a professional development seminar, we know how vulnerable one feels reflecting on one's teaching with a group of colleagues, so it is small wonder that we were not able to arrange this. On the other hand, participants found it easy to empathize with the presenters, so self-reflection among the group was possible. From this we have concluded that as much as possible it should be emphasized in all phases of CDP exchanges that the goal is genuine exchange among the participants and that the interpretations and results of these exchanges are for the benefit of the participants, not to be taken out of context or used for other purposes.

The important message to emphasize is that it is never necessary to insist on uniformity either in the CDPs themselves or in the process. One method will work well in one setting or environment, but not in another. A resumé may be easy to get in one culture, but difficult in another. We had no problem in getting Beijing focus group members to talk and make comments, but the Finnish focus group members talked very little. Their comments were relatively limited. Of course we know the somewhat stereotyped characterizations of Beijing people as quite voluble and Finnish people as preferring reticence. So even the amount of discussion within the focus groups is likely to be quite varied. If we just imagine doing a CDP with a group of Brazilians, as we suggested in the opening example in chapter 1, we could expect a highly voluble and energetic focus group which would contrast very dramatically with the ones we observed in Finland. The key to overcoming such differences and other obstacles is to be flexible and have back-up plans. You will need to have a clear idea of what you want to know and remember that items in the CDP are there to get people in other sites to react to them and make comments. If you fail to get one item, you can try some other items to achieve that effect.

Toward the Future: Technologies of Communication

An article "What the Internet cannot do" begins with an enthusiast acclaiming technology as a panacea: "It is impossible that old prejudices and hostilities should longer exist, while such an instrument has been created for the exchange of thought between all nations of the earth" (1858 writer cited in *The Economist*, August 19, 2000, p. 11). When the first transatlantic telegraph cable was laid, observers had great hopes for alleviation of international provocation through the communication made possible by the new technology. The writer concludes that the lesson of history is that however the Internet may transform the way we do things, it cannot help us eliminate wars, pollution, and inequality any more than the transatlantic cable did over a hundred years ago.

As we argued in chapter 2, the telegraph and then the telephone opened up the development of the C–B–S style of communication, which increasingly dominated international communication in business and the professions through much of the twentieth century. This C–B–S ideal was shaped by a technology that limited communication to one channel or mode and restricted time allotted for speaking while simultaneously saving time by moving signals across space. With new technologies providing multimodal communication at unimagined speeds across the globe, this ideal is becoming increasingly difficult to approximate. The challenge of being clear in multifaceted changing contexts, being brief when differing assumptions require greater explanation, and being sincere when sincerity means different things to different people is producing unprecedented levels of stress as we enter a new century.

We have not dealt directly in our research or in this book with new technologies of communication such as e-mail, though we have been documenting and researching such communication for two decades, for two reasons. First of all, these did not arise as important media in the actual project we conducted. Then also, we have not treated these new media in any detail simply because they are mushrooming so rapidly. Our approach has been rather to document forms of communication that are fairly representative in order to show how the Dale Carnegie style of communication originated in the unique environment of the northeastern United States in the period of optimism following World War I, and is not very widespread even in the United States, although textbooks and wizards still uphold it as the way to success.

Whether dealing by telegraph or Internet, there is no simple formula for successful communication, but there are rewards for exchanging information and comparing approaches to see what works wherever we find ourselves.

Appendices

Reflective Self-Assessment

To help our readers develop the method of self-reflection, we have designed a training workshop showing how to do CDP exchanges and how to elicit comments useful for self-assessment. The appendices contain information and activities to reach this goal, providing practical materials to support the reader in making Communication Display Portfolio (CDP) exchanges. There are three appendices:

1 *The Communication Display Portfolio Exchange Planner.* Appendix 1 consists of a series of questions that will guide the reader in planning the sequence and procedures of the exchange. It is a step-by-step checklist of things that might be done in each phase of the process described in chapter 6.

2 *Presenting Across Cultures.* Appendix 2 is a handbook which may be used in conducting a training program as preparation for a CDP exchange. The four workshop activities are based on the discussions in chapters 2 (telephone calls), 3 (resumés), 4 (presentations), and 5 (meetings).

3 *Suggestions for Users.* Appendix 3 provides suggestions for users who are planning a CDP exchange on how to:
   (a) conduct a language audit
   (b) collect corporate documentation
   (c) make a video of a presentation
   (d) view a video for focus group discussion
   (e) have a successful focus group discussion.

Who Can Use the Material

The material in the appendices, like the rest of the book, can be used by different readers for various purposes depending on their needs. Appendix

3 gives suggestions for all readers planning a CDP exchange, whether as individuals, trainers, consultants, or human resource managers:

- *for trainers.* People giving in-service or pre-departure training to groups from the same corporation working or preparing to work in another country, or to groups of individuals from different organizations, can tailor the materials and develop their own materials according to their particular needs. The facsimiles of PowerPoint® slides can be used as a model for an introductory presentation or a lecture on meetings in other countries. The activities and worksheets can also be adapted to fit the types of documentation being used or recommended.
- *for professionals.* Professionals working with immigrants or colleagues from other countries or preparing to go overseas can use the CDP exchange planner and the suggestions for documentation and exchange to initiate their own reflective self-assessment. The materials in the workshop handbook can serve as a guide to selection.
- *for researchers.* Researchers can use the documentation in the workshop handbook to stimulate research questions. For example, the question of how and when telephone callers are put on hold and with what results can lead to research on the use and meaning of time for the various participants inside and outside the office. Problems arising from the use of presentation technologies, whether in large meetings or in, say, medical consultation, might be suggested by the presentation activity. Wherever workers sit behind terminals at counters that interface with entering clientele, eye contact is made problematical by having to focus on the screen as well as on the faces of people.

  The suggestions on how to do language audits and collect and use documentation in focus group discussions come from the authors' experience in research, consultation, and training over three decades, and reflect changing circumstances in diverse settings, especially with the media expansion and geopolitical mobility of the last decade. Whether one wants to find out how children learn to use palm pilots or how handycams can be used to document work practices in factories by workers from diverse communities, useful ideas can emerge from examining these materials.
- *for students.* This method can also be used in business communication courses for students, either for class sessions arranged by students among themselves or as an aid to study individually or in small groups. Students who are also working professionals but cannot easily arrange exchanges among their colleagues might use the appendices to find ways to achieve reflective self-assessment by interacting with classmates.

Students who work in jobs with little challenge can imagine themselves in roles more to their liking and set about documenting their activities in those roles.

Everyone deals with professionals in their daily lives and wonders why they aren't more effective. Students who do not have any particular professional role they want to improve on themselves can find out how difficult it would be for those who annoy them to modify their behavior, and might even be able to provide suggestions to family and friends.

As we all enact multiple roles as observers as well as clients and professionals, and cannot be aware of these roles and reflect upon them as we carry them out, we can use these materials to reflect on various aspects of our communication as the need arises.

Appendix 1

The Communication Display Portfolio Exchange Planner

This checklist for the process of developing a Communication Display Portfolio (CDP) exchange makes reference to the discussion in chapter 6.

CDP Exchange Planner: A Checklist

1 *Origination*
   - By whom is the exchange originated?
     Individual or a corporation?
   - If by an individual, what are the individual's needs?
   - If by a corporation, what are the corporation's needs?
2 *Participants*
   - Whom are you going to exchange CDPs with?
   - Are you going to do it within your own network or go through a formal channel?
   - If within your own network, how many people are you going to contact?
   - If through a formal channel, how are you going to make the arrangements?
3 *Outline of the CDP*
   - What items are you going to include in your CDP and why?
   - Are you going to include:
     resumé
     name card
     photo of yourself
     brochure
     business letter

e-mail message
company information
language audit
videotape of your presentation
presentation slides
videotape of meetings
audiotape of telephone conversations
writing sample
sales report
other items:

_____

_____

_____

- What are your reasons for including the items you have selected?

4 *Schedule*
- When will you complete the whole procedure?
- Steps in the procedure:
  deliver the first CDP to other participants: complete by _____.
  arrange the first focus group discussion: complete by _____.
  exchange focus group responses: complete by _____.
  self-assessment: complete by _____.

5 *Cost*
- Initial contact:
  telecommunications: $ _____
  postage: $ _____
- Materials preparation: $ _____
- Reproduction of materials: $ _____
- Payment for focus group participants: $ _____
- Assistants: $ _____
- Travel:
  airfare: $ _____
  hotel: $ _____
  meals: $ _____
  local transportation: $ _____

TOTAL COST $ _____
COST PER PARTICIPANT $ _____

Appendix 2

Presenting Across Cultures

The handbook which follows has been used by the authors in conducting our own workshops. While it may be used in the form given here, we suggest that readers will want to use this handbook as a guide to the development of their own training sessions and workshops.

In each of these formats, the actual conduct of the workshop will depend to some extent on the number of participants. A group of six to eight should be kept together as a single group for all activities. If the group is larger, it should be divided into smaller groups of four to six participants each for activities 1, 2, 3, and 4, but preferably with a different group composition for each one.

In all of these formats the presenters of the training should be alert to the need to extend the discussion when interesting and important insights are being developed. If space needs to be made by eliminating a section, we suggest "The Meeting" can be cut and participants can be referred to chapter 5 for reading. On the other hand, if a group is being prepared for meetings in China, the detail in chapter 5 may be usefully presented.

Introduction to the Handbook

In today's global business, governmental, and social environment professional communication across cultures has become the normal situation, not an exception to be dealt with only by a few members of each organizational group.

"Presenting Across Cultures" is based on two ideas:

1   everyone in an international organization needs to be prepared with the knowledge and the practical skills to communicate successfully across cultural boundaries of languages, styles, and values and

2   the necessary knowledge and practical skills are constantly in the process
    of change.

"Presenting Across Cultures" focuses our attention on the main points
of contact between members of organizations who are culturally different
– the points at which they present themselves to representatives of other
organizations. We focus on four such moments – resumés (and business
cards and letters), presentations, telephone calls, and meetings. Because of
the rapid change in each of these areas of international communication
through new media technologies and new international contacts, we focus
on developing a personal process of assessing one's own knowledge and
skills and basing personal development and change on that self-assessment.
This workshop and this handbook can, therefore, be used successfully both
by corporate groups for internal training programs and by individuals for
professional self-development.

How to Use the Handbook

This handbook contains training materials for a one-day workshop. There
are five activities in the workshop: the resumé, the presentation, the telephone call, the meeting, and the portfolio exchange. Of course, these
have been structured to follow the plan of the book, which the reader
can use as a backup and for supplementary material in giving this workshop. Worksheets are provided for each activity, including reflective
questions for participants to answer and suggestions for further points of
analysis.
    We have also included suggestions by which the workshop material
can be used in different ways: one-day, half-day, or two-day versions. For
example, a typical full-day workshop could be completed in a 9-to-4 format.
That format would include coffee and lunch breaks. Alternatively, a
shorter, half-day format could be achieved by selecting just one of the
activities and then going directly to activity 4, the portfolio exchange and
evaluation.
    For a longer, two-day format we recommend separating the two days by
an interval of at least one week, if possible. In this format the first day would
conclude with the assignment for participants to prepare their own actual
materials – a real resumé, an actual presentation, etc. – to bring to the second
day workshop for group debriefing. The second day of the two-day format
would then be based on the participants' own materials.

Agenda

* *Presenting Across Cultures: Professional Communication in International Settings* (p. 166)
  Suggested timing: 30 minutes
* *The Resumé: Activity 1* (p. 170)
  Suggested timing: 45 minutes
* *The Presentation: Activity 2* (p. 184)
  Suggested timing: 45 minutes
* *The Telephone Call: Activity 3* (p. 189)
  Suggested timing: 45 minutes
* *The Meeting: A Talk* (p. 194)
  Suggested timing: 45 minutes
* *The Portfolio Exchange: Activity 4* (p. 202)
  Suggested timing: 90 minutes
* *Topics for Further Discussion* (p. 204)
  Suggested timing: 15 minutes

Presenting Across Cultures: Professional Communication in International Settings

This introduction to presenting across cultures is a presentation covering these points:

* All cultures, groups, corporations, and organizations are dynamic.
* Knowing how to communicate means learning how to change.
* The best source of knowledge about what's right are the people you need to communicate with.
* The professional Communication Display Portfolio (CDP) is a useful tool for exchanges of information about how to communicate effectively across cultures.

Space is provided next to each slide for note-taking.

Presenting Across Cultures

**Professional Communication
in International Settings**

Presenting Across Cultures

- **Our environment is international**
  - business
  - diplomacy
  - personal travel
- **Preparing to communicate across
  cultural boundaries**
  - languages
  - styles
  - values

Cultures are Dynamic

- **All practices are constantly
  changing in our contemporary
  world**
- **Static ideas and practices are a
  dead end**
- **Dealing with constant change**
  - knowledge
  - skills

Conflict Between Belief and Action

- **For ourselves**
- **For others**
- **We assume we know our own
  practices and those of others**

What Can We Do?

- Can't rely on textbooks
- Need to develop our own way to generate observations of real professional communication

How We Do It

- Portfolio exchange
- Develop self-assessment skills
  - increase awareness of the expected practices of other
    - cultures
    - situations
    - corporations
    - organizations

Professional Communication Across Cultures

- Three sites: Finland, Beijing, and Hong Kong
- Develop a professional Communication Display Portfolio (CDP)
- Exchange CDPs
- Focus group discussions

Two Steps

- Prepare a CDP
- Exchange feedback from other cultural (organizational) sites based on the CDP

The Communication Display Portfolio (CDP)

- **Documentation of**
  - your best (or typical) presentations
- **Open-ended and may include**
  - name card
  - resumé
  - sales reports
  - product brochures
  - letters, faxes, other writing samples
  - presentational slides and overheads

Non-Standard

- **Corporate and personal identity means CDP will differ across**
  - individuals
    - CEO, sales personnel, cleaning staff
  - corporations and organizations
    - high technology, medical, diplomatic
  - professions
    - business, government, academic
  - social and national groups
    - monolingual and bilingual business cards, etc.

Getting Feedback

- **Evaluating and commenting on CDP**
- **Discovering "normal practice" in the other cultural group, situation, company**
- **Exchanging ideas on how to accommodate to different practices**

Methodology

- **Self-reflection and development of the CDP**
- **Exchanges of CDPs among colleagues, counterparts in other sites**
- **Assisted focus groups for study and reflection**
- **Developing new CDP materials, styles, format**

This Workshop

• Training manual
• How to run the workshop

The Resumé: Activity 1

Outline of activity

- *Purpose of activity (1 min.).* There is no standard way of writing a resumé for all jobs. We will look at two very different resumés, both successful for the individuals who prepared them in obtaining jobs and opportunities for career advancement. We will discuss different reactions to these resumés and the criteria for evaluation put forth by participants in our focus groups. The purpose of this exercise is to alert participants to the different ways resumés can be evaluated by professionals in different international settings, so that they can learn to tailor their preparation and evaluation of resumés to the particular function being served in a particular organizational setting.
- *Documents provided (two resumés).* The resumés are actual documents provided by professionals. The names of the participants and identifying institutions have been changed to protect their confidentiality. The content and format remain the same.
- *Evaluation of the resumés (20 min.).* Work in small groups of three or so to evaluate and record comments on the resumés provided and how they compare with resumés you are familiar with. A separate worksheet for the evaluation is provided on p. 183.
- *Reports from small groups (15 min.).* Each group will report on their evaluations of the resumés and related discussion.
- *Debriefing by presenter (9 min.).* The presenter will lead a discussion integrating comments from the group reports with comments by professionals in Hong Kong, Beijing, and Finland found in *Professional Communication in International Settings.*
- *Conclusion: what is a good resumé?*

The first resumé

The first resumé was provided for the authors by an administrator for a major American computer manufacturer working in Beijing. The information provided is authentic, but as far as we know the person was not looking for a job. We presume she used a similar resumé to obtain her position.

RESUMÉ

Linda Chen

Room 2003, Building 26
Haidan Qu, Dong Cheng District
Beijing 100000
P.R. China
(86 10) 68224451, 62775034 (H)

Professional Experience

Dec. 1996 to present

China Hewlett-Packard Co., Ltd.

Export Administrator, in charge of compliance with American rules and regulations and control of export licenses issued by US government.

Nov. 1995 to Dec. 1996

Allen & Overy, Beijing Office

Legal assistant, in charge of legal documents translation and liaison with relevant authorities.

I have translated legal documents and other materials relating to JV Contract, AOA, Technical Assistance Agreement and Trademark Licence Agreement, etc.

Aug. 1995 to Nov. 1995

Legal Department of Ciba-Geigy (China) Ltd.

Legal assistant, in charge of legal documents translation and file keeping.

I mainly translated internal legal documents of CCC's Joint Venture companies.

July 1990 to Sep. 1993

Institute of Policy and Management, Chinese University of Sciences

Interpreter

Education

Sep. 1993 to
July 1995

Law Department of Chinese First University
BA

Courses: Jurisprudence, Constitution, Criminal Law,
Criminal Procedural Law, Civil Law, Civil Procedural
Law, Administration Law, Administration Procedural
Law, Economic Law, Corporation and Enterprise Law,
Intellectual Property Law, Environment Law,
International Law, International Private Law,
International Trade Law, International Investment Law,
Finance and Bank Law, Hong Kong Basic Law, History
of Chinese Legal System, etc.

Sep. 1986 to
July 1990

**English Department, Beijing Foreign Languages
and Culture University**
BA

Courses: English Reading, Writing, Listening, and
Speaking; Interpretation and Translation; American
Culture and Society; British Culture and Society;
Applied Linguistics, etc.

Other Experience

1994

*Interpreter for the concluding negotiation of the Technology
Transfer Agreement between AT&A and CEIEC.*

*Interpreter of the Corporatization Seminar sponsored by
China Industrial and Economic Association, Salomon
Brothers McKinsey & Company, Inc., Arthur Anderson-
Hua Qiang Certified Public Accountants and Cleary,
Gottlieb, Steen and Hamilton.*

The second resumé

Eric Fung (a pseudonym), who worked for another big computer company in their Hong Kong office, produced a resumé which covers eight pages and was actually successfully used to find himself another job.

Resumé

Fung Zse Tung (Eric) Page 1

PERSONAL DETAILS

Full Name	:	FUNG Zse Tung (Eric)
Postal Address	:	25D Block 2 Harbor View Garden Tai Wai, NT, Hong Kong
Current Employer	:	Microsoft China/HK Limited
Telephone Number	:	94226666 (Mobile) 28663359 (Business)
Facsimile Number	:	26880066 (Home)
Date of Birth	:	18th May, 1960
Education	:	Graduate Diploma in Commerce University of New South Wales completed in 1994
		Bachelor of Engineering (Electrical) University of New South Wales – completed in 1986
		Higher School Certificate Christian Community High School – completed in 1986 Aggregate – 444
Language Abilities	:	English, Chinese (Cantonese and Mandarin)

Resumé

Fung Zse Tung (Eric)   Page 2

CAREER SNAPSHOT

Dec 1995–Jan 1996   **Advisory IT Specialist**
                       IBM China/HK Corporation

Dec 1993–Dec 1995   **Senior Communication Officer**
                       First Bank Australia

Feb 1992–Dec 1993   **AS/400 System Programmer**
                       First Bank Australia

Feb 1990–Jan 1992   **Network Analyst**
                       NRMA Information Services Pty. Ltd.

Apr 1988–Jan 1990   **Software Engineer**
                       IBM Australia Ltd.

Apr 1984–Dec 1987   **Systems Engineer**
                       IBM China/Hong Kong Corporation Systems
                       Software Support Center (Data Communication
                       Team)

Jul 1983–Apr 1984   **Systems Engineer**
                       IBM China/Hong Kong Corporation
                       Customer Education Center

Dec 1982–Feb 1983   **Trainee Engineer**
                       Thos. Clark & Son Pty. Ltd., Sydney

AWARD ATTAINED

1989–1990   Achievement Award from IBM China/Hong
                       Kong Corporation

Resumé

Fung Zse Tung (Eric) Page 3

TECHNICAL SKILLS

Operating Systems	:	UNIX, MS-DOS, Windows 3.1, OS/400, MVS, TSO, CISCO IOS
LAN Operating Systems	:	Window for Work Group, Win95, Win NT
High Level Languages	:	RPG/III or RPG/400, C, Visual/Borland C++, PASCAL
PC Packages	:	Most PC Packages e.g. MSOFFICE, MSKERMIT, TELIX etc.
SNA Products and Protocol	:	VTAM, NCP, NETSPY, LANSPY, HCF, DDM, ICF, SNADS, 3270 and 5250 EMULATION, DSPT, TOKEN RING LAN, APPN, APPN/LU6.2, SDLC, TCP/IP, ATM, X25, Frame Relay
Database	:	AS/400 Native database and SQL/400
Telephone Information Management System (TIMS)	:	Orbiel, CADSII/III
PABX	:	GPT ISDX
Other Software	:	Most of AS/400 IBM systems software
Telecommunications	:	Timeplex Link/2 Multiplexer, CISCO Routers, Ungerman Base Hubs, Synoptics Hubs, AT&T Cabling System (Premises Distribution System), All kinds of modems (Sync or Async)
WAN Network Management Package and Protocol	:	NetView/6000, Sniffer, SNMP

Resumé

Fung Zse Tung (Eric)   Page 4

CAREER DETAILS

Advisory IT Specialist	**Main Responsibilities**
IBM China/HK Corporation Dec 1995–Jan 1996	* Presales support for all IBM Networking related product including LAN/WAN, SNA, TCPIP and ATM
	* Give consultancy to customer on IBM communications products and perform customer demonstration, executive presentation to show the strength of IBM products
	* Formulate solution to market IBM communications products
	* Carry out SNA revamp program to help IBM customer to convert the legacy SNA network to a multi-protocol network
	* Respond Tender for IBM communication product
Senior Communication Officer	**Main Responsibilities**
Commonwealth Bank Australia Dec 1993–Dec 1995	* Design, implementation and project management of the bank's voice, data and tcp/ip (WAN) networks and infrastructure.
	* Convert IP addresses in the Commonwealth Bank intranet to be Internet compliant
	* Development of network management and operational procedures for the support of implemented systems
	* Provision of high level support and consultancy for existing networks

Resumé

Fung Zse Tung (Eric) Page 5

* Be a member of the CBA overseas network upgrade project team, coordinating and implementing the migration of telecommunication services between Auckland and Sydney from the old lease line Multiplexer based network to a new frame relay based network

AS/400 System Programmer

Main Responsibilities

Commonwealth Bank
Australia
Feb 1992–Dec 1993

* Perform system tuning, tailoring and maintenance for AS/400s in the Commonwealth Bank of Australia

* Provide technical support and consultancy on all aspects of AS/400s including application development and software/hardware evaluation/recommendation

* Provide technical support on all aspects of connectivity between AS/400 networks and the SNA network in Commonwealth Bank including network configuration, problem determination/resolution and performance analysis/tuning

Resumé

Fung Zse Tung (Eric)   Page 6

Network Analyst   **Main Responsibilities**

NRMA Information   * Formulate strategies in monitoring the
Services Pty. Ltd.   performance of Lan
Feb 1990–Jan 1992
                      * Evaluate and acquire a suitable Lan
                        Management package for NRMA LAN

                      * Use Orbitel to generate monthly traffic
                        statistics for the NRMAA Corporate Voice
                        Network: analyze the NRMA monthly
                        voice traffic statistics to produce monthly
                        voice report and make recommendation on
                        areas of improvement

                      * Assist NRMA Network Support team to
                        identify and solve customers' telephone
                        problems

                      * Be a member of the NRMA New Voice
                        Network Replacement team, coordinating
                        and implementing the migration of old
                        NRMA TIMS (Orbitel) to the new NRMA
                        TIMS (CADS III)

                      * Formulate strategies in monitoring the
                        performance of the New Voice Network
                        (based on ISDN) using CADSIII from
                        Phoneware Communication systems

                      * Produce monthly Voice Network charge
                        back report for the whole NRMA
                        Corporation

Resumé

Fung Zse Tung (Eric)   Page 7

Software Engineer

IBM Australia Ltd.
Apr 1988–Jan 1990

Main Responsibilities

* Network Administrator and Technical
  Support on token ring LAN using OS/2
  and AS/400

* System management on AS/400 including
  system backup, disaster recovery and
  connectivity using APPN

* Programming using RPGIII and CL
  Language

* Perform functional and acceptance tests on
  IMAS/400 related package

System Engineer

IBM China/HK Corp.
(System Software
Support Center)
Apr 1984–Dec 1987

Main Responsibilities

* Conduct technical seminar and provide
  user training to customers and IBM
  systems engineers in IBM
  telecommunication products e.g. AS/400
  networking, SNA, APPN, Token Ring
  Lan etc.

* Support voice communication products,
  including DirectTalk/6000 and IDNX

* Customer technical support on the
  following IBM telecommunication
  products:
  – IBM midrange system connectivity
  (AS/400, S/36 and S/38) using
  APPN/APPC, LAN, ANS and X.25 to
  other IBM systems eg AIX, OS/2, DOS
  and VTAM/NCP

  – Most SNA products e.g. VTAM, NCP,
  HCF, SNADS, 3270 and 5250 emulation,
  DSPT etc.

  – Token Ring Lan on most IBM systems

* Pre- and post-sales support on major IBM
  telecommunication products

Resumé

Fung Zse Tung (Eric)   Page 8

REFEREES

Mr Y. K. Wong
Senior Technical Specialist
Computer Operation Specialist
Multimedia Terminals Limited
Berth Three, Tai Wai, N.T. Hong Kong
Ph: 852-27788371

Mr Siu Lam
Senior Network System Programmer
Australian National Bank
Ph: 9936-3040 (w)

Mr Harry Chun
Advisory IT Architect
Sinotech Corporation
Ph:9633-7878 (mobile)

HOBBIES AND OTHER INTERESTS

1991	Open water II Scuba Diver – NAUI
1987	Choir member of Chinese Presbyterian Church
1994–1995	Vice President, Peter Fellowship, Chinese Presbyterian Church, Surry Hills, Sydney
1995–1996	President, Peter Fellowship, Chinese Presbyterian Church, Surry Hills, Sydney

Worksheet on Resumés

1 How do the two resumés differ from each other in terms of the following dimensions?
   • length
   • style
   • format
   • content
   • focus

2 What kind of information is provided in each resumé: general vs. particular?

3 Are there any differences relating to personality, job, task, and type of business presented in the two resumés?

4 What organizational and sociocultural group differences can you observe from the two resumés?

5 How do your own criteria compare with these? With the standards provided in textbooks?

The Presentation: Activity 2

Outline of activity

- *Purpose of activity (1 min.).* Presentations for business and other purposes are increasingly using new media technologies. The audience is asked to focus their attention on one or more screens where images, words, graphs, charts, and videos are being presented. At the same time there remains a strong belief that a successful presenter should engage his or her audience with eye contact and keep the audience's attention through expressive gestures. These two forms of presentation are now in conflict because the media are in competition with the presenter for the audience's attention.

    In this activity, we will illustrate this conflict by giving a presentation using presentation software and discuss how this conflict can become an issue in professional communication in international settings.

- *PowerPoint Presentation (15 min.).* The PowerPoint presentation (copies of PowerPoint slides are provided below) discusses the presentation paradoxes in today's professional world, and different reactions to and evaluations of the use of visual aids and technologies in presentations by different cultural groups.

- *Group evaluation and discussion (20 min.).* In small groups of three to four people, evaluate and discuss the presentation from the point of view of analyzing the possible contradictions and competitions for attention. A separate worksheet for discussion is provided on p. 188.

- *Reports from small groups (9 min.).* Each small group will choose one spokesperson and report to the whole group on their topics of discussion.

Presentation Paradoxes

**Eye contact or
multimedia production?**

Current Presentation Style

- **Hong Kong**
  - presentation software
- **Finland**
  - presentation software
  - overhead projector
  - slides
- **Beijing**
  - overhead projector
  - slides

Speaker-Centered vs. Visual Aids-Focused

- **Traditional (American style)**
  - interactive
  - face-to-face
- **Use of visual aids and technologies**
  - constrains the movement of the speaker
  - competing eye focus

Traditional Study of Oral Presentation and Intercultural Communication

- **Speaker-centered**
- **Face-to-face**
- **Verbal**
  - language
  - tone
  - contextualization cues
- **Nonverbal**
  - body movement
  - gestures
  - eye gaze
  - space

Technological Erosion of Oral Presentation

- **Oral presentations**
  - more technologically oriented than before
  - being replaced by other means of communication
    - fax
    - mobile phone
    - e-mail
- **Technologies introduce new semiotic basis**
  - strong departure from the speaker-centered presentations

Technology-Based Presentations

- **Speakers' focus**
  - screen or slides
- **Presenter**
  - voice-over narrator and technician to run the show
- **Audience's eye focus**
  - screen, slides

Slides

- **Symbols**
- **Charts**
- **Texts, high information load**
- **No clear indication of relationship between points**

Intercultural Communication?

- Not an interaction between person and person, but between an audience and a media production

- Assumptions and expectations of oral presentation remain the same, influenced by the standardized practice

How the Problem Arises

- Interpretation of presentation style based on an assumption about the need for face-to-face interaction with the audience, with the presenter as the center

- The presenter is still being judged on these terms and often receives negative evaluation

- Not being evaluated in terms of influence of visual aids or technologies

- Nor in terms of cultural practice, but in terms of professional performance, competence, or knowledge

Conflict Between Belief and Practice

- **American standard, or world-wide standardized business practice**
  - face-to-face interaction with the speaker as the center of interaction
- **Center has shifted to the mediational means of presentation software, OHTs, and other technologies**

Worksheet on Presentations

1 Does the presenter achieve his or her purpose in the presentation?

2 Please comment on the style, format, and focus of the presentation.

3 Did the use of visual aids and technologies in the presentation help or hinder the delivery of information and interaction with the audience? Could the presenter have done it any other way?

4 What is your reaction to the use of visual aids and technologies in professional presentation? Why?

5 What can you tell from the presenter's eye gaze, gesture, dress, and speed in the presentation?

6 How important do you think the interaction between the presenter and the audience is? What kind of interaction do you think is necessary? Why?

7 What do you think is a good presentation? What criteria?

8 What would you do if you were to give a professional presentation?

The Telephone Call: Activity 3

Outline of activity

- *Purpose of activity (1 min.)*. There are many types of telephone calls – those you make to get business information from other business colleagues, those you make to friends, still others to clients and customers or to other businesses from which you are buying services and goods. Each of these types of calls is arranged differently. The purpose of this activity is to examine three actual telephone calls to see how easily we can distinguish what type of call it is on the basis of the language used and the topics which are discussed. Then, more importantly, the aim is to examine them to see if you can come to a common agreement about such intangibles as politeness, effectiveness, and professionalism, which we know are very different from company to company and from cultural group to cultural group.
- *Review of three telephone calls (3 min.)*. Please review the transcripts of three telephone calls provided on the following pages. These are actual calls made by business people in our research projects, which is why we have just one side of the call to examine.
- *Small group discussion (25 min.)*. In small groups of three to four people, discuss these calls to evaluate them for politeness, effectiveness, and professionalism. A separate worksheet for small group discussion is provided on p. 193.
- *Reports from small groups (11 min.)*. Select one spokesperson to report back to the whole group for discussion on these topics.

Three telephone calls

Following are three telephone calls made in his office by an IBM networking representative. These calls were recorded by this representative as part of his professional portfolio. The names of participants have been changed to protect their confidentiality. The three calls were made in Cantonese. They are transcribed and translated by the authors. The following conventions have been used in presenting the transcription:

01	The number before each line indicates the turn taken by the caller.
italic	Words in the conversation in *italics* were said in English by the participant in the original.
＿＿＿	A long dash represents indecipherable speech.

Telephone call 1

Eric is an IBM networking representative making an inquiry call to a retailer asking about the price of a product.

01	Hello, may I ask, is this CEC?
02	Yes, excuse me. I have something that I want to just *check check*. Do you have ____ ?
03	I need one with BMC on one side and UTP on the other.
04	$1100 each? Wow, that's so expensive, so . . .
05	Oh, oh, wow, that's very expensive. Do you have anything less expensive?
06	No? I really need BMC to transfer . . .
07	Yes, yes.
08	Have to use ____ ?
09	*OK*, then. That's alright. Well, thank you anyway. *OK?* Oh, *bye–bye*.

Telephone call 2

Eric is an IBM networking representative calling his client.

01	Hello, good morning. May I ask if Frank is there?
02	Oh, he is at a meeting. I'm with IBM networking. My name is Eric Fung. Do you know when he will finish the meeting?
03	Oh, OK. My number is 91308894.
04	Eric Fung.
05	Yes, ah. Is Tim there?
06	Has gone to the branch office. Then, then, maybe, can I bother you to ask him to return my call?
07	OK, thank you. Thanks! *Bye-bye.*

Telephone call 3

Eric is an IBM networking representative making a call to a customer for after-sale service.

01	Good morning. May I speak to Carrie?
02	Hello, Carrie.
03	This is Eric from IBM networking.
04	I'm calling to *confirm* with you. You connected your computer yesterday, and are now running *World One Image*, right?
05	Then this afternoon about three o'clock, we, Tom, William and I will go to your place, then . . .
06	Oh, *OK*, OK, OK. We hope we can fix it this afternoon. In *worse case*, if we can't finish it, we will bring all the stuff back and ask our *overseas expert* to fix it. Actually, *for your information*, I *sent* a *fax* yesterday to make inquiry. He asked me for *return code*, and things like that, because I didn't copy it down last time. But they said it is *unlikely* that the *system* has *problem*. It's most likely the *configuration* has some problem, so . . .
07	Yeah, we hope that is the problem.
08	Yes, yes. We also found something. We'll go to your place to try some *scenario* first.
09	OK, we'll see you in a while.
10	OK. Thank you. *Bye!*

Worksheet on Telephone Calls

1 What was the purpose of the call?

2 Did the caller achieve his purpose? Could he have been more effective? How?

3 Does the caller sound professional? What criteria do you use in making this judgment?

4 Does the caller sound polite? Why do you think so?

5 What do you notice about how the call is structured?

6 What do you miss by not hearing the party being called?

7 How does this call compare with the others?

8 Is this call similar to or different from your own business calls? In what way?

The Meeting: A Talk

Meetings are very different in business and in government, in banking and in advertising, in the US and in Japan. Because they are so different in all of these different settings, it is impossible to give a set of fixed principles by which meetings are organized or by which they *should be* organized.

This presentation uses research from the US, Japan, China, and Europe to show just some of the ways in which meetings can be different. We first developed this presentation for one of the world's leading manufacturers of telecommunications equipment, a European company working in China. They had requested consultation on meetings because they felt they had been understanding what was happening at one level, but at another level completely failing to achieve their goals. We were able to show them that the primary difference was that they were expecting to use the meeting as the main place in which they would discuss ideas and problems and arrive at decisions, whereas their Chinese counterparts were expecting these decisions to be arrived at *outside of* the meeting format.

While this presentation was first developed for an international commercial telecommunications company, we have also given it to diplomatic audiences in China, and to professional audiences in Hong Kong, Finland, and the US.

The presentation begins with a few brief comments about US–Japanese differences, based on research by Dr Haru Yamada and Dr Yoshiko Nakano, and then turns to focus on our own research as well as that of Professor Gu Yueguo of the Chinese Academy of Social Sciences.

Chinese Cross-Situation Comparison

- Service encounters
- Family/personal events
- Meetings

Service Encounters

- Shopping
- Taxis
- Meals in a restaurant
- Paying bills
- Routine banking

Inside/Outside

- Relationship (*guanxi*) is most important dimension
- "Facework" or form of politeness

Outside (*No Guanxi*)

- Direct
- No opening comments
- No closing comments
- Instrumental
- No small talk

Inside (With *Guanxi*)

- Opening comments (to establish or remind of relationship)
- Small talk before getting to business
- Much "face" politeness, "family" relationship talk

State-Owned Business

- Use "Outside" pattern

Private Sector (*Ge Ti Hu*)

- Use "Inside" pattern

Family/Personal Events

- Age and gender dominate
- Use "inside" pattern
- *Guanxi* is very important

Meetings

- **Formal and official**
- **Official rank dominates**
- **Much less important**
  - age
  - gender
  - connections (*guanxi*)

Meeting Opening Flow

- **Person 1 starts topics, passes to person 2 for discussion**
- **Person 2 opens the discussion**
- **Period of open discussion follows**
  - mostly without person 1

Meeting or Topic Closing

- **Person 1 shows his or her own view**
- **Person 2 says he or she supports**
- **Others show their support**
- **Person 2 summarizes and confirms group's agreement**
- **Person 1 finalizes the decision**

Summary

- **Service encounters**
  - inside/outside (*guanxi*) most important
- **Family/personal events**
  - older males dominate topics and opinions
- **Meetings**
  - official rank most important, person 1 controls

Japanese/American Business Meetings

Japanese	Americans
• Relationship over information	• Information over relationship

Function – Meetings

America	Japan
• Negotiate and develop positions	• Publicly state and legitimate positions

Structure – Business Meeting

Japan	America
• No formal agenda • No topical ownership	• Formal agenda • Topic designation

Three Kinds of Power

Leadership
Administrative
Expertise

Two Traditional Forms of Power in China

- "Leadership power" (*lingdao quan*)
- "Administrative power" (*xingzheng quan*)

"Leadership Power" (*Lingdao Quan*)

- Chairman Mao: "Leadership power comes out of the barrel of a gun"
- Based on national, political, unquestionable power

"Administrative Power" (*Xingzheng Quan*)

- Theoretically kept separate from "leadership power"
- The power to implement decisions, not to make decisions

Expertise (the New Power)

- A third power base
- Related to reform movement
- Not yet fully understood or used

Domains of Power

- **Leadership power**
  - pre-meeting planning
  - conduct of the meeting
- **Administrative power**
  - post-meeting implementation
- **Expertise power**
  - small role in meetings
  - strong role in implementation

Four Ways to Use Power

- **Walk the upper road (follow the leadership)**
- **Walk the lower road (cultivate subordinates)**
- **Be clever on all sides (somehow do both: *very rare*)**
- **Oily mouth (work only for your own good and advancement)**

Power and Meetings

- **Pre-meeting**
- **Meeting**
- **Post-meeting**

Pre-Meeting

- **Leadership power**
  - initiation
  - agenda fixing – may be used to expose or embarrass as well as for decision making
  - participation – must include all who hold leadership power
  - meeting site – must favor higher in leadership power
  - notification of meeting – must come from equal ranks
  - seating

Seating, Walking, and Entering

Power Positions	**Subordinate Positions**
• Up	• Down
• Front	• Back
• First	• Later
• Central	• Sideways

Post-Meeting (Before Departure)

- *Implementation* – administrative and expertise power
- Six main activities

Post-Meeting Activities

- Discussion of implementation of actions and decisions
- Further private and individualized discussions
- Minor followup meetings, small groups
- Off-agenda items or impossible items
- Interpersonal *guanxi* development
- Entertaining meals

Summary

- Each form of power has a preferred situation for use
- If your power is not official, most effective is
  - influence pre-planning through expertise
  - post-meeting implementation with expertise and administration

The Portfolio Exchange: Activity 4

Outline of activity

- *Purpose of activity (5 min.).* The professional Communication Display Portfolio (CDP) helps focus attention on points of contact between individuals as representatives of corporations, government agencies, or other organizations. The contents of the CDP will depend on the nature of the communication engaged in by the person who prepares it. For sales representatives, presentations using PowerPoint® or some other presentation software, computer graphics, and other technological support may be a salient part of day-to-day communicative activity. For customer service representatives, telephone activity may be most salient. The resumé may be important for consultants who have to sell their services. In the changing international environment, it is not easy to find out how one's communicative practices come across to the people one works with.

  The purpose of this exercise is to get participants to work together in small groups to role-play the following:
  - developing a portfolio and arranging an exchange
  - arranging and conducting focus groups
  - reporting the results of focus group evaluation
  - debriefing.
- *Procuring portfolios (15 min.).* If possible it is best to have portfolios prepared beforehand. You may want to look at the sample portions of portfolios provided in activities 1, 2, and 3 to get an idea what they might look like. There is no fixed format, and some items may be difficult to obtain because of considerations of confidentiality.

  If no portfolios are ready beforehand, each participant can work on his or her own to decide what are the important items to be included in a CDP, on the basis of the worksheet provided opposite.
- *Exchanging portfolios (small group activity) (10 min.).* Assuming you have some form of CDP, the next step is to arrange for these to be exchanged among the different organizations whose representatives are doing business with each other. Work in small groups to decide on how and when the CDPs are to be exchanged.
- *Arranging and conducting focus groups (small group, role-play) (20 min.).* Now that you have CDPs from the other group members, arrange and conduct focus groups to evaluate them. Supposing you are in a focus group discussion, evaluate, and comment on the CDPs of the other members.
- *Reports on evaluation by focus groups (20 min.).* Choose a spokesperson from each group to report on how they evaluated the CDPs of the other group members.

Worksheet on Communication Display Portfolio (CDP)

Check the appropriate boxes to indicate the importance of items to be included in your CDP.

Items	Importance		
	Absolutely necessary	*Necessary*	*Not necessary*
Resumé	☐	☐	☐
Name card	☐	☐	☐
Photo of yourself	☐	☐	☐
Brochure	☐	☐	☐
Business letter	☐	☐	☐
E-mail message	☐	☐	☐
Company information	☐	☐	☐
Videotape of your presentation	☐	☐	☐
Presentation slides	☐	☐	☐
Videotape of meetings	☐	☐	☐
Audiotape of telephone conversations	☐	☐	☐
Writing sample	☐	☐	☐
Sales report	☐	☐	☐
Other items:			
_____	☐	☐	☐
_____	☐	☐	☐
_____	☐	☐	☐
_____	☐	☐	☐

Topics for Further Discussion

We would very much appreciate your thoughts about this workshop, which you could give us by responding to one or more of the following:

1　If we planned a followup workshop for this one, what kinds of information and activities would you like to see included?

2　Do you have any personal examples that you think would help to extend or develop or clarify any of the concepts that we have discussed in this workshop?

3　If you would like followup information about further training or other materials which we have prepared, please give us your preferred contact information:

Name: _____

Address: _____

　　　　_____

　　　　_____

Telephone contact: _____

Fax contact: _____

E-mail contact: _____

Suggestions for Implementation: The Agenda

A typical full-day workshop could be completed in a 9-to-4 format as suggested here. This format includes morning and afternoon coffee breaks and a lunch break of one and a half hours.

9:00	Presenting Across Cultures: An Introduction
9:30	The Resumé: Activity 1
10:15	*Coffee break*
10:30	The Presentation: Activity 2
11:15	The Telephone Call: Activity 3
12:00	*Lunch break*
1:15	The Meeting: A Talk
2:00	*Coffee break*
2:15	The Portfolio Exchange: Activity 4
3:45	Workshop Evaluation: Suggestions for Improvement
4:00	Close Workshop

Appendix 3

Suggestions for Users

This appendix consists of five subsections with suggestions on how to:

*   conduct a language audit (this page)
*   collect corporate documentation (p. 216)
*   make a video of a presentation (p. 217)
*   view a video for focus group discussion (p. 219)
*   conduct a successful focus group discussion (p. 219).

How to Conduct a Language and Communication Audit

A language and communication audit may be individual or corporate. That is, one might use a language audit to undertake a self-assessment in relationship to a position in a company or to a specific task. For example, if you are applying to a position in a company which does business in Holland, you would want to know if that company would require you to know Dutch. In the same way, a company or organization might want to undertake a survey (or audit) of its own needs for communication skills both within the corporate structure and between the company and its clients or the public.

In a previous book by two of the authors, *Intercultural Communication: A Discourse Approach*, we suggest that a language and culture audit might begin with a survey of seven main components of typical modes of communication:

*   scene
*   key
*   participants
*   message form

- sequence
- co-occurrence patterns
- explicitness.

Scene   You would want to know what settings (times, places, or locations) would require what kinds of language or communication use. For example, in chapter 5 we noted that in Hong Kong meetings might be conducted in English but all of the surrounding side-conversations are likely to be in Cantonese. A personal audit would show that full participation in meetings would require not only formal, business-meeting English competence, but also casual Cantonese conversational ability.

The scene would also include an analysis of the purpose or function of an event or document as well as its topic and style or genre. One study showed that in Macau faxes were actually more successful when the English in which they were written was *less* formal and *less* standard than common business correspondence. And we all know that casual notes to office mates should be written in a different style from the report of a committee to the management.

Key   This means that you need to know what the expected tone is – serious or joking, casual or formal – for documents and events within your work performance. Many second-language users are quite capable in formal uses of the language but are unable to joke or to speak causally. The reverse may also be the case. Your personal audit should include an analysis of whether your ability with a language allows you to switch styles and tones as you need.

Participants   *How* you speak or write depends, of course, on *whom* you are speaking to or writing to. Many people in international settings discover the hard way that their language ability is quite good for conducting ordinary business affairs but is extremely limited when it comes to showing extra levels of respect. In many societies this has the effect of creating a "politeness ceiling" on the person's ability to work with higher levels of management or ownership.

Message form   Most individuals are uneven in their capacity to use all forms of communication. We may speak better than we write or vice versa. Many can use traditional forms of business or organizational speaking and writing but have little or no capacity to use new media communication technologies, such as presentation software, video, or hypertext and Internet software. A personal audit would be certain to include which message forms and technologies are one's fortes and which are better avoided.

Sequence Your knowledge of language and communication includes not only the ability to listen, speak, read, and write, but also many more complex structures of expectation. For example, in one major company studied by one of the authors it was found that three levels of management power carried with them three different closing sequences for a committee document. The lowest-level committee concluded their committee reports by outlining a set of options for taking action. The middle-level committee concluded reports by making a specific recommendation to choose one of the options. The highest level of management ended its reports by making a decision to take a particular action. A language and communication audit would include an assessment of whether or not the individual knows the distinctions among different types of documents or conversational sequences or structures.

A further example of this was discussed in chapter 5. We noted that the "proper" sequence of discussion in an American business meeting is to follow a pre-set agenda, with each person speaking primarily on his or her own topic of expertise. In a Japanese meeting it was seen that the "proper" sequence is to follow the development of interpersonal relationships. In a Brazilian meeting the "proper" sequence is to carry on multiple discussions simultaneously. A good audit would focus the individual's attention on his or her knowledge of such sequences for the situations in which he or she expects to work.

Co-occurrence patterns When we discussed the telephone call in chapter 2, we noted that early telephones were poor in transmission and reception and so shouting became typical of the "telephone voice." In chapter 3 we said that in some situations a resumé is expected to include personal information and in others it is not. In chapter 5 we told of a colleague who took up smoking so that he could join in causal (but very important!) business discussions outside of the office. Chinese and Hong Kong movies frequently portray people speaking and eating at the same time, yet this is almost never depicted in a movie made in America. All of these are patterns of "co-occurrence." Everybody eats and everybody talks. The question is under what circumstances or in what situations is it acceptable or even expected to do them together or separately. Ability in language and communication should also include a knowledge of such co-occurrence patterns, as they are very different from one international setting to another.

Explicitness All of these features of communicative situations, of course, may be either explicit or implicit. An important aspect of one's language and communication audit is to assess the extent to which one knows whether or not the "rules" for language use are made explicit in a particular situation, or if they are only implicit.

In the course of a typical work day a person will engage in many different communicative events. Some may be routine, while others pose problems. For a language audit, either personal or corporate, you would want a fairly detailed survey of the many types of communication using different media in different settings. However, if you are not an ethnographer but simply want to improve your own skills and become more flexible in communicating across cultural or professional boundaries, your task becomes much simpler. It is still worth training yourself to pay attention to as many of these elements as you can. As we have repeatedly emphasized, in today's global environment people travel so far and organizations change so rapidly that you need to look very specifically at the salient aspects of your own communicative environment. A change in one component may reverberate in other areas. Having to speak German instead of English, for example, might limit your participation or require an interpreter.

To give an example, which is based on our own consultation work, say your job is to train, monitor, and evaluate sales or customer service representatives for a telecommunications company in the United States. These customer service representatives are calling people who speak many different languages, and so the personnel you supervise speak several different languages as well. Each of them works in a cubicle four feet square, sitting at a desk with a computer, switchboard, pen, and notepad, wearing a headset for an 8-hour shift beginning at 8 in the morning or 4 in the afternoon. If you are bilingual in French and Italian you would do training sessions for the service representatives in each of these languages. Still, you would communicate with other trainers and your supervisor in English, as that is the language of the company.

Perhaps your first language is Italian. You studied English but just picked up French informally and never learned to write it. Your job requires you to translate documents into French and Italian. You may need help writing but would be able to read well enough to see whether your scribe had prepared a suitable translation. Your language audit (in the simplest form) might look something like this, with job requirements on the left and your skills on the right:

	Job requirements	**Personal skills**
English		
	Listening	Acceptable
	Speaking	Acceptable

	Reading	Acceptable
	Writing	Acceptable
French		
	Listening	Acceptable
	Speaking	Acceptable
	Reading	Acceptable
	Writing	Poor
Italian		
	Listening	Excellent
	Speaking	Excellent
	Reading	Excellent
	Writing	Good

An example of a CDP exchange

What follows is an example of how a professional trainer might do her CDP, which in this case includes a language and communication audit. This example is based on our own consultation work.

Background   A newly established telecommunications company in North America is working to reach customers of different ethnic groups. People speaking languages other than English are hired as sales representatives for the company. A training program is set up to train the newly hired and to monitor the performance of sales representatives. The training team consists of a training manager, a trainer who can speak the target language, and a contracted language and culture specialist. In the Chinese training program, the training manager is an American who speaks only English. The trainer is an American Chinese who speaks Cantonese Chinese (her native language), English, and Mandarin Chinese.

Problems   The trainer in the Chinese program encounters difficulties in the training program. She feels that it is not very effective. The language and culture specialist, who speaks Cantonese, Mandarin, and English and specializes in cross-cultural communication, is hired by the training manager on a contractual basis to monitor and evaluate the progress of the training program and the performance of the sales representatives.

- *Problem 1.* The training manual is in English. The trainer has to deliver the training in Chinese, but the Chinese trainees are from two very different regions of China, the north and the south. The northern Chinese speak Mandarin Chinese, and the southern Chinese speak Cantonese.

These two variants of Chinese are mutually unintelligible; they are as different as Italian and French. Because the training manager, who speaks only English, does not know this, the sales representatives speaking Mandarin and Cantonese Chinese are grouped together in the Chinese training program. In conducting the training, the trainer has to switch back and forth between the two languages of Mandarin and Cantonese. This would be equivalent to training speakers of Italian and French together: some but not all of the Italian speakers would understand French.

- *Problem 2.* The script for promotional calls used by the sales representative is in English. The sales representatives are required to follow the script step by step, but they can't read English. The script has to be translated into Chinese, but the trainer can only speak Chinese, not write it. She has to ask her trainees to write the script in Chinese for her to use.

- *Problem 3.* The trainees, after they have completed the training program, show slow progress in their job performance. There is some resistance from the Chinese sales representatives to following the instructions specified by the company.

The trainer is frustrated by these problems. She wonders how other telecommunications companies get their Chinese-speaking sales representatives to reach a high standard of performance. She recalls that she has received several calls from different sales representatives of a telecommunications company, and they all showed the same level of professionalism and followed the same sequences. She learns that an acquaintance has a friend who works as a trainer in another telecommunications company. She decides to conduct a CDP exchange with the acquaintance's friend. Here is what she decides to include in her CDP:

1   a videotape of herself conducting a training session
2   the English script of the questions and sequence that a sales representative should ask and follow
3   the Chinese translation of the script
4   the training manual (in English)
5   an audiotape of a conversation between a sales representative and a customer
6   an evaluation form outlining the criteria for evaluating the professional performance of sales representatives
7   a language and communication audit of how sales representatives do business over the phone (see audit 1 below)

8   a language and communication audit of how she trains sales representatives (see audit 2 below).

Audit 1: A language and communication audit of a sales talk in a
telecommunications company
• Scene:
    – Time: 4 p.m. to midnight
    – Place: A cubicle 4 feet square, sitting at a desk with a computer,
      switchboard, pen, and notepad, wearing a headset. This workstation
      would be one among dozens located in a large hall in a corporate
      building
    – Purpose: To answer incoming calls and to get callers to sign up for
      services
    – Topic: Telephone services offered by the company
    – Genre: Business telephone conversation (sales)
• Key:
    – Serious, professional, and friendly
• Participants:
    – Who they are: Sales representative and potential customers
    – Roles they play: To sell services (sales representative) and to pur-
      chase services (potential customers)
• Message form:
    – Speaking: Two persons speaking in Mandarin or Cantonese
    – Writing: Sales representative taking notes on notepad in Chinese
      characters
    – Other media: Key information into the computer, switchboard, tape
      recording of the conversation
    – Silence: When not receiving calls
• Sequence:
    – Set agenda: The sales representatives must follow the script and
      sequence of questions
    – Taking notes in Chinese after the call is terminated
• Co-occurrence patterns:
    – Typing into the computer in English (very limited English) while
      speaking and listening in Mandarin or Cantonese
    – Tape recording while call is being made
    – No eating, drinking, or smoking while taking the calls
• Explicitness:
    – Explicit instruction from the trainer and explicit explanation to the
      potential customers

- Implicit understanding that sales representative will follow the script (in Chinese) and at the same time be able to key in information in English
- Implicit understanding that the sales representative will be given a bad evaluation for taking notes, as she is expected to key in the requisite information when she is on the line. Taking notes is seen as an inefficient use of time

Discussion This detailed audit shows the expectations of the company, i.e. members' generalizations. This can be compared with the tape recording of a sales representative actually carrying out a sales talk, an objective record. It represents one person's experience and can be shown to neutral observers to obtain a comparative perspective. From the point of view of the sales representative, she can see how well she measures up to her trainer's expectations.

From the point of view of the trainer, this audit distills the requirements for hundreds of phone calls she is required to monitor and evaluate. There may be a mismatch between this description and what she is competent to monitor. For example, the audit shows that callers write notes in Chinese, which she cannot read. Though it is a major part of her job, it does not cover other important aspects of her work, which show up in the second audit below. First we do a simple language audit:

	Requirements	**Personal skills**
English		
	Listening	Acceptable
	Speaking	Acceptable
	Reading	Acceptable
	Writing	Acceptable
Cantonese		
	Listening	Acceptable
	Speaking	Acceptable
	Reading	Acceptable
	Writing	None
Mandarin		
	Listening	Acceptable
	Speaking	Acceptable
	Reading	Acceptable
	Writing	None
Translation		
	English into written Chinese	English into spoken Cantonese or Mandarin

The gaps are filled by asking trainees who have to write the scripts for the trainer. A fuller audit done by the first author, who was hired as the language/culture specialist, shows that simple literal translation of politeness formulas from English into Chinese does not work, as we detailed in chapter 2. Her audit shows up conflicts between the expectations of the training manager and the sales representatives that make it difficult for the trainer to work harmoniously with both.

Audit 2: Training program
- Scene:
  - Time: 4 p.m. to midnight
  - Place: Conference room (for presentation), training manager's office (for monitoring session and evaluation session), and a cubicle 4 feet square where a sales representative is sitting at a desk with a computer, switchboard, pen, and notepad, wearing a headset. This workstation would be one among dozens located in a large hall in a corporate building. Individual training takes place in this kind of workstation
  - Purpose: To train newly hired sales representatives to conduct professional business calls with customers over the phone
  - Topic: Professional behavior over the phone
  - Genres: Group training session, monitoring live phone calls, evaluation meeting, individual training
- Key:
  - Serious: Presentation
  - Professional: Phone conversation, monitoring session, individual training
  - Friendly: Phone conversation, individual training
  - Joking: Individual training, monitoring session
  - Resentful: Individual training, monitoring
- Participants:
  - Who they are: Training manager, trainer, language/culture specialist, sales representative, potential customers
  - Roles they play:
    ◦ Training manager and trainer: To teach the new sales representatives the company's standards and business procedure, and to evaluate their performance
    ◦ Language/culture specialist: To monitor and evaluate the professionalism and appropriateness of sales representatives' performance

- ○ Sales representative: To sell services
- ○ Potential customers: To inquire about and purchase services
- Message form:
  - – Speaking:
    - ○ Trainer's presentation of how to use the script and how to perform over the phone (in Mandarin or Cantonese, or both)
    - ○ Sales representative's phone conversation with potential customers (in Mandarin or Cantonese)
    - ○ Trainer's evaluation meeting with sales representatives (in Mandarin or Cantonese)
    - ○ Monitoring session with the language/culture specialist (in English, Mandarin, and Cantonese)
    - ○ Individual training and feedback (in Mandarin or Cantonese)
  - – Writing:
    - ○ English script and Chinese translation of questions and procedures for sales representatives
    - ○ English training manual
    - ○ Evaluation form (in English)
    - ○ Marking criteria (in English)
    - ○ Evaluation report (in English)
    - ○ Notes of the monitoring session (in English)
  - – Other media:
    - ○ Computer
    - ○ Switchboard
    - ○ Tape recording
- Sequence:
  - – Set agenda in training presentation and monitoring session. Certain steps to be followed in each session
  - – Open agenda in individual training and feedback: individualized interaction between the trainer and a sales representative
- Co-occurrence patterns:
  - – Taking notes while monitoring
  - – Tape recording sales calls
  - – No eating, drinking, or smoking while taking the calls
- Explicitness:
  - – Explicit instruction from the trainer in how to conduct a sales phone conversation
  - – Explicit explanation of how sales representatives are evaluated
  - – Implicit understanding that the trainer knows how representatives should speak

Discussion   The audit by the language/culture specialist gives the trainer some clues about what to include in her CDP. After putting together these documents, she has her CDP ready for exchange with her acquaintance's friend for feedback and evaluation. She may also want to design a list of questions to elicit comments and feedback based on her needs.

How to Collect Corporate Documentation

The language audit indicates what documents play a key role in the business of the corporation or agency and in the particular professional's work. For the trainer in the telecommunications company it included training manuals, scripts for sales calls, evaluation forms with marking criteria, and evaluation reports, all in English, a language that her trainees have limited control of.

The documents you collect will depend on the nature of your work, which may require only a few or many types. The list below shows the somewhat bewildering array of documents listed in an actual audit of a major corporation. (Some document types have been deleted because of confidentality.)

advertising reports
applicant assessment
   reports
assessment reports
benefits papers
biannual reports on
   approved banks
booklets on services
briefing notes
briefings for the steering
   committees
budgets
capital authorization
   proposals
comments on memos
committee minutes
committee papers
complaint letters
contracts
discussion papers

e-mail messages, many
   genres
end-of-year reports
evaluation reports
faxes
financial reports
functional
   specifications
housing benefits
   reviews
human resources office
   policy
improvement
   proposals
incident reports
instructions
interview reports
investigation reports
investigative reports
IT documents

justification papers
legal advice
letters
malpractice reports
management papers
manpower papers
marketing plans
memos
minutes for
   departmental
   meetings
monthly reports
operating
   procedures
operation manuals
operational reports
papers on
   acquisitions
pay-rate reviews
policy papers

policy proposals
procedures
progress reports
project management
 deliverables
project plans
project preparations
project statements
project status reports
proposals
quality assurance
 performance
 reviews
quality assurance
 reports
quality newsletters
quarterly reports
recommendations

recruitment
 advertisements
recruitment reports
recurrent audits
reference letters
rental assessments
replies to customers
reports
reports on disciplinary
 cases
reports to committees
reports to management
 requesting funds
requirements for a
 system
responses to audit
responses to requests
requests for proposals

scientific publications
short notes
standard formal letters
system development
 deliverables
system review reports
system specifications
technical
 specifications
tenders
training programs
training rundowns
university scholarship
 reviews
user management
 deliverables
user manuals
users' requirements

Select documents that are salient in your normal activity but do not contain sensitive information and are relatively distinctive yet easy to obtain.

How to Make a Video of a Presentation

The focus of the video is the presentation, not the video itself, and so there is no need to try to achieve a professional production-quality video. Good quality in the image, lighting, and coloring will keep the other participants in the CDP exchange from being distracted or from making unconscious negative evaluations of the presenter, but we believe that it is entirely sufficient for the CDP exchange to make a good-quality but decidedly "amateur" video of a presentation.

There are two major issues to consider first:

- *permission.* You must make sure that the video is made with the permission of all of the participants who can be viewed. This includes not just the presenter but other members of the audience who might take an important role. This would occur, for example, in a Q & A (question and answer) session.

- *confidentiality*. The confidentiality of participants can be assured in several ways. The most common way is to limit the viewing of the videos to just the participants in the CDP exchange and to provide them all with a briefing on the importance of maintaining mutual confidentiality for all members of the group. In some cases editing of the video can remove sections of sensitive matter. In most cases even an edited video will give plenty of material for CDP exchange discussions.

The following are several steps in the process along with a few points to consider which have come out of our own CDP exchange projects:

- Select a kind of presentation, internal or external. Generally speaking, "internal" presentations (i.e. within your own company) are easier to control but have a great risk of breaching confidentiality. The choice (if only one is included) should be based on the importance of these pre-sentations to your own self-assessment, not on how easy it is to get the presentation recorded.
- Videotape one's own presentation. It is preferable to ask a colleague or a friend to help you make the videotape of yourself. It is difficult to manage the video equipment at the same time you are presenting. What is most important, however, is that you and others see it as your choice to videotape yourself. There is power in recording and many people resent being recorded by others. Gaining permission to use the materials will also be less of a problem if you are recording your own presentation.
- Record about 10 to 20 minutes of presentation. You may need to cut out sensitive materials. That will leave 5 to 10 minutes of presentation. Be sure to include the beginning, the closing, and crucial transitional moves. These changes of the scene are very important in showing how we take up and lay down different styles and roles. In many ways the transitions are more important than the body of the presentation.
- In some cases it is impossible to make a videotape. In such a case use visual materials such as overhead transparencies (OHTs), slides, Power-Point® slides, handouts, brochures, or other visual materials. You can often use an audiotape to get comments on the quality of the voice and the speed or pace of the presentation.
- Overall, try to get a comparable quality in each site to avoid negative evaluation because of the video quality. It is more important to get com-parable quality than to get very high-quality recordings in some places and poor-quality recordings in others. There is a tendency for the tech-nology to become "invisible." We don't see a poor-quality videotape, we see a poor presentation. As long as the quality among the CDPs being

exchanged is about equal, this factor is evened out in the discussions and assessments.

• Edit or select the parts that you want people to react to or that show your best representation. The purpose is to try to show yourself at your best. The goal of the CDP is not psychological counseling but professional development. As in the resumé, one wants to show others the best that one has. The goal is to seek to improve this quality.

How to View a Video for Focus Group Discussion

The biggest problem with using video is that we already have so much experience watching movies and television that we look at *any* video in about the same way. There is a tendency in focus groups for participants to just sit back when the video comes on and to look at it as if it were a television program – a particularly bad or dull one. Generally speaking, it is very difficult to get participants to look at a video analytically. The suggestions we offer here, then, are to try to counteract this tendency to just watch.

• Use short pieces which are stopped frequently. You need to break up the rhythm of just watching. Overall in a focus group you would not want to use more than a total of 5 to 10 minutes of continuous video.
• Prepare the group for viewing. You should be sure everyone in the group knows what you are about to see and why you are looking at it.
• Prepare discussion questions or points for each segment of the video. This will assist you in preparing the group for viewing.
• View the whole video once through (after preparation) so that the group will have an idea of the continuity.
• View segment by segment, using your discussion questions or points, and allow ample time for discussion after each segment.

In a focus group of 1 hour to 90 minutes, it is very difficult to get the participants to concentrate on more than 5 to 10 minutes of video, and even then they cannot usually focus their attention for more than about 30 minutes. Be sure to keep the focus group focused on the points you want to think about and discuss.

How to Conduct a Successful Focus Group Discussion

Many people in business and other organizations will have experience with focus groups, as they are used in marketing, public opinion gathering, or still other uses. As we use the idea of a focus group for making

CDP exchanges, it is important to remember that these are really small, voluntary, and mutually reflective discussion groups. The purpose is not to develop a product or an opinion *to be used outside of the group*. The purpose is self-study or self-reflection for members of the group itself. This difference in function means that the attention needs to be continually returned to this main purpose.

To keep the attention focused on the reflective purposes of the CDP exchange, we suggest the following general principles:

- *Participants*. The ideal number of participants is six to eight. They should be of similar background and mixed in gender. This is not a scientific study; the purpose is to get feedback from one's peers and colleagues. This should be the guiding principle. Participants should either be one's colleagues and counterparts or people very much like them.
- *Time frame*. Two hours is the maximum for a comfortable focus group. Set a clear time that is convenient for the participants. Naturally, conversation sometimes "spills over" into the period after the focus group, but people should be allowed to leave at a fixed time.
- *Site*. The site should be convenient for all of the participants. If possible, it is good to have a site that is "neutral" to all of them. Meeting in the conference room of one of the participants may be necessary, but it gives this person a "home court" advantage. Research has shown that people who are in their "own territory" tend to speak faster, take more of the conversational space, and generally dominate the discussion.
- *Seating arrangement*. It is most comfortable for discussions for people to sit around a table or in a circle so that the participants can face one another, not the video recorder. While you will want to record the focus group, the most important thing is not the quality of the recording but the quality of the discussion. Always keep the camera and recording equipment in a secondary position.
- *Materials preparation*. To keep the focus group's attention focused on the CDP exchange and the discussion, be sure to arrange the CDP materials in advance and to have a plan for what to present first and what to follow with. You want the discussion to be as free and open as possible. This can be assured by making it clear at the outset what you all want to accomplish rather than wasting focus group time by sorting through materials.
- *Questions*. The questions for discussion should be well organized to follow the materials presented to the focus group. If possible they should

be sorted into questions about each of the aspects of the CDP, such as documents, resumés, and videos.

- *Language.* A mini-language audit should be made before the focus group. As far as possible, the participants should be able to use their native languages for the discussion. In any international exchange a language audit will show much complexity. We had cases of Mandarin Chinese participants discussing in a mixture of Mandarin and English. The videos and audios were in Cantonese and English in one case and in Finnish and English in another.
- *Moderator.* The moderator should, of course, be able to speak the language(s) of the participants but also be able to translate or interpret the materials on the exchange CDPs. This will rarely be entirely possible. The moderator should at least be comfortable in the participants' language and as far as possible be demographically like the participants – similar age, position, or status in the corporate or organizational world. The moderator or facilitator should lead by asking the discussion questions but not talk too much. The goal is to facilitate, not to arrive at any preconceived conclusions.
- *Note-taking.* One observer (preferably not the moderator) should take notes during the focus group discussion. The participants themselves should be entirely free to focus their attention on their own reflections about the CDP exchange. Like the moderator or facilitator, the observer should be demographically much like the participants.
- *Recording.* Audiotaping and videotaping together are ideal. Videotaping of a focus group is very useful for viewing reactions and the interactions of the participants, but it is often difficult to get a sound recording that is adequate for transcription. An audiotape which is made at the same time is useful for this. While it is not essential, many participants will find a transcript of the discussion very enlightening. Also, for exchanges with the other sites a transcript may be needed to guide making a translation. At the other sites, participants can read the translated transcript along with viewing the video for nonverbal aspects of the discussion.
- *Refreshment.* In order to lighten up the atmosphere it is useful to provide refreshments, depending on the time of day and other aspects of the situation. Providing refreshments can also alter the definition of the situation so that it is not perceived as "another meeting" but rather as an informal conversation.
- *Gratuity.* The focus group that is convened for CDP exchange is not a commercial focus group for marketing purposes, and so it is probably not appropriate to directly pay participants. Nevertheless, some small

souvenir or other gift which shows gratitude for participation can help with continuing involvement in the project over time. We found it very useful to invite the participants in our focus groups to have dinner together with us after the focus group discussion. Not only was this a token of our appreciation, but we found that the discussion over dinner were in many ways more fruitful than those in the focus group itself.

Further Reading

We have made reference throughout the book to sources across a wide range of fields from business communication and intercultural communication to linguistics and psychology. In this further reading section we give the details of the references from this research literature which we have used in the text of the book. The reference section that follows is a citation list of these sources. That list includes other sources in addition to the ones cited here or in the text for the reader who is interested in following up any particular topic.

The Research Base

Chapter 1   Analyzing Communication in the International Workplace

The research project *Professional Communication Across Cultures* was supported by a City University of Hong Kong strategic grant. Reports based on this project have been presented as Pan et al. (1998), R. Scollon et al. (1998), and Pan (2000c), and published as R. Scollon et al. (1999).

An interesting study of Brazilian communication patterns in business negotiations which includes a description of the conduct of meetings is Garcez (1993).

As the work of Gumperz and others (Gumperz 1977, 1982a, 1982b; Tannen 1984, 1989; R. Scollon and Scollon 1981, 1995) has demonstrated, perceptions are responses to contextualization cues that are habitual and largely out of conscious awareness.

The methodology of our project was based on the classical interactional sociolinguistic method of recording authentic data, analyzing that data, and then returning that material including the analysis to original participants for cross-checking (Gumperz et al. 1979; Tannen 1984). To this research method we added a further triangulation by having the data and analyses of each site cross-culturally compared in two other sites and then having the responses in those sites returned to the original locations. Thus by adding the methodology of Tobin et al. (1989) to standard interactional sociolinguistic methodology, we believe we were able to provide a second level of perceptions which greatly enriched both the theoretical and practical training perspectives of this project.

Differences in language are often handled through simple translation, but research in interactional sociolinguistics (Gumperz 1977, 1982a, 1982b; Tannen 1984, 1989; R. Scollon and Scollon 1981, 1995) has indicated that more often problems arise from other aspects of communication. Among the features of communication that research has demonstrated set the stage for communicative cross-purposes are:

- body language, dress, tone of voice (Hall 1959, 1969; Hall and Hall 1987)
- use of space, layout, and design of both physical spaces and publications (Hall 1959, 1969; Hall and Hall 1987)
- the use of colors to reflect subtle impressions (Hall 1959, 1969; Hall and Hall 1987)
- timing at the face-to-face level as much as the degree of punctuality in meeting deadlines (R. Scollon 1985; Hayashi 1988, 1990; Auer 1992, 1995)
- the use of meetings for negotiation as opposed to ratification of already agreed positions (Pan 1995, 1996a, 1996b, 2000a; Gu in press; Yamada 1992)
- leading with main topics as opposed to leading with social relationships (Young 1982, 1994; R. Scollon and Scollon 1991, 1995)
- talking vs. silence (Tannen and Saville-Troike 1985; R. Scollon 1985; Lehtonen and Sajavaara 1985; Lehtonen 1986; Salo-Lee et al. 1996; Pörhölä et al. 1997)
- formal agendas vs. open discussion (Maynard 1989; Yamada 1992).

The Finnish references are from R. Scollon et al. (1999), recommended by our Finnish colleagues.

Research on "human knowledge" and "institutional knowledge" and the concepts of gatekeeping were developed by Erickson and Shultz (Erickson 1976; Erickson and Shultz 1982).

Lanham (1974, 1983) has written about what he calls the C-B-S style, C for "clarity," B for "brevity," and S for "sincerity." The C-B-S style has been shown by two of the authors to have developed as part of what we have called *the utilitarian discourse system* (S. Scollon 1994b; R. Scollon and Scollon 1995, 2001), which is in conflict with the social practices of many groups including Native Americans (R. Scollon and Scollon 1981) and Asians. It is inculcated in schoolchildren in part by means of the written essay.

The four perspectives from which we approach the study of communication are adapted from Ruesch and Bateson (1968 [1951]), S. Scollon (1998), R. Scollon (1998) and R. Scollon and Scollon (2001).

The rules of thumb for Carnegie-style communication are abstracted from Arredondo (1991), Bergin (1995), Curtis et al. (1992), Holcombe and Stein (1996), Lambert (1989), Levy (1995), Smith (1984), Staley and Staley (1992), and Thrash et al. (1984).

Chapter 2   The Telephone Call: When Technology Intervenes

The citation about the ear and the excerpt from the contest-winning essay are from Fischer's social history of the telephone (1992:70).

Gillen's (2000) research on children shows that before there is any substance to their conversation or before they have any conception of there being someone at the other end of the phone line they have learned the attitudes and social practices of using the instrument.

Martin (1991) has shown that certain formulas such as "hello," "please," and "thank you" were prescribed by telephone companies in their instructions to users, who were also advised not to make callers wait. In keeping with her focus on gender and culture in the formation of social practices of telephone usage, she points out that women were the main target of exhortations on telephone etiquette and were considered to make excessive use of the instrument for social calls during business hours.

In chapter 1 we introduced the C-B-S style, which is the basis of conventional wisdom about "getting down to business," speaking clearly and succinctly without fooling around or wasting time. Here we would include under the heading of "sincerity" the idea that the telephone user or the person in business more generally should show courtesy through formal openings and closings. This was particularly important in the early days of the telephone because the low level of technology required one to shout, which would sound very rude. The courtesy formulas were derived, in part, to offset the rudeness of this rough talk.

We also mentioned the utilitarian discourse system, which developed during the period of industrialization along with the use of the telephone. This includes the idea that one should at least appear to be speaking only about facts and not trying to persuade through rhetoric, the idea that one should put the topic of what one has to say right at the beginning of either conversations or written documents (*deductive presentation*), and the idea that one speaks and makes decisions as an equal individual. While these seem like commonsense ideas within at least a "western" business environment, we have shown that this "common sense" has a historical beginning in the Enlightenment period and was given strength, as we have argued here, through the new communication technologies of the telegraph first (clarity and brevity were necessary) and then the telephone.

The references to the book by Bateman and Sigband (1989) are used here as an example of standard approaches to business telephone calls. We do not mean to say that they give bad advice or that such books in general should be avoided. Our point is simply that in specifically international settings, where communication styles and patterns can be very different and based in different social and cultural histories, this type of advice can be quite misleading. Jones and Alexander's (1989a, 1989b, 1989c) *International Business English*, like the Bateman and Sigband book, upholds some of these same ideals of international business communication, which are, in real situations, impossible to carry out.

The QWERTY phenomenon has been described by Wertsch (1998). The history of the technology of sound performance is detailed in van Leeuwen (1999). Singers now train their voices in radically different ways from the old music hall perform-ers. Hall (1959, 1969) studied interpersonal distances and showed that if we use the voice of intimate distance in speaking across a formal distance, we convey a much more complex message than just using a loud voice.

The study of client and colleague telephone calls is reported in R. Scollon (1995a, 1995b, 1998, 1999). Schegloff (1972, 1986) was the first to develop a sociological study of the language used in telephone calls. Now there is a very large literature which looks in close detail at how telephone calls are actually originated, developed, and closed. See Houtkoop-Steenstra (in press) for recent studies in the framework of conversational analysis.

The study of "face" relationships has been expanded by Pan's (1995, 2000a, 2000b) research. She found, for example, that the relationships among people in China were very different in three different situations – service encounters (such as between customers and sales clerks in a fashion boutique), official meetings, and family dinners. Different sources of power were recognized in these settings and people's politeness behavior varied accordingly. This work also covers the use of politeness formulas in common day-to-day speech.

The observations on Dutch telephone calls are from Houtkoop-Steenstra (1991, in press) and those on Swedish from Lindström (1994). The comments about "low-trust" and "high-trust" environments are from Heritage (1999). Research on tele-phone answering in intimate relationships is reported in Schegloff (1986) and R. Scollon (1998).

Chapter 3   The Resumé: A Corporate "Trojan Horse"

The story on the "Killer Resume" virus is from the *Washington Post* website (Ho 2000).

In preparing this chapter, we made reference to several books on resumé writing including Beatty (1995), Eyler (1999), Noble (2000), Provenzano (2000), Pontow (1999), Tepper (1998), and Troutman (1999).

Gumperz (1977, 1982a) first developed the idea of conversational inference, namely that as we speak we make ongoing inferences about not only *what* people are saying but also *why* they are saying it. These inferences, according to Gumperz, are mostly based on previous assumptions we make about ourselves and the people with whom we are speaking. Mostly, however, we do not pay attention to the actual inferential process but jump immediately to conclusions about the character and attitudes of those with whom we are speaking (Gumperz et al. 1979; R. Scollon and Scollon 1981; Tannen 1984, 1989).

Our own research on institutional and personal knowledge was first reported in R. Scollon (1981). We have continued to examine these problems in R. Scollon and Scollon (1995, 2001). Erickson and Shultz (1982) is our source on the role of co-membership in gatekeeping and the power of personal knowledge to override pro-fessional/institutional information. Lave and Wenger (1991; Wenger 1998) touch on issues very similar to these in their analysis of the idea of a community of practice.

Chapter 4   *The Presentation: From Dale Carnegie to Ananova the Avatar*

The story about "Ananova" is by Farhi (2000). The material about Dale Carnegie comes from his original book as well as the "Carnegie Coach" installed in Microsoft PowerPoint® in Microsoft Office 2000. *Dilbert* on August 16, 2000, depicts a character gagging because of "'POWERPOINT' poisoning." The story about Tung Chee-hwa, chief executive of the Hong Kong Special Administrative Region, appeared in the *South China Morning Post*, June 4, 1997, in a story by C. K. Lau under the title "Hollowness in Tung's words."

Finnish communication style is discussed by Sajavaara and Lehtonen (1985, 1997). Reticence and silence are the salient characteristics of Finnish communication, at least in traditional settings among older Finns. Our Chinese source on public speaking is Li and Zou (1997). Some aspects of the relationships among multiple parties to a communicative task are discussed in R. Scollon (1985) on the basis of research on news media organizations.

Suggestions for the use of visual aids and presentation style are discussed by Kupsh and Graves (1993), Robbins (1997), Kalish (1997), Asher and Chambers (1997), and Zelazny (2000).

Research on the "faces of world English" in television news presenters is found in S. Scollon (1995, 1999).

Chapter 5   *The Meeting: Action or Ratification?*

Burgess (1984) contains various tidbits about the history of coffee in the development of our contemporary world. Toussaint-Samat (1992) is a much more thorough-going history of the role of coffee in the rise of commercial organizations in England and in Europe beginning in the seventeenth century. Yamada's (1992) comparative study of Japanese and American bank meetings is the basis for our analysis in this chapter. Other related research has been done by Maynard (1989). The study of negotiation in a Japanese–American interaction was done by Nakano (1995), who also cites Tsuda (1984) on Japanese and American sales talk. The first author of this book, Pan (1995, 1996a, 1996b, 2000a, 2000b), provides one source for the studies of Chinese business meetings as well as the comparative study of meetings, family dinners, and service encounters. This research has been supplemented by Gu's (in press) research. Garcez (1993) is our source on Brazilian meetings.

Chapter 6   *The Reflective View: Seeing Ourselves as Others See Us*

Research on which the language audit is based includes S. Scollon (1996), where she notes the practice of using Cantonese discussions to produce English documents in Hong Kong businesses. Cremer (1991) also discusses the use of "bad" English as the most effective style in common trade negotiations such as faxes.

References

Arredondo, Lani. 1991. *How to Present Like a Pro: Getting People to See Things Your Way*. New York: McGraw-Hill.

Asher, Spring and Wicke Chambers. 1997. *Wooing and Winning Business*. New York: John Wiley & Sons.

Auer, Peter. 1992. Introduction: John Gumperz' approach to contextualization. In P. Auer and A. di Luzio (eds), *The Contextualization of Language*. Amsterdam: Benjamins, pp. 1–37.

Auer, Peter. 1995. Ethnographic methods in the analysis of oral communication. In Uta M. Quasthoff (ed.), *Aspects of Oral Communication*. Berlin: Walter de Gruyter, pp. 419–40.

Augé, Marc. 1995. Non-places: Introduction to an anthropology of super-modernity. London: Verso.

Bateman, David N. and Norman B. Sigband. 1989. *Communicating in Business*. Glenview, IL: Scott, Foresman.

Beatty, Richard H. 1995. *The Resume Kit*. New York: John Wiley & Sons.

Beatty, Richard H. 2000. *The Resume Kit*. Fourth edition. New York: John Wiley & Sons.

Bergin, Francis. 1995. *How to Make a Perfect Presentation*. Upper Saddle River, NJ: Prentice-Hall.

Burgess, Jillian. 1984. *The Coffee Book*. London: Kato Press.

Carnegie, Dale. 1964. *How to Win Friends and Influence People*. New York: Simon and Schuster. (First published 1937.)

Cremer, Rolf D. 1991. Stock in trade: The role of English in international trade proceedings. *Journal of Asian Pacific Communication* 2(1):103–16.

Curtis, Dan B., James J. Floyd, and Jerry L. Winsor. 1992. *Business and Professional Communication*. New York: HarperCollins.

Erickson, Frederick. 1976. Gatekeeping encounters: A social selection process. In Peggy Reeves Sanday (ed.), *Anthropology and the Public Interest: Fieldwork and Theory*. New York: Academic Press, pp. 111–45.

Erickson, Frederick and Jeffrey Shultz. 1982. *The Counselor as Gatekeeper: Social Interaction in Interviews*. New York: Academic Press.

Eyler, David R. 1999. *Resumes that Mean Business*. New York: Random House.

Farhi, Paul. 2000. The newscaster who's pixel-perfect. *Washington Post*, May 30, A33956-2000 May30.html.

Fischer, Claude S. 1992. *America Calling: A Social History of the Telephone to 1940*. Berkeley: University of California Press.

Garcez, Pedro de Moraes. 1993. Point-making styles in cross-cultural business negotiation: A microethnographic study. *English for Specific Purposes* 22: 103–20.

Gillen, Julia. 2000. The acquisition of speech genres: A study of young children talking on the telephone in pretence and dialogic modes. Paper presented at Sociolinguistics Symposium 2000, University of the West of England, April 27–9.

Gu, Yueguo. In press. Guan (Chinese officialdom) at work in discourse. In Colin Barron, Nigel Bruce, and David Nunan (eds), *Discourse Practices and Social Change*. London: Addison Wesley Longman.

Gumperz, John. 1977. Sociocultural knowledge in conversational inference. In M. Saville-Troike (ed.), *28th Annual Round Table Monograph Series on Language and Linguistics*. Washington, DC: Georgetown University Press, pp. 191–212.

Gumperz, John. 1982a. *Discourse Strategies*. New York: Cambridge University Press.

Gumperz, John. 1982b. *Language and Social Identity*. New York: Cambridge University Press.

Gumperz, John, Tom C. Jupp, and Celia Roberts. 1979. *Crosstalk: A Study of Cross-Cultural Communication*. Southall: National Center for Industrial Language Training.

Hall, Edward T. 1959. *The Silent Language*. Garden City, NY: Doubleday.

Hall, Edward T. 1969. *The Hidden Dimension*. Garden City, NY: Doubleday.

Hall, Edward T. and Mildred Reed Hall. 1987. *Hidden Differences: Doing Business with the Japanese*. Garden City, NY: Doubleday.

Harris, P. R. and R. T. Morgan. 1987. Japan, doing business with Asians – Japan/China/Pacific Basin. In P. R. Harris and R. T. Morgan (eds), *Managing Cultural Differences*. Houston: Gulf, pp. 387–98.

Hayashi, Reiko. 1988. Simultaneous talk: from the perspective of floor management of English and Japanese speakers. *World Englishes* 7(3):269–88.

Hayashi, Reiko. 1990. Rhythmicity sequence and synchrony of English and Japanese face to face conversation. *Language Sciences* 12(2/3):155–95.

Heritage, John. 1999. Conversation analysis at century's end. *Research on Language and Social Interaction* 32(1&2):69–76.

Ho, David. 2000. FBI: New computer virus spreading. *Washington Post*, May 26, A16544-2000 May26.

Holcombe, Marya W. and Judith K. Stein. 1996. *Presentations for Decision Makers*. New York: Van Nostrand Reinhold.

Houtkoop-Steenstra, Hanneke. 1991. Opening sequences in Dutch telephone conversations. In Deirdre Boden and Don H. Zimmerman (eds), *Talk and Social Structure: Studies in Ethnomethodology and Conversation Analysis*. Cambridge: Polity, pp. 232–51.

Houtkoop-Steenstra, Hanneke. In press. Sex differences in Dutch telephone openings. In P. Glenn, C. LeBaron, and J. Mandelbaum (eds), *Excavating the Taken-for-Granted: Studies in Language and Social Interaction*. Mahwah, NJ: Lawrence Erlbaum.

Jin Ren. 1940. Dianhuaji pang [Over the telephone]. In *Tanhua de yishu* [*The Art of Conversation*]. Hong Kong: Da di tushu gongsi yinhang, pp. 112–15.

Jones, Leo and Richard Alexander. 1989a. *International Business English: Teacher's Book*. Cambridge: Cambridge University Press.

Jones, Leo and Richard Alexander. 1989b. *International Business English: Student's Book*. Cambridge: Cambridge University Press.

Jones, Leo and Richard Alexander. 1989c. *International Business English: Workbook*. Cambridge: Cambridge University Press.

Kalish, Karen. 1997. *How to give a Terrific Presentation*. New York: AMACOM.

Kupsh, Joyce and Pat R. Graves. 1993. *How to Create High Impact Business Presentations*. Lincolnwood, IL: NTC Business Books.

Lambert, Clark. 1989. *The Business Presentations Workbook*. Upper Saddle River, NJ: Prentice-Hall.

Lanham, Richard A. 1974. *Style: An Anti-Textbook*. New Haven, CT, and London: Yale University Press.

Lanham, Richard A. 1983. *Literacy and the Survival of Humanism*. New Haven, CT: Yale University Press.

Lave, Jean and Etienne Wenger. 1991. *Situated Learning: Legitimate Peripheral Participation*. Cambridge: Cambridge University Press.

Lehtonen, Jaakko. 1986. Puhekasvatus ja sosiaaliset taidot [Communication education and social skills]. In L. Kirstinä (ed.), *Puhumalla paras. Äidinkielen opettajan litton vuosikirja XXXIII*. Helsinki: ÄOL, pp. 20–40.

Lehtonen, Jaakko and Kari Sajavaara. 1985. The silent Finn. In Deborah Tannen and Muriel Saville-Troike (eds), *Perspectives on Silence*. Norwood, NJ: Ablex, pp. 193–201.

Levy, Mike. 1995. *The Professional Presentation Pack*. Ely: Wyvern Crest.

Li, Yuanshou and Zou Kunshan. 1997. *Yan Jiang Xue* [*Public Speaking*]. Wuhan: Huazhong Ligong Daxue Chubanshe.

Lindström, A. 1994. Identification and recognition in Swedish telephone conversation openings. *Language in Society* 23:231–52.

Martin, Michele. 1991. *"Hello, Central?" Gender, Technology, and Culture in the Formation of Telephone Systems*. Montreal and Kingston, London, Buffalo: McGill Queen's University Press.

Maynard, Senko Kumiya. 1989. *Japanese Conversation: Self-Contextualization through Structure and Interactional Management*. Norwood, NJ: Ablex.

Nakano, Yoshiko. 1995. *Frame Analysis of a Japanese–American Contract Negotiation*. Ann Arbor, MI: UMI Dissertation Services.

Noble, David F. 2000. *Professional Resumes for Accounting, Tax, Finance and Law.* Indianapolis: JIST Works.

Pan, Yuling. 1995. Power behind linguistic behavior: Analysis of politeness phenomena in Chinese official settings. *Journal of Language and Social Psychology* 14(4):462–81.

Pan, Yuling. 1996a. Discourse patterns and politeness in the Chinese workplace. Paper presented at Sociolinguistics Symposium 11, University of Wales, Cardiff, September 5–7.

Pan, Yuling. 1996b. Speaking for the other: Power recognition in Chinese official settings. Paper presented at Georgetown Linguistics Society, Georgetown University, Washington, DC, October 11–13.

Pan, Yuling. 2000a. *Politeness in Chinese Face-to-Face Interaction.* Stamford, CT: Ablex.

Pan, Yuling. 2000b. Facework in Chinese service encounters. *Journal of Asian Pacific Communication* 10(1):25–61.

Pan, Yuling. 2000c. Powerpoint: The visual semiotics of business presentations. Paper presented in the colloquium "Visual Semiotics in Business and Public Discourse: Literate Technologies of Representation," Georgetown University Roundtable, Washington, DC, May 4–6.

Pan, Yuling, Ron Scollon, and Suzanne Scollon. 1998. The corporate construction of the global person. Paper presented in the session "Globalism in Hong Kong Public Discourse: Post-Modern Ideology and Local Resistance" at the Annual Meetings of the American Anthropological Association, Philadelphia, December 2–6.

Pontow, Regina. 1999. *Proven Resumes.* Berkeley: Ten Speed Press.

Pörhölä, M., A. Sallinen, and P. Isotalus. 1997. Culture as communication context: Finnish cultural characteristics in political television programs. In J. L. Owen (ed.), *Context and Communication Behaviour.* Reno, NV: Context Press.

Provenzano, Steven A. 2000. *Top Secret Executive Resumes.* Franklin Lakes, NJ: Career Press.

Robbins, Jo. 1997. *High-Impact Presentations: A Multimedia Approach.* New York: John Wiley & Sons.

Ruesch, Jurgen and Gregory Bateson. 1968 [1951]. *Communication: The Social Matrix of Psychiatry.* New York: W. W. Norton.

Sajavaara, Kari and Jaako Lehtonen. 1997. The silent Finn revisited. In Adam Jaworski (ed.), *Silence: Interdisciplinary Perspective.* New York: Mouton de Guyter, pp. 263–83.

Salo-Lee, L., R. Malmberg, and R. Halinoja. 1996. *Me ja Muut: Kulttuurienvälinen Viestintä [We and Others: Intercultural Communication].* Helsinki: YLE Educational Programmes.

Schegloff, Emanuel. 1972. Sequencing in conversational openings. In John Gumperz and Dell Hymes (eds), *Directions in Sociolinguistics.* New York: Holt, Rinehart, and Winston, pp. 346–80.

Schegloff, Emanuel. 1986. The routine as achievement. *Human Studies* 9:111–51.

Scollon, Ron. 1981. Human knowledge and the institution's knowledge. Final report to the National Institute of Education on grant No. G-80-0185 "Communication Patterns and Retention in a Public University."

Scollon, Ron. 1985. The machine stops. In Deborah Tannen and Muriel Saville-Troike (eds), *Perspectives on Silence*. Norwood, NJ: Ablex, pp. 21–30.

Scollon, Ron. 1995a. From Pidgin English to Professional Communication: English Teaching and the Utilitarian Discourse System. In Paul Bruthiaux, Tim Boswood, and Bertha Du-Babcock (eds), *Explorations in English for Professional Communication*. Hong Kong: City University of Hong Kong, pp. 21–39.

Scollon, Ron. 1995b. International English and Chinese women: Clients or colleagues in the international utilitarian discourse system? *Asian Journal of Women's Studies* 1(1):87–99.

Scollon, Ron. 1998. *Mediated Discourse as Social Interaction: A Study of News Discourse*. New York: Longman.

Scollon, Ron. 1999. Mediated discourse and social interaction. *Research on Language and Social Interaction* 32(1&2):149–54.

Scollon, Ron and Suzanne Scollon. 1981. *Narrative, Literacy and Face in Interethnic Communication*. Norwood, NJ: Ablex.

Scollon, Ron and Suzanne Wong Scollon. 1991. Topic confusion in English–Asian discourse. *World Englishes* 10(2):113–25.

Scollon, Ron and Suzanne Wong Scollon. 1995. *Intercultural Communication: A Discourse Approach*. Oxford: Blackwell.

Scollon, Ron and Suzanne Wong Scollon. 2001. *Intercultural Communication: A Discourse Approach*. Second edition. Oxford: Blackwell.

Scollon, Ron, Suzanne Wong Scollon, Yuling Pan, and Ming Li. 1998. Intercultural differences in professional communication: Professional communication between Hong Kong and Beijing. Paper presented at SIETAR Congress 98: Asia/Pacific Basin, Tokyo, November 19–24.

Scollon, Ron, Suzanne Wong Scollon, Wenzhong Hu, Liisa Salo-Lee, Yuling Pan, Li Ming, Cecilia Leung, and Zhenyi Li. 1999. Professional communication across cultures: A focus group based, three-way cross-cultural comparison. *SIETAR International Journal* 1(1):97–108.

Scollon, Suzanne. 1994a. Hong Kong women in the workplace: Conflicting discourses of the self. Paper presented at the American Association of Applied Linguistics, Baltimore, MD, March 7.

Scollon, Suzanne. 1994b. The utilitarian discourse system. In David Marsh and Liisa Salo-Lee (eds), *Europe on the move: Fusion or fission? Proceedings 1994 SIETAR Europa Symposium*. Jyväskylä: SIETAR EUROPA and University of Jyväskylä, pp. 126–31.

Scollon, Suzanne. 1995. The faces of world English: Nonverbal contextualization cues in TV news broadcasts. Paper presented at Second International Conference on World Englishes, Nagoya, May 25–8.

Scollon, Suzanne. 1996. Cantonese discussion, English documents: Professional communication in Hong Kong. Paper presented at the conference on Knowledge and Discourse, Hong Kong University, June.

Scollon, Suzanne. 1998. Methodological assumptions in intercultural communication. In Bates L. Hoffer and John H. Koo (eds), *Cross-Cultural Communication East and West in the 90s*. San Antonio, TX: Institute for Cross-Cultural Research, Trinity University, pp. 104–9.

Scollon, Suzanne. 1999. The study of gaze as critical semiotics. Paper presented at the Critical Discourse Analysis seminar, Birmingham, April 6–7.

Scollon, Suzanne and Vicki Kit Yee Yung. 1997. Hollywood east and west: Participation frameworks in Hong Kong and Hollywood academy awards. Paper presented at the Second Symposium on Intercultural Communication, Beijing Foreign Studies University, October 10–15.

Smith, Terry C. 1984. *Making Successful Presentations: A Self-Teaching Guide*. New York: John Wiley & Sons.

Staley, Constance Courtney and Robert Stephens Staley. 1992. *Communicating in Business and the Professions: The Inside World*. Belmont, CA: Wadsworth.

Tannen, Deborah. 1984. *Conversational Style: Analyzing Talk Among Friends*. Norwood, NJ: Ablex.

Tannen, Deborah. 1989. *Talking Voices: Repetition, Dialogue and Imagery in Conversational Discourse*. Cambridge: Cambridge University Press.

Tannen, Deborah and Muriel Saville-Troike (eds). 1985. *Perspectives on Silence*. Norwood, NJ: Ablex.

Tepper, Ron. 1998. *Power Resumes*. New York: John Wiley & Sons.

Thrash, Artie Adams, Annette N. Shelby, and Jerry L. Tarver. 1984. *Speaking Up Successfully: Communication in Business and the Professions*. New York: Holt, Rinehart, and Winston.

Tobin, Joseph J., David Y. H. Wu, and Dana H. Davidson. 1989. *Preschool in Three Cultures*. New Haven, CT: Yale University Press.

Toussaint-Samat, Maguelonne. 1992. *History of Food*. Oxford: Blackwell.

Troutman, Kathryn Kraemer. 1999. *The Federal Resume Guidebook*. Indianapolis: JIST Works.

Tsuda, Aoi. 1984. *Sales Talk in Japan and the United States*. Washington, DC: Georgetown University Press.

van Leeuwen, Theo. 1999. *Speech, Music, Sound*. London: Macmillan.

Wenger, Etienne. 1998. *Communities of Practice: Learning, Meaning, and Identity*. Cambridge: Cambridge University Press.

Wertsch, James V. 1998. *Mind as Action*. New York: Oxford University Press.

Yamada, Haru. 1992. *American and Japanese Business Discourse: A Comparison of Interactional Styles*. Norwood, NJ: Ablex.

Young, Linda Wai Ling. 1982. Inscrutability revisited. In John Gumperz (ed.), *Language and Social Identity*. New York: Cambridge University Press, pp. 72–84.

Young, Linda W. L. 1994. *Crosstalk and Culture in Sino-American Communication*. Cambridge: Cambridge University Press.

Zelazny, Gene. 2000. *Say it with Presentations*. New York: McGraw-Hill.

Index

agenda 112
  Chinese meetings 119
  Japanese meetings 114
agent *see* avatar
Alexander, Richard 29
American style of presentations *see*
  Dale Carnegie model of
  presentations
American/British style of meetings *see*
  C-B-S style
Ananova 79, 80, 94
anchor point, in telephone calls 40
audience dynamics and presentations
  90
audiotapes 11–12
  presentations 83
avatar 79, 80, 88, 94
  model of presentations 88

Bateman, David N. 28, 29, 30, 50
Beijing 18
  CDP exchanges 9
  focus group 47, 69–72, 95, 99, 100,
    101
  presentation style 97, 98
  presentations 96, 97–8, 99
  resumés 6, 62, 63, 65–6, 69–72, 77
  telephone calls 47
Bell (Alexander Graham) 34
bio statement *see* resumés

biodata *see* resumés
body language 11, 82, 86, 95, 98, 99
British/American style of meetings *see*
  C-B-S business style of
  communication
Burgess, Jillian 107
business card 55, 56, 149

"Carnegie Coach" (PowerPoint®
  wizard) 79
Carnegie, Dale *see* Dale Carnegie
Carnegie model of presentations 82–6,
  84, 85, 86, 89
Carnegie standard in presentations
  103
Carnegie style of presentations 100–2
case histories 19, 21, 24, 142
case study, resumé 62–6
C-B-S business style of communication
  14–15, 23, 27–8, 34, 38–9, 42, 49,
  77, 97, 111, 114, 115, 123, 126–8,
  129, 143–6, 158
  resumés 58–9, 73–4, 76–7
  telephone 34–8, 40, 42, 51
  telephone calls 32–8, 40, 42
  telephone practices 28, 34
  see also communication styles
CDP exchanges 5–10, 15, 43, 75–6,
  78, 125, 130, 147, 157, 202–3, 218
  checklist for developing 162–3

cost 153
example 210–16
knowledge (professional and
    personal) 75–7
Planner *see* Communication Display
    Portfolio Exchange Planner
process 151
setting up and making 22–5, 148–50
suggestions for users 159, 206–22
CDPs 5, 7, 24–6, 43, 76, 97, 108,
    137–9, 141–2, 159
communicative effectiveness of
    materials 5–6
evaluation 9–10
items 152–7
language audit 136
meetings 130–1
preparation 9
procedure 147–50
production 24–6
schedule 152
self-assessment 152
cell phones *see* mobile telephones
cellular telephones *see* mobile
    telephones
China
focus group 68
language 97
meetings 23–4, 115–25, 126, 146
post-meetings activities 121
presentations 89
public speaking 89
resumés 21
clarity-brevity-sincerity style *see*
    C-B-S business style of
    communication
commonsense view *see* conventional
    wisdom
Communicating in Business (Bateman
    and Sigband) 28–9
communication 105, 110
analysis 1–26
clarity 15
conflicts 143

mode 104
paralinguistic aspects 12
practices 3, 4, 142
self-reflective understanding of
    processes 5, 25, 137
spoken 55–7, 76–7
standardization 3–4
styles 38–42, 102
technologies 143
written 55–7
communications and cultures 104–5
Communication Display Portfolio
    Exchange Planner 138, 159, 160,
    162–3
Communication Display Portfolio
    Exchanges *see* CDP exchanges
Communication Display Portfolios *see*
    CDPs
communication practices 3–4
communicative image 9
communicative situations 142
communicative style
    computer-generated visuals 83, 84
    technological transformation 39
contextualization cues 11, 12
contrastive studies 16–17, 19–20, 24
conventional wisdom 15, 16, 17–19, 20
    telephone calls 27–30
corporate documentation collection
    216–17
courtesy in telephone calls *see*
    telephone usage, courtesy
cultural assumptions 156
cultural behavior and resumés 72
cultural boundaries and resumés 73
cultural considerations and resumés
    63–4, 72
cultural differences 2, 155, 165
    evaluation of telephone calls 52
    Finnish about resumés 64–5
    telephone calls 48–50, 52
cultural practices 4, 109–10
cultural values and business meetings
    109

cultures 102–3
curriculum vitae *see* resumés
CV *see* resumés

Dale Carnegie 4, 18, 22, 79, 81, 145,
    158
Dale Carnegie model of presentations
    82–6, 84, 85
Dale Carnegie presentation style 101
delivery of presenters 93
documentation 5, 9, 20
    personal 149
documents 141
    business card 55, 56
    resumés 55–7, 61
double relationship model of
    presentations 89, 90

English language 4, 94, 96, 97, 99,
    103–4
    world language 92–4
Erickson, Frederick 75

Finland 8, 18, 68
    business practices (telephone) 43
    CDP exchanges 9
    focus groups 25, 73, 95, 98, 99, 100,
        134–5, 219–22
    presentations 98–9
    resumés 6, 62–5, 68, 73
focus groups 5–6, 20, 24, 47, 70, 74,
    75, 130, 134, 149, 150, 153, 156
    Beijing 21, 69–74, 95, 96, 97–9
    discussions 5, 20, 24
    Finland 95, 98–9, 131
    Hong Kong 21, 66–9, 74, 95, 98–9,
        131
    language 66
    perceptions 66–73, 96–7, 100–1,
        102
    presentations 95
    resumés 63, 66–73
    telephone practices 47–8
    see also individual focus groups

"gatekeeping" situations 75
gestures 82, 86, 95, 99
Gu, Yueguo 119–21, 135

handbook for "Presenting Across
    Cultures" 159, 164–205
Hong Kong 8, 155
    broadcast styles 92
    CDP exchanges 9
    CDPs 43
    focus group 62, 66–9, 95, 98, 99,
        100, 103, 134–5
    meetings 128–30
    presentations 94–5
    resumés 6, 62–3, 65–7, 69, 70, 72
    telephone calls 40, 43–8
    telephone practices 43
*How to Win Friends and Influence
    People* (Dale Carnegie) 79
human knowledge *see* information

ICT *see* information and
    communication technology
information 22, 24, 68, 74, 146
    CDP exchange 25
    institutional *see* information,
        professional
    personal 12–14, 21–2, 24, 43, 67–9,
        74–8, 146
    professional 7, 12–14, 21–2, 75–8,
        143
    professional communication 22
    resumés 73, 74–5
    technology 87
information and communication
    technology (ICT) 31–2, 36,
    38–40
interaction with audience in
    presentations 99, 103
*Intercultural Communication: A
    Discourse Approach* (Scollon and
    Scollon) 28
intercultural differences, presentations
    8–9

International Business English (Jones and Alexander) 29–30
international workplace 3–5

Japan
  style of business relationships 127
  style of decision making 115
Japanese business meeting 23, 111–12, 146
  American perceptions 115
  negotiation process 113–14
  topics 115
Jones, Leo 29
Jyväskylä, Finland *see* Finland

knowledge, human *see* information
knowledge, institutional *see* information, professional
knowledge of new technologies, impact in China 118
knowledge, personal *see* information, personal

language 4, 17, 30, 46, 47, 63, 66, 130, 149, 150
  registers 140, 141, 142
  spoken genres 140, 141
language analysis 11–12
language audit 25, 135–6, 137, 138, 139–42, 160, 206–10
  meetings 140
  resumés 63
language and communication technologies 104
language in telephone calls 47
language usage 10–11, 43
  see also nonverbal communication
language use 10, 62
  business 129
  focus groups 66, 103–4
  meetings 129–30
  telephone calls 30, 31, 46, 47
languages 92, 141, 142
  meetings 135

Lanham, Richard 14, 15
law and resumés 21, 68, 76
Li, Yuanshou 89, 90
linguistic analysis 10–12
linguistic expression, nonverbal elements *see* nonverbal communication
Lloyd's of London 107

Martin, Michele 35
meetings 17, 20, 25, 106–36, 142, 148
  agenda 112, 114, 119
  American 23, 111–13, 115, 146
  assumptions 23–4
  Chinese 24, 119–20
  cultural variations 108–11
  definition 107–8, 121, 122
  expectations 127
  film portrayals (reactions) 131–5
  function 108–9, 112
  linguistic strategies 113, 122
  perceptions 1–3, 23–4
  presentation across cultures 194–201
  procedures 109
  sociolinguistic analysis 129
  structural properties 109
  methodology 10
Microsoft Word® resumé wizard 59–61
mobile telephones 7, 27, 28, 31, 35
  practices 28
multiple relationships model of presentations 91

Nakano, Yoshiko 126–7
nonverbal communication 11, 17–20, 22, 25, 83, 86
  presentations 99

objectivity 15, 16, 19
OHTs *see* overhead transparencies
overhead transparencies (OHTs) 83, 99, 100, 104

paralanguage 19, 20
perceptions 10
  meetings 12, 125–8, 129
  presentations 9
  professional communication 22
  resumés (by focus groups) 6
perspectives on professional
    communication 15–18, 19–20,
    147
politeness in telephone calls *see*
    telephone usage, courtesy
power in Chinese society 116, 118
  leadership 119–20
  types 118, 119
power flow in Chinese meetings 116,
    118, 124
  see also power relationship in
    Chinese meetings
power hierarchy in meetings 146
  Chinese 118, 121, 123, 125
PowerPoint® 87, 94, 95, 98, 100, 104
power relationship in Chinese meetings
    24, 116, 121, 122
  administrative 120–5
  expertise 120–5
  see also power flow in Chinese
    meetings
Power Resumes (Tepper) 58
practice, institutional 146
practices 6, 145, 148
  North America 144
  presentations 101
  studying 42–8
  telephone calls 28–9, 44–5, 49–50
presentation software 81, 143
presentation technologies 79–81, 87,
    100, 102, 160
presentations 8–9, 20, 22–3, 79, 102,
    103, 142, 148
  across cultures 164–205
  cultures 94–9
  Dale Carnegie model 22–3, 82–7
  delivery 82
  double relationship model 89, 90

language 94–5
length 83
linguistic expression (verbal and
    nonverbal elements) 86
multiple relationships model 91
news 92–4
questions 83
relationship between speaker and
    audience 83, 85, 89, 90–1
research 82
self-reflective understanding 25
styles 9, 80–7, 94, 95, 104, 145
teams 83
technology 80, 87
technology-based 86–8
visual aids 83
presenter in presentations 100–1
presenter's style 87, 92–4, 95, 97, 98
procedure in CDPs 150
procedures *see* practices
processes of communication, self-
    reflective understanding 5
Professional Association of Resumé
    Writing 56
professional communication style, four
    perspectives 15–17, 139
Provenzano, Steven A. 59

QWERTY keyboard 20–1, 36–7

rank hierarchy in Chinese meetings *see*
    power hierarchy in meetings,
    Chinese
reflective analysis 138
reflective self-assessment 159–61
reflective view 137–58
registers (language) 140, 141, 142
  telephone usage 31
relationship building and meetings 114
relationships 92
research base in intercultural
    communication 8–10
research methodology 10–11
resumé writers (professional) 56

resumé writing 56–7, 58–9, 67, 73
  legal questions 68
  literature 57
  professional evaluation 77
  standardized practices 73
  wizards (word-processing) 59–61
  word-processing software (wizards) 59–61
resumés 5, 6–7, 8, 21–2, 54–78, 142, 149
  America 71, 77
  Beijing 6, 58–9, 62, 69
  Beijing focus group 69–72
  case study 62–6
  chronological 57, 77
  content 58, 60, 70, 71, 73
  cultural considerations 72
  evaluation 21, 57, 77–8
  Finland 6, 62, 63–4, 73
  focus 73–4
  functional 57, 67
  history 54–5
  Hong Kong 6
  impact 56
  international settings 55
  legal constraints 21, 68, 76
  length 70, 71, 73
  perceptions 6, 56, 64–5
  personal information 21, 22, 67–9, 72–4, 75, 77–8
  presentation 61–2
  presenting across cultures 170–82
  privacy of employees 71
  professional information 68–9, 77–8
  quality 73–4
  standards 21, 73–4
  see also resumé writing, wizards

schedule of CDP 152
self-assessment 138, 147, 149, 152–3
  communicative image 9–10
self-presentation in professional communication in international settings 69

Shultz, Jeffrey 75
Sigband, Norman B. 28, 29, 30, 50
software (in presentations) *see* PowerPoint®
speech and writing 55–6
standardization in communication practices 3–4
status display 24
  Chinese meetings 120
styles
  meetings 134
  presentations 22–3, 92–4, 100, 104

technological transformation of communicative style 39
technologies 27, 86, 143
  communication 157–8
  new 102, 104
  presentation 25, 80–2, 84, 86, 102, 145
  styles of communication 38
technology 31, 46, 101, 102, 157
  communication 102
  Dale Carnegie style 81
  presentations 87, 95, 96
  telephone 30, 111
telegraph 37, 157
telephone 36, 143, 158
  C-B-S business style 32–8
  history 30
  ICT 31–2
  see also mobile telephones
telephone calls 22, 29, 46, 105, 142, 144, 145
  analysis 20
  business styles 47
  C-B-S business style 34–8
  cultural differences 48–50, 52
  endings 29–30, 41–2
  making 27–32, 42
  meetings 135
  openings 30–2
  presenting across cultures 189–92
  sociocultural conditions 50–1

telephone calls *cont.*
  standards 42
  structure 45, 47
  technology 27, 30–2, 33–4
  types 40–1, 42
  see also Beijing, telephone calls;
    Finland (business practices);
    Hong Kong, telephone calls
Telephone Engineer (1910) 30–1
telephone etiquette *see* telephone
  usage, courtesy
telephone language 37
telephone practices 7, 27–8, 33, 42, 52
  America 43
  Europe 43
  Finland 8, 18
  (identification) 49
  sociocultural environment 50–1
  studying 42–8
telephone technology 27, 32, 51, 144
telephone usage 21, 30, 32, 36–43, 47
  C-B-S style 34
  children 31
  courtesy 35, 37–8, 41, 43, 44–6,
    48–50, 51–2
  efficiency 51–2
  gender 29, 35–6
  history 33–5
Tepper, Ron 58, 59
three-culture reflective model 10–12
topic in meetings 112–15

verbal communication 83
verbal cues in presentations 99

see also nonverbal communication
videos 19, 137, 148, 156
  focus groups 219
  meetings *see* meetings, film
    portrayals (reactions)
  presentations 217–19
  visual aids 83
visual aids 3–6, 87, 104
  overhead transparencies 83, 100
  presentation styles 87
  presentations 83, 100

Windows 98® PowerPoint® Wizard
  79
wizards (word-processing)
  presentations 22, 79–80
  resumés 21, 59–61
workplace (international) 3–5
worksheets
  CDPs 203
  presenting across cultures 188
  resumés 183
  telephone calls (presenting across
    cultures) 193
workshops
  handbook for "Presenting Across
    Cultures" 138, 160, 164–205
  presenting across cultures 165–6
  topics for further discussion (form)
    204–5

Yamada, Haru 111–16

Zou, Kunshan 89, 90